Autonomy and Liberalism

Routledge Studies in Contemporary Philosophy

Autonomy and Liberalism

Ben Colburn

Routledge
Taylor & Francis Group
New York   London

First published 2010
by Routledge
270 Madison Avenue, New York, NY 10016

Simultaneously published in the UK
by Routledge
2 Park Square, Milton Park, Abingdon, Oxon OX14 4RN

Routledge is an imprint of the Taylor & Francis Group, an informa business

Typeset in Sabon by IBT Global.

Library of Congress Cataloging-in-Publication Data
Colburn, Ben, 1982–
    Autonomy and liberalism / by Ben Colburn.
       p. cm.—(Routledge studies in contemporary philosophy ; 19)
    Includes bibliographical references and index.
    1. Liberalism.   2. Autonomy (Philosophy)   I. Title.
    JC574.C644 2010
    320.51—dc22
                                               2009037979

ISBN10: 0-415-87596-X(hbk)
ISBN10: 0-203-85533-7 (ebk)

ISBN13: 978-0-415-87596-7 (hbk)
ISBN13: 978-0-203-85533-1 (ebk)

Anne Whyte 1924–1990
Pat Colburn 1913–1999
William Whyte 1914–2007

We have given to thee, Adam, no fixed seat, no form of thy very own, no gift peculiarly thine, that thou mayest feel as thine own, have as thine own, possess as thine own the seat, the form, the gifts which thou thyself shalt desire. A limited nature in other creatures is confined within the laws written down by Us. In conformity with thy free judgment, in whose hands I have placed thee, thou art confined by no bounds; and thou wilt fix limits of nature for thyself. I have placed thee at the centre of the world, that from there thou mayest more conveniently look around and see whatsoever is in the world. Neither heavenly nor earthly, neither mortal nor immortal have We made thee. Thou, like a judge appointed for being honourable, art the moulder and maker of thyself; thou mayest sculpt thyself into whatever shape thou dost prefer.

PICO DELLA MIRANDOLA "Oration on the Dignity of Man"

Contents

Acknowledgments

This book developed out of my PhD thesis, which I wrote in Cambridge between 2004 and 2007 with the help of a doctoral grant from the AHRC. I completed it during a Junior Research Fellowship at Corpus Christi College, Cambridge, between 2008 and 2009. Some material in Chapter 2 has appeared in slightly different form as 'Forbidden Ways of Life' in *The Philosophical Quarterly* 58 (2008).

My thesis was written under the supervision of Serena Olsaretti and Hallvard Lillehammer. My very great thanks for their time, wisdom, and encouragement. My thanks also to my examiners, Matthew Clayton and Jonathan Wolff. I hope that I have done justice to at least some of their insightful objections.

Amongst others, especial thanks are due to my dear friends and colleagues Matthew Clark, Jane Clossick, Daniel Elstein, Lorna Finlayson, Brian King, and Mark Ynys-Môn, who have been well-springs of both inspiration and support. And for help in various different ways, I should like to thank the following: Harry Adamson, Tim Button, Fabian Freyenhagen, Raymond Geuss, Ross Harrison, Matthew Hodgetts, Jules Holroyd, Luca Incurvati, Lesley Lancaster, Keith Lark, David Liggins, Stuart and Jan Macdonald, Chris Mann, Hugh Mellor, Neil Sinclair, Peter Smith, Tim Storer, Diktynna Warren, Nathan Wildman, Colin Yardley, and Margaret Young. I am also grateful for useful comments from audiences in Bristol, Cambridge, Glasgow, London, Manchester, Montreal, Pavia, Southampton, and Warwick.

Finally, I should like to register my love and gratitude to my parents, Eric and Liz Colburn, my sister Hannah Colburn, and my godmother Noëlle Mann; also to my grandfather William Whyte, who didn't quite see this book completed, and to whom it is dedicated.

Introduction
What is Liberalism?

There is no clear answer to this question. That fact reveals twin dangers for those who wish to think of themselves as defenders of liberal political theory. On that theoretical level, there has been no clear and unified understanding of what a liberal political philosophy is committed to. Hence, liberalism as a political philosophy has been vulnerable to a charge of internal incoherence. And these theoretical problems have made the practical debate about liberal policies almost impossible to conduct in a clear and systematic way. Ought a liberal state to accommodate illiberal minority practices? Should providing freedom of choice be the main aim of such a state, or should its emphasis be upon supporting an extensive system of welfare? The term 'liberal' is applied at different times—both by proponents and opponents—to all these different policies, and in the resulting cacophony, the chance of identifying a clear and coherent liberal voice is lost.

I am going to try to bring order to this chaos. This must be done with an eye on policy, for ultimately our concern should be with what we must do, and hence with providing a theory adequate to give clear practical direction. However, this is a work of political *philosophy*, not just a blue-print for policy. The confusion in the policy debate arises due to the different competing philosophical interpretations of what the foundations of liberalism should be understood to be. So, it is to those foundations that we must first turn our attention.

I shall argue that we should understand liberalism as the political philosophy that is committed to the promotion of individual autonomy. In what follows I spell out more what this means, and show that the intuitive heart of the ideal can be traced in a number of writers. Pico della Mirandola's 1486 *Oration on the Dignity of Man* imagines God speaking to Adam and giving him this charter:

> thou mayest feel as thine own, have as thine own, possess as thine own the seat, the form, the gifts which thou thyself shalt desire . . . In conformity with thy free judgment, in whose hands I have placed thee, thou art confined by no bounds; and thou wilt fix limits of nature for thyself . . . Thou, like a judge appointed for being honourable, art the

moulder and maker of thyself; thou mayest sculpt thyself into whatever shape thou dost prefer.[1]

Though rarely stated again in such exalted terms, this ideal recurs throughout the history of Western thought. The great Prussian philosopher and educationalist Wilhelm von Humboldt defended an ideal of human individuality as an ideal of shaping one's life according to what one deems valuable.[2] Thus also John Stuart Mill, who said that

> Human nature is not a machine to be built following the style of a model, and set to do exactly the work prescribed for it, but a tree, which is required to grow and develop itself on all sides, according to the tendency of the inward forces which make it a living thing.[3]

Finally, amongst contemporary political philosophers, Joseph Raz calls this ideal 'autonomy', saying that the ideal of personal autonomy is that people should make their own lives. The autonomous person is a (part) author of his own life. The ideal of personal autonomy is the vision of people controlling, to some degree, their own destiny.[4]

More precise analysis of this ideal will come in what follows. However, the golden thread running throughout is this: What is distinctive and valuable about human life is our capacity to decide for ourselves what is valuable in life, and to shape our lives in accordance with that decision. That is, to live autonomous lives. The proper aim of politics should therefore be to enable people to live lives embodying that ideal, and the proper political philosophy is that which has this aim at its core: autonomy-minded liberalism.

This book is concerned with both the foundations and consequences of this position. It has three aims: first, to make clear what autonomy is, and why we should consider it valuable; secondly, to indicate what consequences follow from taking this to be the ideal at the heart of one's liberal theory; and third, to show that such a theory is the best way of finding a stable set of commitments that are recognisably liberal in character.

Mindful that 'autonomy' is an ambiguous and contested term, in Chapter 1 I engage in a critical examination of the various historical and contemporary accounts of autonomy. This leads me, in Chapter 2, to develop my own account: autonomy consists in an individual deciding for herself what is valuable and living her life in accordance with that decision. I explain in detail what I believe the relevant notion of 'decision' to be, and flesh out this conception of autonomy by describing various lives that illustrate different ways in which one might be autonomous. In so doing, I not only make clearer what my theory amounts to, but also offer some motivation for taking autonomy, so understood, to be valuable.

Both tasks continue in Chapter 3, where I show that the claim that the state should promote autonomy both implies, and is implied by, anti-perfectionism about state action. This provides support for my position by embedding it within a network of other commonly held positions: primarily anti-perfectionism, as mentioned, but also certain types of pluralism and value-relativism. I thereby raise the theoretical costs faced by someone who denies that the state should promote autonomy. The equivalence thesis also refutes the two principal alternative accounts of liberalism. Neutrality-based liberals are committed to anti-perfectionism but deny that the state should promote autonomy, while perfectionistic liberals are committed to the promotion of autonomy and the denial of anti-perfectionism. I show that neither position is tenable; hence, such liberals must either accept my theory or reject whichever one of those claims they take to be constitutive of their theories.

Having carved out a space for autonomy-minded liberalism in this way, Chapter 4 teases out the implications of this commitment. It outlines the political morality of liberalism, showing the connections between autonomy and the other purported liberal values of freedom and equality. I argue that in addition to giving people freedom (meaning a range of choices in their actions), the autonomy-minded state should ensure that people are well-informed about their options and that those options are such that they could be chosen voluntarily. I also argue that if the state is to promote autonomy, it must aim for equal access to autonomy for all, which is to say a system in which the only inequalities of autonomy that arise must be ones for which individuals are responsible. This entails further egalitarian commitments, such as equality of opportunity for as wide a range of goods as possible.

In Chapter 5 I conclude by considering the possibility left open by my conclusion in Chapter 3, namely that a liberal might deny both that the state should be autonomy promoting and that it should be anti-perfectionistic. I focus my attention upon multicultural liberals, since they are the main contemporary inhabitants of that theoretical territory. I argue that there is almost no distinctive ground for a liberalism of this sort, and that what little there is involves endorsing claims which are extremely unattractive. Hence, I conclude that mine is the strongest possible liberal political theory: someone who wants to be a liberal should be an autonomy-minded liberal.

1 Three Conceptions of Autonomy

For all that it is a concept in common use in political philosophy, there is little consensus about what autonomy actually is. Clearly, this is a dangerous state of affairs if one is trying to justify a theory of liberalism based on a commitment to the value of autonomy. Justification is apt to be misunderstood, with different readers taking 'autonomy' to mean different (sometimes wildly different) things. Opponents of such a theory run the risk of attacking it on an understanding of autonomy different from that on which it is actually based; a parallel danger for me will be unwittingly playing upon equivocations to make justifications seem more plausible than they in fact are. These dangers cannot entirely be avoided. The best that can be done is briefly to survey the territory, then clear the undergrowth a little by clarifying what I shall mean by 'autonomy' in what follows, and why. This chapter deals with that task.

Before I start, it will be useful to make clear two distinctions between ways of understanding autonomy. First, we might distinguish between autonomy conceived of as a *local* property—that is, as a property of a person at a particular time and perhaps in respect of particular decisions or actions—and as a *global* property, meaning a property of a person's life as a whole. Secondly, we can distinguish between different types of properties that one might take autonomy to be. Some conceptions take autonomy to be a *condition* that someone can be in, and others take it to be a *capacity* that one might possess, the possession of which is itself valuable (independently of its exercise, for example). These distinctions will prove significant later on, especially when I show how my conception of autonomy differs from the others I examine.

Despite the lack of consensus surrounding contemporary conceptions of autonomy, I suggest that we can identify a common thread running through them all. Following John Christman, I suggest that the core concept of autonomy is something like self-governance, or control of one's commitments.[1] Each of the conceptions autonomy that I examine below is a different understanding of a concept of self-governance.

There are three dominant conceptions of autonomy currently in circulation. First, there are conceptions of autonomy as rational self-legislation, most famously (though not exclusively) espoused by Kant and his intellectual successors. Secondly, there are conceptions that rely upon the notion of a hierarchy of motivations advanced by Harry Frankfurt and by Gerald Dworkin. Finally, there are conceptions built on a notion of self-authorship or individuality, such as that employed by Joseph Raz. Considering these three conceptions separately should not imply that they are necessarily in direct conflict with each other. As we shall see, I adopt my conception of autonomy partially in response to the flaws of the other positions, but I do not assume from the outset that it is impossible that the three families of conceptions examined here might coexist. There may just be three different and compatible ideals at work, each indicated by a different conception of autonomy.

1.1 AUTONOMY AND REASON

One family of substantive conceptions of autonomy understands self-governance to consist in rational self-legislation or determination. So, on these views, the concept of autonomy is to be fleshed out as an ideal of a condition possessed by agents at particular times: for an agent to be autonomous is for them to act with self-control in accordance with reason. Such conceptions fall into two main categories, which I shall call Kantian and non-Kantian rationalism respectively.

According to Kant, a person is autonomous if his will is self-ruling.[2] To be self-ruling, the will must be 'efficient independently of alien causes determining it,' where alien causes include not only the agency of others (as, for example, if one were being controlled by hypnosis) but also the laws of nature. The latter includes things like desires and impulses: such mental phenomena are part of the causal chain of nature, and therefore constitute alien causes. Kant also wanted to exclude lawless action, for that too is a sort of slavery (though to chaos, rather than to alien causes). So, the autonomous will must be in accordance with laws of a special kind, namely those that have as their source nothing other than the will itself. That, Kant said, meant behaving in accordance with the Categorical Imperative, for that is the only law that can be derived just from pure reason. To be autonomous, the will must not act on anything that might be an alien cause. Alien causes derive from the particular, contingent circumstances of individuals: desires, impulses, adverse conditions and pressures, and so on. To avoid these, the will must act in a way completely undetermined by the particular circumstances under which it is acting. That means, though, acting on motives that one might will that anyone—including those who don't share one's particular circumstances—could also will. So, in Kant's theory, the autonomous will is just one that acts in accordance with the Categorical Imperative.

Kant's theory, as sketched here, has two components. First, there is the concept of autonomy for which he argued: autonomy is a property of a person's will which consists in that will being determined only by laws given by the will itself. Secondly, there is the particular conception of autonomy that comes from his claim that the only law so given is the Categorical Imperative. It would be possible for someone to endorse the first component, but not the second. That is, we could agree that autonomy consists in acting only on laws given by the will itself, while thinking that the Categorical Imperative is not the only law that can be so given. We might, for example, disagree with Kant that all contingent factors count as alien causes in the relevant sense, and discriminate between different types of desire. Perhaps certain types of desire might not be alien to us, and that acting on those desires would not vitiate autonomy. Or, we might agree that all desires are alien causes, being part of the natural chain of causation, but think that there is nothing to stop the will from choosing autonomously to take them into consideration in its deliberation.

This gives us various possible Kantian conceptions of autonomy. The strictest position is that held by Kant himself: autonomy is equivalent to the behaviour demanded by morality, which is to say acting in accordance with the Categorical Imperative. Conceptions can vary in strictness by allowing that there might be other things than the Categorical Imperative that are non-alien in the relevant sense.

Contemporary philosophers who have used a Kantian conception of autonomy vary in their strictness. Jonathan Jacobs, for example, takes a position at the stricter end of the spectrum: he argues that someone who acts freely and voluntarily might nevertheless fall short of autonomy because they might fail to follow the moral law.[3] Others defend conceptions that are less strict, sometimes considerably so. David Richards, for example, takes himself still to be a Kantian, but says that the requirement that the will is not determined by alien causes is satisfied by a weak endorsement condition: it is sufficient for autonomy to have exercised 'the higher-order capacity of the agent to choose her or his ends, whatever they are' for those ends to count as non-alien.[4] Richards' variant of the Kantian conception brings it close to collapsing into the conceptions I examine in Section 1.2, which emphasise higher-order endorsement as the key to autonomy. However, Richards' view remains distinct insofar as—like Kant—he takes the non-alienness of causes to be centrally important, and endorsement important as the means to guaranteeing non-alienness.

At this point, we might worry whether Richards, Jacobs and Kant are really all using the same conception of autonomy. Indeed, we might even worry whether a Kantian conception of autonomy can properly be applied to political philosophy at all, since in Kant's own theory its role is just to identify the quality that the will must have if it is to be able to act in accordance with morality. Kant's conception of autonomy is sometimes called *moral autonomy*, and is contrasted with *personal autonomy* (which is normally equated with one of the other conceptions of autonomy I examine in this chapter). Drawing this distinction is often intended to motivate our avoiding moral autonomy as a potential subject for political philosophers to consider. This sometimes seems to be the position of John Rawls, for example.[5] Even if we grant that a Kantian conception of autonomy can play a role in political philosophy, there is dispute about whether the people who take themselves to be Kantians are working within such a framework. Onora O'Neill argues, of positions such as Richards', that they badly misrepresent their own foundations if they claim Kantian support.[6]

These are interesting problems, and they have received some attention in recent literature.[7] However, they are somewhat tangential to our present business. As a matter of fact, there *are* political philosophers who adopt a Kantian conception of autonomy and apply it to political philosophy. So, they are worth examining here, even if we worry about their Kantian pedigree. To put it another way, regardless of whether we think them genuine interpretations of Kant, Kant-inspired, or only pseudo-Kantian, they all share the core thought that autonomy consists in acting only from non-alien causes, which they all identify roughly as acting only in accordance with *reason*. Another group of conceptions of autonomy exist, which while they do not trace a lineage to Kant, still place emphasis upon the notion of rational self-legislation or direction. So, for example, Robert Ladenson sketches a conception—which he attributes to Dewey—on which autonomy is identified with a life lived in accordance with reason, understood as

> a set of abilities and capacities whose coordinated operation tends to result in a person's attaining goods and avoiding evils, both on particular occasions and over the long run.[8]

These 'more developed' capacities are contrasted with lower ones such as emotions, instincts and habits. Hence, we suppose, for Ladenson being autonomous consists in being guided by reason and eschewing those lower capacities. Ladenson's ideal has a teleological air—that is, it identifies an end-state condition which is valuable, and identifies autonomy with what is needed to get to it. Other proponents of rationalist autonomy avoid this teleological character and instead take the value of autonomy to be the exercise of a capacity. Some writers on Stoicism, for example, take autonomy to be a condition consisting of control over one's urges and impulses, either through the exercise of willpower,[9] or by the use of the capacity for reason.[10] Others use a similar conception of autonomy, though they don't identify it as especially Stoic in nature. So, George Sher says that an autonomous agent is self-governing in the sense of 'exercising their will on the basis of good reasons';[11] Keith Lehrer suggests that autonomy consists just in being governed by reason;[12] John Benson says that to be autonomous one must 'put oneself in the best position to answer for the reliability of one's beliefs';[13] and Lawrence Haworth says that to be autonomous an agent must display 'full rationality', which consists in both means-end reasoning and exercise of critical appraisal of the ends they adopt.[14]

In all these conceptions of autonomy there is a common emphasis upon rational behaviour. The concept of autonomy as self-governance is interpreted as an ideal of the exercise of reason. It is in respect of this emphasis on reason that the conceptions in this family are distinct from those I consider later. And because of this, these conceptions are all in danger of unjustifiably lionising reason over other possible sources of action and motivation. Why, we might ask, should we think that acting on reason is valuable, or at least the same sort of ideal as autonomy? Why should we think that only acting on reason can count as self-governance?

One consistent answer—but one which we might be reluctant to accept—was given by Kant. Kant gave an objective criterion by which he judged that pure reason was the only non-alien cause. According to Kant we should distinguish between the phenomenal world, in which our desires are bound within a causal chain that destroys freedom, and the noumenal world, in which we are free from such causal determination. It is only insofar as we act without being determined by the tyranny of causation that we govern ourselves. So, Kant's motivation for identifying autonomy with acting on pure reason flowed from his broader metaphysical theory, and it serves as a motivation *only if* we accept that metaphysics.

Suppose that we reject Kantian metaphysics, or at any rate want to avoid basing our political philosophy on such controversial territory. What then? I suggest that, with Kant out of the picture, there *is* no justification for placing such weight on the exercise of reason in our account of autonomy. After all, introspection suggests that there are other motivations which seem, as much as acting on reason does, to derive from the 'self'. So, if our core concept of autonomy is that of self-governance, it is unclear why those other motivations mightn't also count. In the absence of a positive argument for abandoning common sense here (and assuming that we do not want to adopt the whole of Kant's metaphysical position), this should make us wary of understanding autonomy in this way.

Admittedly, pointing out the absence of an argument for the emphasis on reason hardly refutes the rationalist conceptions of autonomy. However, there are other reasons to think that there is something unattractive about autonomy understood in this way. All the conceptions considered in this section take self-governance to mean self-governance *according to what is demanded by reason*. They differ in quite how stringent and specific they take those demands to be, but they are all committed to taking those demands to be binding. Hence, they recognise no authority for individuals over questions of what will make their lives go well. As we shall see in Section 1.3 I take this to a core component of the ideal of autonomy I defend; and it is for this reason that I distance myself from Kant, his successors and his imitators. This is not to suggest that reason will play no role in my conception of autonomy: I do place importance upon the possibility of reflecting (rationally) upon what one considers valuable. However, in my own conception reason will not have the pre-eminence it enjoys in the views discussed here.

1.2 AUTONOMY AND MOTIVATION

A second family of conceptions of autonomy springs from the work of Harry Frankfurt and Gerald Dworkin. On this view, self-governance is understood to consist in our motivations being structured in a certain way. Frankfurt and Dworkin note that we can distinguish between different types of attitudes—by which they mean preferences, desires, wishes and the like—by seeing that such attitudes sit in a hierarchical structure.[15] So, we have first-order attitudes concerning particular actions we might perform: a preference for playing tennis, perhaps, or a desire to eat a bacon sandwich. We also have higher-order attitudes, concerning which first-order attitudes we want to have or to follow. For example, I might prefer to follow preferences which will involve exercise, or desire to desire less fatty foods. These higher-order attitudes might themselves generate first-order attitudes (so, my preference for exercise-preferences might lead to my developing a preference for running in the morning). On the other hand, first-order attitudes can arise which don't derive from any higher-order attitude, and may indeed conflict with some such attitude. For example, if I desired to eat a bacon sandwich, that desire might conflict with a higher-order desire to desire healthy foods. A given individual's attitudes will thus be of different orders, and arranged in a hierarchy of motivations: a structure of first- and higher-order motivations, with some first-order motivations arising out of higher-order motivations, and some motivations in tension with each other.

Working within this hierarchical model of motivation, Dworkin defines two slightly different conceptions of autonomy. The notion that is central to both is identification. In one place, Dworkin defines autonomy thus:

> A person is autonomous if he identifies with his desires, goals, and values, and such identification is not influenced in ways which make the process of identification in some way alien to the individual. Spelling out those conditions of procedural independence involves distinguishing those ways of influencing people's reflective and critical faculties which subvert them from those which promote and improve them.[16]

The two conceptions that can be found in Dworkin's work differ in respect of what they take identification to be. Note, however, that both differ significantly from the rationalist conceptions discussed earlier: unlike those conceptions, Dworkin's two views each allow that one's motivations need not be rational to contribute to our autonomy. Hence, he escapes one of the criticisms I made of that view earlier, which was that it lionised reason without justification.

His earlier position was that identification consists in one's hierarchy of motivations being arranged in a particular way: first-order attitudes must be congruent with one's higher-order desires: that is, we must *identify* with our desires.[17] So, my autonomy is hindered in a situation where I desire both to eat a bacon sandwich and desire to desire healthy food. Experiencing the latter (higher-order) desire means that I do not identify with the former (first-order) desire. In order to become more autonomous, I might bring my first-order desire in line with my higher-order desire: perhaps by ceasing to desire the bacon sandwich and instead desiring salad.

Dworkin later repudiated this view of identification in response to three limitations, all of which reveal unpalatable consequences of understanding autonomy this way.[18] First, autonomy so understood would be a local property, which would have implausible consequences. For example, a drug addict might conceivably identify with his addiction one day then feel it alien the next day. Does this shift in his higher-order desires mean that we take him to shift back and forth between autonomy and non-autonomy? Dworkin's response is 'surely not'. Secondly, that conception of autonomy allows that one could become more autonomous not by revising one's first-order attitudes, but rather one's higher-order attitudes. So, I need not abandon my first-order desire to eat a bacon sandwich, but might instead jettison my higher-order desire to desire healthy food. Dworkin takes this possibility to be a sign that the proposal inadequately captures our intuitions about autonomy: a conception of autonomy ought to privilege keeping higher-order attitudes constant and revising first-order attitudes, rather than *vice versa*. Thirdly, Dworkin worries that his earlier view of autonomy is consistent with an agent being unable 'to make certain desires effective in our actions.' A drug addict who identified with his addiction would, with *that* view, be autonomous, despite his being unable to change his first-order desires (and not merely being unwilling to, as in the previous case). Dworkin assumes that this is unacceptable: one must be able 'not only to scrutinize critically their first-order motivations but also to change them if they so desire.'

In response to these problems, Dworkin changed his conception. His later formulation was as follows:

> Autonomy is conceived of as a second-order capacity of persons to reflect critically upon their first-order preferences, desires, wishes, and so forth and the capacity to accept or attempt to change these in light of higher-order preferences and values.[19]

Moreover, he says that 'by exercising such a capacity, persons define their nature, give meaning and coherence to their lives, and take responsibility for the kind of person they are.' Dworkin does not spell out precisely what this amounts to in practical terms, but his criticisms of his earlier conception give us some idea. To be autonomous, we must live lives in which we generally identify with our first-order attitudes, as a result of exercising the capacity for critical reflection and bringing those attitudes in line with our higher-order commitments.

Dworkin's conception of autonomy has attracted significant criticism. For example, Gary Watson and Irving Thalberg complain that the crucial notion of identification is sufficiently vague to make one skeptical about the whole theory.[20] Since I do not defend Dworkin's conception of autonomy myself, I shall not discuss most criticisms in detail. However, one line of attack *is* relevant, since it motivates my own conception of autonomy.

Marilyn Friedman suggests that, in some cases where an individual has a conflict between higher- and lower-order attitudes, we might think (contrary to Dworkin's suggestion) she is more autonomous if she acts on the latter and attempts to revise the former.[21] Consider, for example, an individual conditioned into a desire for some oppressive level of obedience to a spouse. Such an individual might have a strong first-order desire not to wash the dishes, and a strong higher-order desire not to have such disobedient desires. From the point of view of promoting autonomy, it is not at all clear that the first-order desires should be overridden: indeed, our intuitions rather favour the opposite. Since Dworkin's conception of autonomy implies the first course, it is (says Friedman) implausible.

In response to criticisms like Friedman's, the debate over Dworkin's conception of autonomy has become somewhat stuck in a baroque fugue between critics (who propose cases as counterexamples to the conception) and proponents (who offer small modifications to address each counterexample as it arrives). The debate is inconclusive, and its details need not concern us here. However, the fact that Dworkin's conception has become enmired in such a fruitless debate reveals a deeper worry about that conception. Why, we may ask, should we care whether people have their hierarchies of attitudes arranged in the particular way he describes? Why should higher-order attitudes be authoritative? Insofar as the hierarchical theory leaves such questions open, it is inconclusive, since it fails to account for why autonomy so conceived is something we should think valuable.

One possible answer is suggested by Friedman, who notes that both Dworkin and Frankfurt seem to be motivated by the thought that autonomy consists in being true to our 'true selves', and that our true selves should be identified with our higher-order desires. If this is right, though, it means that the hierarchical conception of autonomy suffers from a problem analogous to one that I identified in the rationalist conceptions above, namely that it seems to identify too narrow a subset of our possible motivations as what counts as self-governance.

What else might we say on their behalf? One answer brings us back to another point discussed in the previous section. Perhaps Frankfurt and Dworkin describe an ideal of rationality: to be ideally rational one's attitudes must be in harmony, and the mechanism for restoring harmony must be one which causes lower-order attitudes to defer to higher-order ones. If this were the motivation for endorsing Dworkin's conception of autonomy, then my earlier concern still holds: we need some independent reason to assign rationality this pre-eminent place at the core of autonomy.[22]

On the other hand, one might think that this particular arrangement of the hierarchy is something to aim for because it is the best guarantee of some other important condition to be realised. If *that* is so, however, the proponent of the hierarchical conception still has to identify the plausible idea at its core. In Chapter 2 I describe what I take to be such a conception, based on the notions of autonomy and individuality I consider in the following section. Adopting *that* conception of autonomy might give us reasons to accept what Dworkin says. However, the previous discussion suggests that the hierarchical conception does not identify a free-standing ideal in its own right. Hence, I discuss the matter no further.

1.3 AUTONOMY AND INDIVIDUALITY

In *The Morality of Freedom* Joseph Raz identifies a conception of autonomy as an ideal different from what we have considered so far. Raz's central notion is self-governance is to be understood as an ideal of 'self-creation'. He says that

> [t]he ruling idea behind the ideal of personal autonomy is that people should make their own lives. The autonomous person is a (part) author of his own life. The ideal of personal autonomy is the vision of people controlling, to some degree, their own destiny, fashioning it through successive decisions throughout their lives.[23]

Later, he says that it is central to the conception of autonomy that 'the autonomous person has or is developing a conception of himself.'[24]

In these passages Raz identifies an ideal of autonomy distinct from anything in the two families considered so far. Unlike the rationalist conceptions considered in Section 1.1, pursuing Raz's ideal does not demand that one acts only on laws the rational will can give to itself: there is no particular reason to think that self-authorship demands that we act only rationally. And unlike the hierarchical conceptions considered in Section 1.2, it does not appear to require any particular configuration of one's hierarchy of attitudes: it remains neutral on the question of whether the Frankfurt-Dworkin model of motivations is appropriate or not.

Admittedly, theorists of autonomy within those other families might disagree that this is a separate category. Both the rationalist and the supporter of the hierarchical model might say that they too endorse an ideal of self-authorship, but understand that to amount to rational self-legislation or higher-order endorsement respectively. That is, they might take 'self-authorship' just to be another name for the core concept of self-governance shared by all conceptions of autonomy.

More detailed discussion of Raz's conception—and in particular of its historical precedents—will, I hope, serve to make the distinction clearer.

However, something can be said now in more general terms. The conceptions examined so far take self-governance to be in some sense a constraint. To be autonomous in Kant's sense one must act only on certain maxims, and to be autonomous in Dworkin's sense one's motivations must be organised in a certain way. Raz takes self-governance to be something different, in which the conditions that determine whether or not one is autonomous are decided by the agent herself. On Raz's view a life is judged as autonomous or not depending on whether the person concerned shapes that life as she sees fit.[25] So, it is indeed significantly different from the two families of conceptions considered earlier.

I should note, though, that even if these conceptions of autonomy are distinct as understandings of a basic concept of self-governance, there may well be a practical connection between them. For example, it would be coherent to hold that to be an author of one's own life one must, in practical terms, strive to bring one's first-order attitudes in line with one's higher-order attitudes. (As we shall see, I do indeed use some of Dworkin's apparatus in elucidating my own views). Even if there were this practical convergence, though, my basic point would still stand. Considered as understandings of the content of the concept of self-governance, they are clearly different, because they take that arrangement of the motivational hierarchy to be valuable in different ways: intrinsically valuable on Dworkin's view, and either constitutively or instrumentally valuable on Raz's.

Raz's ideal is very influential, especially amongst modern liberal thinkers who (like him) seek to justify a perfectionistic liberalism based on a state commitment to the promotion of autonomy. It is also an expression of an idea with a long historical pedigree, in particular the writings of Wilhelm von Humboldt and John Stuart Mill. Although neither mentioned autonomy explicitly, each placed great importance upon a notion of individuality. In what follows, I argue that these notions (especially once they are revised somewhat in response to some apparent contradictions) are significantly similar to the conception of autonomy described by Raz, and to the conception that I myself will develop in the next chapter. Hence, examining Humboldt and Mill in some detail will be useful both to tell us something about the history of the conception of autonomy I adopt, and to help make that conception more vivid.

Wilhelm von Humboldt (1767–1835) was a polymath who, in addition to reforming the Prussian education system, wrote on topics in philosophy, linguistics, history, psychology and the natural sciences. The relevant work here is *Ideen zu einem Versuch, die Gränzen der Wirksamkeit des Staats zu bestimmen*, published in 1810, and known in English as *The Limits of State Action*, in which—amongst many other things—Humboldt describes a striking ideal which lies behind his detailed political prescriptions, namely an ideal of the development and exercise of human individuality as the highest good.[26]

Humboldt's conception of individuality has various independent aspects, only some of which I take as inspiration for the view of autonomy under examination. In particular, it is important to separate two major components. The first is that individuality involves being self-directed: it is a value that can be achieved only by someone acting freely and on their own initiative. So, he says that 'whatever does not spring from a man's free choice . . . does not enter into his very being, but still remains alien to his true nature; he does not perform it with true human energies.'[27] By 'free choice' here Humboldt means not just that individual actions must be free, but also that there must be freedom in respect of the principles on which we act, which is to say that individuals must determine for themselves what is valuable in their lives, without it being imposed on them from some other source.[28] Secondly, individuality involves the avoidance of 'one-sidedness': that is, a pursuit of single goals imposed from without for an entire life. So, Humboldt writes that

> man has it in his power to avoid this one-sidedness, by attempting to unite the distinct and generally separately exercised faculties of his nature, by bringing into spontaneous cooperation, at each period of his life, the dying sparks of one activity, and those which the future will kindle, and endeavouring to increase and diversify the powers with which he works . . . [29]

The difference between these two aspects is illustrated by two things Humboldt might have thought we should avoid. 'One-sidedness' could be bad because it involves pursuing only a single goal, or it could be bad because that goal is imposed from outside.

Understood as addressing the former concern, individuality seems like a rather restrictive ideal. Whatever an individual's views on the matter, the ideal they must strive for is all-roundedness: the integration and development of the various talents they possess. On the other hand, we might understand Humboldt's main concern to have been the second: that is, the effect upon individuality of one's goals being imposed from outside. On this reading, it is easier to see how individuality might be an ideal of autonomy. Humboldt said that the ideal condition for humans is

> that in which each individual not only enjoys the most absolute freedom of developing himself by his own energies, in his perfect individuality, but in which external nature itself is left unfashioned by any human agency, but only receives the impress given to it by each individual for himself and of his own free will, according to the measure of his wants and instincts, and restricted only by the limits of his powers and his rights.[30]

There is an element of unattractive solipsism in the passage just quoted, and I don't mean to suggest that this ideal of total *independence* is one that

I endorse. However, it does tell us what Humboldt's concerns were, and hence how to interpret the ambiguous passages above. In the passage just quoted, it sounds rather as though it is the *self*-direction and *self*-development that Humboldt valued in individualism, not especially the perfection of the talents of individuals irrespective of the attitudes of the individuals whose talents they are.

The same is indicated by his insistence that there is no particular end that we should have in mind when considering the ideal of individuality:

> There is no pursuit whatever that may not be ennobling and give to human nature some worthy and determinate form. The manner of its performance is the only thing to be considered . . . [31]

The 'manner' referred to is a matter of the attitude with which we undertake these pursuits: if they are to contribute to the ideal of individuality, must be ones which people engaged on them consider valuable. Otherwise, the self-same activities will not contribute to their individuality; and hence will either not benefit them, or have an influence that is 'pernicious'.

This gives us two interpretations of Humboldt's theory. One takes the value of individualism to the fact that it is needed to promote the perfection of individual talents. The other takes the value of individualism to consist in charting one's own path through life through pursuits that one considers valuable. It is unclear which of these is the best interpretation of Humboldt. In the following paragraph, I suggest reasons why in Mill's case we might consider an analogue of the latter position best. Insofar as Mill's theory is clearly inspired by Humboldt's, it might give us reason to prefer the latter reading in the present case as well. Even if that is wrong, however, my main point still stands. Whatever Humboldt intended, we can find in his writings an expression of an ideal rather similar in its main parts to the conception of autonomy sketched by Raz, and on which my conception too is based.

Humboldt's thought became known in the English-speaking world mostly through the activities of John Stuart Mill (1806–1873), in particular his essay *On Liberty*, originally published in 1859. Mill's principal concern was anti-paternalism. He argued for severe restrictions on how far the state can intervene in people's lives to make them better. A central reason for this is that it would fail necessarily if it tried to do so, because 'it really is of importance, not only what men do, but what manner of men they are that do it.'[32] For our lives to be valuable, according to Mill, we must live them with individuality: 'In proportion to the development of his individuality, each person becomes more valuable to himself'.[33] That is, we must be self-governing, determining our plans of life for ourselves. Someone who does not do this, and 'lets the world [i.e. other people, or social convention] choose his plan of life for him', fails to live the sort of life that is fully good for humans: 'one whose desires and impulses are not his own, has no character, no more than a steam-engine has a character.'[34]

Recognising the importance of individuality, for Mill, meant allowing people to control their own commitments and develop their own plan of life in response to their experience of the world and their reflections upon questions of value:

> [I]t is the privilege and proper condition of a human being, arrived at the maturity of his faculties, to use and interpret experience in his own way. It is for him to find out what part of recorded experience is properly applicable to his own circumstances and character.[35]

The development of individuality depends upon individuals asking themselves 'what do I prefer? Or what would suit my character and disposition? Or, what would allow the best and highest in me to have fair play, or enable it to grow and thrive?'[36] That is, individuality depends not only upon one's plan of life not being imposed from without, but also upon reflection about the preferences that one has, and also questions of what is valuable.[37]

Individuality can issue in a huge diversity of ways of life, with no particular pattern that someone must follow:

> Human nature is not a machine to be built after a model, and set to do exactly the work prescribed for it, but a tree, which requires to grow and develop itself on all sides, according to the tendency of the inward forces which make it a living thing.[38]

So long as a life is guided by 'inward forces'—by which I take it Mill meant the processes of self-governance and determination described previously—then it will be one lived with individuality: its precise shape determined by the individual themselves. Mill's words here echo Humboldt's insistence that there is 'no pursuit whatever that may not be ennobling and give to human nature some worthy and determinate form',[39] and are echoed in Raz's claim that autonomy can be 'described without commitment to the substance of the valuable forms of life with which it is bound up.'[40] Mill's notion of individuality, so understood, is a vital source of inspiration for the conceptions of autonomy I examine here.

There are two problems with taking Mill himself to have endorsed an ideal of autonomy in the sense that we would recognise it. The first is that in places he seemed to endorse claims about what is valuable for humans that are inconsistent with parts of the theory of individuality sketched above. The second is that it is unclear how far Mill would actually have endorsed individuality as an ideal in its own right.

A significant mark of the influence on his thought by Humboldt is that Mill too, in places, stated that the good of individuality consists in the full development of each individual's talents and capacities. So, for example, Mill said that a theist ought to believe that the divine being 'gave all human faculties that they might be cultivated and unfolded, not rooted out and consumed, and that he takes delight in every nearer approach made by his creatures to the ideal conception embodied in them, every increase in any of their capabilities'.[41] That is, the best life for an individual is the full development of all their talents and capacities.

As I proposed in discussing the identical position held by Humboldt, this suggests that there are two readings of Mill's theory, only one of which supports my identification of the roots of a conception of autonomy in this ideal of individuality. In respect of Mill, however, I can go further than I did previously. Perfectionism about talents sits uneasily with the rest of what Mill said about individuality, for it raises the spectre of a tyranny of capacities: if we seriously believe that individuality consists in the full development by an individual of the talents and capacities that they happen to possess, then we should think that this is valuable regardless of their views on the matter. Someone with a strong latent talent for playing the piano lives a worse life if they do not develop that talent, even if they don't want to play the piano (or even consider playing the piano disvaluable). However, there is no significant difference between such an imperative and the more familiar social conventions that Mill attacked in discussing the ills of an individual's plan of life being determined from without. So, on Mill's own terms there are reasons to jettison the perfectionism about talents inherited from Humboldt. As before, though, it does not matter if this is unconvincing as an account of Mill's own intended theory: even if it is against his intentions, it seems we can find something akin to a conception of autonomy in his writings.

A second problem is that it is unclear why Mill took individuality to be valuable. In places, Mill seemed to regard individuality as something just instrumentally valuable for various reasons. So, for example, he said that individuality is useful as part of our enterprise to find the best way to live:

> As it is useful that while mankind are imperfect there should be different opinions, so it is that there should be different experiments of living; that free scope should be given to varieties of character, short of injury to others; and that the worth of different modes of life should be proved practically, when any one thinks fit to try them.[42]

He also famously said that societies must encourage people of great individuality and genius because it is only by the activities of such people that happiness and progress can be advanced for society as a whole.[43] Such utterances sit uneasily with thinking of individuality or autonomy as an intrinsic good, rather than one justified instrumentally by its beneficial social effects. And certainly Mill never claimed to be providing an ideal which is supposed to be a source of moral claims independent from the wider utilitarian theory within which he placed it. So, is it a bad misinterpretation to suggest that Mill's notion of individuality is one of the roots of a modern conception of autonomy?

I suggest not. Even if Mill's ultimate focus was on utility, it does not follow that he accorded individuality merely instrumental value. Mill explicitly said that his argument relied upon 'utility in the largest sense, grounded in the permanent interests of man as a progressive being',[44] and individuality appears to be not merely a means to such utility. Mill had a richer notion of human happiness than some of his utilitarian forebears. Consider, for example, his statement that

> the free development of individuality is one of the leading essentials of well-being; that it is not only a coordinate element with all that is designated by the terms civilisation, instruction, education, culture, but is itself a necessary part and condition of all those things.[45]

Mill might just have meant here that individuality is a constitutive *means* to utility. That is, utility is only instantiated when individuality also obtains. However, it is also consistent to take individuality to be a constitutive *part* of utility: that is, individuality is itself part of what human action should aim at. We might at least be able to locate a modest ideal of individuality in such ideas, even if—as a matter of interpretation—we think that Mill subsumed its importance under that of utility.

Some commentators have gone further than this and suggested that the ideal of individuality in *On Liberty* had a role in Mill's thinking independent of his utilitarianism. Some of his utilitarian contemporaries took this to be a damning criticism of *On Liberty*, saying that Mill's argument for the liberty principle failed because he used arguments inaccessible to the true utilitarian and concealed a hidden regard for individuality not dependent upon utilitarian justification.[46]

Other modern readers have identified the same commitment, though on the whole not taken this to be a criticism. Moreover, they have taken Mill's notion of individuality to be identical with an ideal of personal autonomy. So, for example, John Gray says that

> Despite the absence in his writings of any explicit use of the jargon of autonomy and authenticity, I think we are on a firm ground if we include an ideal of personal autonomy among Mill's most fundamental commitments.[47]

Others have read Mill in the same way, as providing in his theory of individuality an account of an ideal which can inspire modern conceptions of autonomy.[48]

For our purposes, the question of how Mill himself saw his theory of individuality is moot. One aspect of the enormous influence of *On Liberty* is the extent to which it has inspired people in ways not clearly linked to Mill's original intentions, and it may be that the foregoing discussion of individuality is an example of that phenomenon. Mill painted a picture of individuality which others have subsequently taken to be an ideal of self-governance, and something to strive for. Hence, it stands as a source of inspiration for the conceptions of autonomy considered in the present section, and sits comfortably within the same family as the ideals expressed much later by Raz and his contemporaries.

Many modern writers on autonomy use notions which seem to be be strongly coloured by Humboldt's and Mill's ideals of individuality. To take three examples: Thomas Hurka says that to be autonomous is 'to direct oneself where different directions are possible' and that it is an ideal of 'self-determination'.[49] Steven Wall defends autonomy as 'the ideal of people charting their own course through life', and of them 'making something out of their lives according to their own understanding of what is valuable and worth doing.'[50] Marina Oshana says that autonomy is an ideal that consists in 'having authority over one's choices and actions whenever these are significant to the direction of one's life.'[51]

The ideal of autonomy I endorse and defend in this volume lies within the same family as these writers. These ideals of autonomy better capture something that is of value than the conceptions discussed in Sections 1.1 and 1.2, and they do not suffer from the failings I identified earlier.[52] Another reason for adopting an ideal within this tradition is that it is clearly an ideal with political relevance. Raz, Hurka and Wall all use autonomy as the foundation for a liberal political philosophy committed to its promotion. As we shall see, I diverge from them about what this commitment actually amounts to. However, the conception of autonomy that will be used is, I think, broadly the same.

That having been said, the ideal as stated by the modern writers above is rather indistinct. So, I propose the following way of characterising it:

Autonomy is an ideal of people deciding for themselves what is a valuable life, and living their lives in accordance with that decision.[53]

It may be, of course, that some of the philosophers mentioned so far in this section would not endorse this as an accurate *paraphrasis* of the ideal they endorsed. Nothing important hinges on whether this is the case or not. It suffices to say that *if* someone wanted to avail themselves of the arguments for liberalism I shall present in the chapters that follow, *then* they must understand autonomy in a way not significantly different to the formulation given before.

CONCLUSION

In this chapter, I have given a brief description of the territory within which my value of autonomy sits. I have suggested that conceptions of autonomy tend to fall into one of three families, which are distinguished by giving emphasis to different aspects of an ideal of self-governance. These are: rationalist conceptions of the sort defended by the followers of Kant; hierarchical conceptions based on the Frankfurt-Dworkin model of motivations; and individualistic conceptions which place importance on a notion of self-authorship understood as a development of individuality. I also noted that my own conception lies within the latter family. This discussion has served two purposes. First, it makes clear where some of the inspiration for my own view lies, and allows me to show in what respects I agree with the philosophers I have mentioned. Secondly, it allows us to make clear some of the different things that one might be committed to in talking about autonomy, not all of which are implied by my conception. So, by explaining the differences between autonomy as I conceive it and as it is conceived by others, I reduce the risk of confusion as I lay out my own theory of autonomy-minded liberalism. Before I do *that*, however, I need to say more about what my conception of autonomy amounts to. The next chapter is concerned with that task.

2 A Theory of Autonomy

In the previous chapter I introduced my conception of autonomy as an ideal of people deciding for themselves what defines a valuable life, and living their lives in accordance with that decision. This, I noted, sits within the same family of views as Raz's conception of autonomy and parts of the ideals of individuality defended by Humboldt and Mill.

One feature of this conception of autonomy is that it is global: on my view, it is *lives* which are autonomous. This means that one of my central tasks is to explain what is the relationship between this global ideal and what are the local features of it, for example the particular decisions people make, and the actions they perform. How must those local properties be, for the global property to obtain? This is a difficult question to answer, and the other philosophers who hold a conception of autonomy like mine have done little to try to tease out these connections. So, for example, the only thing that Raz says which is at all germane to the question is to point out that a life can be autonomous to differing degrees, and that an autonomous life is not necessarily one lived in pursuit of one particular project decided on at its start.[1] Wall says a little more, in that he gives some more examples of how autonomous lives may be more or less variegated, but neither writer addresses the particular problem of the connection between local properties and autonomy directly, and says what it is about the particular things that happen in a life that will lead to its possessing this global property.[2]

In this chapter, I answer these questions, as well as saying something about why I formulate the ideal of autonomy in the way that I do, and what it means to be committed to that ideal as something to guide state action. That is, I offer a *theory* of autonomy, to elaborate on and motivate the conception I have introduced.

My discussion here will necessarily be limited. Explaining in detail the consequences for political morality will have to wait until Chapter 4. So, what follows is intended mainly to provide a sketch of what an autonomous life might be. In so doing, I do not intend to give a conclusive argument for the claim that one ought to be committed to the value of autonomy, or the proposition that the state ought to promote it. My argument to that end resides in the next chapter. However, adding colour to the preceding definition will, I hope, serve to show why we might be attracted to autonomy on my conception.

My formulation of the value of autonomy follows Raz's in placing emphasis upon an individual having control of the shape that their life takes. It also makes more explicit two different parts of what it is to have such control. An autonomous life is one in which an agent decides what values guide it, and also which is lived in the pursuit of those values. So, I shall reflect upon each of these aspects, before concluding with a more general discussion of what is distinctive about autonomy as a basis for political action.

2.1 DECIDING WHAT IS VALUABLE

First, an autonomous life is one in which the values which guide it—an agent's views on what it is important to do, and on what makes their life go well—are ones which that agent has decided upon for herself. This is important because the notion of self-governance seems to have no force if we describe autonomy in a way consistent with someone directing themselves in accordance with values adopted due to manipulation, brainwashing or coercion. If self-direction is important for an individual's life at all, then it must be important also in respect of the most general questions for that individual about what is valuable. In this, I follow in the footsteps of the thinkers described in Section 1.3, recalling Wall's claim that autonomy means 'making something out of their lives according to their own understanding of what is valuable and worth doing',[3] and Mill's insistence that individuality does not consist just in the satisfaction of preferences, but also in the pursuit of a plan of life after reflection on our preferences and on what is valuable.[4]

At this point, I wish to correct some potential misapprehensions about what I mean by an agent *deciding* on what is valuable. It may be thought that this involves one or both of two mistakes: an implausible view of the relation between individuals and society, or a false (or at least narrow and unattractive) view of commitment. Each charge would, as made against my position, be a misapprehension, but it is worth explaining why in some detail because it makes plainer what autonomy on my view does and does not involve.

One criticism famously levelled against liberalism by Michael Sandel is that it presupposes an 'unencumbered self': that individuals start with no commitments, and then acquire commitments through voluntary choice throughout their lives.[5] This, Sandel says, is an unwarranted assumption, since it ignores the fact that individuals (by dint of being born into families, societies and cultures) already have deep and serious commitments that are constitutive of our identities and are non-voluntary. Hence, the self is encumbered, and if liberalism presupposes otherwise, it rests on false foundations. A similar criticism is made by Charles Taylor, though he characterises the mistaken presupposition of liberalism as 'atomism': that is, the view that society is nothing more than an aggregation of individuals who are defined without reference to their context and to the roles that they have in their society.[6]

I shall not here discuss in detail the various liberal responses to Sandel's and Taylor's attacks. My response in respect of my own conception of autonomy is a familiar one. Saying that individuals should decide for themselves what is valuable does not presuppose that they must do so from a position of complete detachment. In some cases, deciding what one values *will* be making a new commitment, going from a position of detachment with respect to a particular end to a position of attachment. However, it need not be so: decision might also be a matter of reaffirming values to which one is already committed. The conception of autonomy described here *does* require that people are able (in a very bare sense, as we shall see) to reflect upon and assess the commitments into which they are embedded; but that is not at all the same thing as denying that such commitments exist. Nor is it to claim that we have some sort of perfectly detached perspective from which we can reassess all our commitments. It just requires that they be like the planks of Neurath's ship: any of them might, in principle, be revised, even if (at any given time) we hold many of them beyond question. That does not mean that they can all be removed together, nor that we presuppose that the ship is something abstract and distinct from its planks.[7]

The second possible misapprehension about my position is this: by saying that individuals should decide upon what is valuable, I mistake the nature of human commitment. Commitment to values, it might be argued, is *not* something that we decide upon. Rather, an individual perceives reasons to act in certain ways, and responds in a way entirely determined by the weight of those reasons. Hence, to imply that individuals can choose or determine their commitments is wrong. Either no commitments can be so chosen—in which case my conception of autonomy can never be satisfied—or only certain shallow commitments can be, in which case my conception loses its attractiveness by ignoring the deep and serious commitments that actually shape people's lives.

It may well be that some conceptions of autonomy *do* favour either an ironic or a shallow attitude to serious commitments, and it may well be that such a bias should make us reluctant to think that autonomy, understood in such a way, is valuable. I remain neutral on these questions here, because as it applies to my conception of autonomy, the criticism is mistaken. This is because it involves an unfeasibly narrow understanding of what 'deciding upon one's values' might mean. The word 'decide' as it is used in ordinary English is ambiguous, and the ambiguity reveals a much larger range of attitudes one might take towards one's commitments than the picking-and-choosing which is the subject of the preceding criticism.

So, for example, we can talk about someone 'deciding' when they make an epistemic judgment, or come to believe something or do something in response to the weight of reasons that they face. We might say 'he decided that the earth goes round the sun', or 'he decided that the left-hand path was the best way to go home'. 'Deciding', in the sense used here, is different from 'deciding' as it appears in sentences such as 'he decided to drink the orange juice' or 'he decided to play the cello'. The phenomenology of the situations is entirely different: there seems (to the agent deciding) to be an act of the will in the latter case, but not the former. Nevertheless, both can sensibly be thought of as species of decision, especially when it is made clear that by describing an epistemic judgment as a decision, I do not commit myself to saying that we are able to decide what to believe. (In ordinary usage, if I say that I *decide that* X, it does not imply that I *decide to believe that* X.)

There may well be yet more senses that we could distinguish, but it should now be clear why the criticism of my concept of autonomy fails. By saying that autonomy involves deciding what is valuable, I do *not* commit myself to understanding the term 'decision' to consist only in the selection of an option. Hence, I do not limit my conception of what is valuable in life to just those things that can be selected in this manner.

Indeed, the reason that I do not presuppose any particular way in which the term 'decide' might be used is that the ambiguity seems rather appropriate. The fact that the term 'decision' has these multiple meanings captures something important about the ideal of autonomy that I describe. Consider, for example, the two senses distinguished previously (that is, decision as selection and decision as responding to the weight of reasons). Some individuals will choose to pursue some project and thereby make its fulfilment valuable: someone could *decide to* become a great concert pianist, and another might *decide to* spend her life travelling the world. By contrast, some will reflect on questions of value, and come to the conclusion that they ought to spend their life doing certain things, for reasons nothing to do with any choice of theirs. So, someone might *decide that* she ought to pursue the cure for cancer, and another might *decide that* he should enter a monastery. The conception of autonomy defined previously aims to be broad enough to encompass such disparate usages.

This shows why my conception of autonomy of autonomy is *not* vulnerable to the charge that it does not take commitment seriously. The linguistic point about the breadth of the word 'decide' reflects something of deeper importance: we want to allow not only that different people consider different things valuable, but that people think about value in different ways. So, using the word 'decide', with its rich ambiguity, allows us to capture the thought that people might live autonomous lives in many different ways, including with deep and serious commitments, though of course not all cases which might be called 'decision' will count as autonomy-generating.

This illustrates what I mean when I say that an autonomous life is one in which an individual decides for herself what is valuable. However, the notion of 'decision' is still rather vague. Hence, I suggest the following way of making it clearer. A life is more or less autonomous depending upon the extent to which the agent in question throughout her adult life decides for herself what is valuable, and at any particular time she decides for herself what is valuable to the extent that the following two conditions hold:

> **Endorsement.** She has a disposition such that if she reflects (or were to reflect) upon what putative values she ought to pursue in her life, she judges (or would judge) of some such things that they are valuable.
> **Independence.** She is in a state where her reflection is, or would be if it took place, free from factors undermining her independence.[8]

These conditions capture in more precise terms just what I mean when I talk about 'decision', and this in turn allows us to say what is required for autonomy (which is, recall, a global property). A life is autonomous to the extent that an agent, over the course of her whole life, satisfies these conditions (both of which admit of degrees). The more time that she satisfies them, and the greater the extent to which she satisfies them, the more that she decides on her values for herself; and, so long as her life is lived on the basis of the decisions that she makes, the more autonomous her life is as a whole. So, the global property of autonomy depends upon the local properties of the commitments she has, and upon her success in pursuing of those commitments.

Only some commitments need satisfy both conditions. Some commitments are derivative, in the sense that the only reason we have them is because they are implied by some other, prior, commitment. So, for example, I might come (derivatively) to think that swimming is valuable because I believe that good health is important and that swimming is a good way of being healthy. Non-derivative commitments are *not* dependent in this way, though that need not make them especially fundamental or important.

It is only *non-derivative* commitments that need to satisfy both the Endorsement and Independence Conditions. Derivative commitments must satisfy the Endorsement Condition—that is, it must be the case that we judge them to be valuable in the light of our non-derivative commitments, or would do if we were to reflect upon them. However, they need not satisfy the Independence Condition: so long as the commitments from which they derive are ones that we make independently, lack of independence need not be a problem (though it may still be). I discuss this point in greater depth in the following section, and will also discuss the two conditions in more detail.

2.1.1 THE ENDORSEMENT CONDITION

The first condition is that of endorsement. Because this condition requires the presence only of a disposition, an agent can satisfy it without necessarily going through the process of consciously reflecting upon her values: it may just be that *were* she so to reflect, in her present circumstances, she would come to the judgments described. Hence, in respect of the Endorsement Condition, the causal history of our commitments is less important to my notion of autonomy than it is to some of the others I considered earlier. One's commitments having gone through a process of reflection might give us more confidence that they satisfy the condition, but it is certainly not necessary.

This is important because it preserves the breadth of the ideal of autonomy. It avoids a bias towards the autonomous life being reflective, rather than active. *If* being autonomous required constant conscious deliberation, then—given the limited mental resources an agent has, and the limited time in which to do things—that deliberation will tend to crowd out action. Requiring only the disposition to endorse one's values, rather than actual conscious endorsement, allows that one might spend most of the time not consciously reassessing and reflecting upon one's values without this being *ipso facto* an indication of a lack of autonomy. That is, it allows the autonomous life to be active, or at least does not require that it be strenuously contemplative.

More generally, saying that it is a *disposition* that we care about is a way of making concrete the notion that the Endorsement Condition can be satisfied either explicitly or implicitly. One might not have consciously reflected upon whether one really takes a given thing to be valuable to be autonomous in its pursuit: instead, one's behaviour might indicate a tacit endorsement of that value. So, consider someone who is a talented geneticist and pianist, and who eventually chooses to pursue the cure for cancer rather than the world of concert performance. It may well be that she never consciously weighs up two different putative values—'curing cancer' and 'producing great music'—and makes an explicit judgment about which one she believes she should pursue. Nevertheless, we might think that her pursuing the cure for cancer is an implicit endorsement of curing cancer as a valuable pursuit: she was aware of what alternatives she had, and might have explained, if we asked her to, why she took that course rather than pursuing the musical life instead. Phrasing the Endorsement Condition in terms of dispositions allows us to say that an implicit endorsement like this also counts as deciding for oneself what is valuable.

2.1.2 THE INDEPENDENCE CONDITION

The second condition needed for an agent to count as deciding for herself what is valuable is that of independence. By this, I mean that she is in a position such that her reflection is, if it takes place, or would be, if it were to take place, free from factors which undermine the extent to which we can say that she is deciding *for herself*.

Note that the Independence Condition, unlike the Endorsement Condition, is *not* satisfied by counterfactuals. To repeat, we only need to have a disposition to judge that something is valuable in order to satisfy the Endorsement Condition. Hence, we need not *actually* reflect in order to satisfy the Independence Condition. However, the conditions under which one has the *disposition* to endorse a given value must preserve our independence. This means that our autonomy is undermined in respect of a particular commitment *whenever* the independence of that commitment is vitiated, and even if I would come to that commitment had the vitiation not occurred. For example, if I take something to be valuable as a result of non-voluntary hypnosis, my independence has been violated, regardless of whether I would have come to take it to be valuable without that hypnosis; and pursuing my commitment will not contribute to my autonomy.[9]

Taking independence to be central to autonomy in this way echoes the work of Gerald Dworkin. Dworkin insists on the importance of procedural independence, as he puts it, but notes just how difficult it is to give a general account of it. He does, however, give a succinct explanation of what sort of account is needed:

> Spelling out the condition of procedural independence involves distinguishing those ways of influencing people's reflective and critical faculties which subvert them from those which promote and improve them. It involves distinguish those influences such as hypnotic suggestion, manipulative coercive persuasion, subliminal influence, and so forth, and doing so in a non ad hoc fashion.[10]

As Dworkin notes, independence in the relevant sense does not mean the absence of *any* influences on our decisions about what is valuable. Taking it to be so would bring my conception perilously close to the unattractive and atomistic positions attacked by Sandel and Taylor. Rather, when we say that someone's judgment is (or would be) independent, we mean that they are free of a *certain sort* of influence. Dworkin fails to give any general account of what this sort of influence is, beyond mentioning the intuitive instances listed before. In the remainder of this section, I try to make some progress towards such a general account, by considering various sufficient conditions for the failure of independence, and reflecting on what is shared between these different threats.

Many such threats (but not all of them) share the feature that they influence the way an individual views their choices (or the range of commitments they might have) by some mechanism of which that agent cannot be fully aware. One way in which this works is by making an individual's reflections concerning a given value or commitment less content-sensitive. That is, the Independence Condition is undermined by circumstances that make the judgment that something is valuable depend on something other than the nature of that thing. Suppose, for example, that someone comes to value what they do as the result of manipulation or brainwashing. We can then explain her decision just by referring to the techniques that have been applied to her, and the actual content of the commitments she arrives at is irrelevant to the explanation. In such cases, the independence of her decision is undermined.

It might be objected that there are cases when content-insensitivity does *not* undermine the Independence Condition, because it is possible to live an autonomous life which involves some—or, indeed, many—of one's commitments being made for content-insensitive reasons. Consider, for example, someone in a relationship who cultivates an appreciation of cricket, because his partner loves the game and he wants them to share as much of their lives as possible.[11] His commitment to cricket is content-insensitive: if his partner preferred football, or lacrosse, or basketball, his commitment would simply follow suit. However, it does seem as though such a process is at least compatible with such commitments contributing to one's autonomy. If my account of independence implies otherwise, then it seems defective.

In reply, I return to a point I made before, which is that some of our commitments are derivative: we hold those commitments because of some other, prior commitment. The explanation for our derivative commitment might be different in different cases—it may be based on a means-end relationship, for example, or our derivative commitment may be to a constitutive part of a good to which we are otherwise committed. In the case previously described, the commitment to cricket is just such a derivative commitment: it derives from his prior commitment to a valuable relationship. As long as that prior commitment is independent, then the content-insensitivity of the derivative commitment is not a problem for his autonomy. So, there is no problem with the cricket-loving partner. So long as his non-derivative commitment to sharing his partner's life is content-sensitive, it does not matter that other commitments dependent upon that commitment are content-insensitive.

The case of the cricket-loving lover is, of course, a relatively mild one. Depending on the individual concerned, it may be that the vast majority of their commitments are content-insensitive. Consider, for example, someone who decides, in a perfectly content-sensitive way, that it is valuable to be a monk. That commitment necessitates most of one's daily activities being determined by dependent commitments: such a person is committed to praying at *this* and *this* and *this* time, and so on. Those dependent commitments may well be content-insensitive, but so long as the general commitment to the monastic life is content-sensitive, such a life can be autonomous.

Cases such as the cricket-loving lover and the monk demonstrate that failing the Independence Condition is not necessarily problematic, so long as the reason that a commitment is content-insensitive is that it is derivative.

I have discussed content-insensitivity as one thing that is sufficient to violate the Independence Condition. That condition can also be violated in another way. Put roughly, independence is also undermined when an agent is in a situation where she endorses (or would endorse) her values for reasons that she herself cannot perceive.

More precisely, consider the contrast between first- and third-person viewpoints on the decisions an individual makes: that is, between the reasons an individual gives for the commitments she has, and the reasons someone would adduce if trying to explain her commitments. Usually, the former will feature in the latter. If someone asks me why I am committed to playing a musical instrument, I might say something like 'Because I chose to devote myself to learning the harp several years ago, and it is important to me to fulfil that ambition', or 'Because playing the harp well is valuable.' In most cases, someone trying to give a third-person explanation of my commitment will echo these answers: 'It is because he wants to fulfil his ambition to succeed in his chosen hobby', or 'It is because he believes that playing the harp well is valuable'. And that is as it should be: when thinking about why someone has the commitments they do, their own perspective on what is valuable and their motivations have some sort of authority.

There are cases, though, in which the first-person explanation features in none of the third-person explanations. In such cases, the third-person explanatory reason for a commitment is opaque from a first-person point of view: more colloquially, we worry that the motivational reason that an individual adduces for their commitment, however sincerely, is not the 'real' reason.[12] Situations which tend to make an individual's reasons for a commitment opaque to themselves are also ones which undermine the Independence Condition, in a way problematic for autonomy even when those commitments are derivative.

The most prominent examples of such cases are ones in which agent's decisions about what is valuable are based on 'sour grapes' reasoning. This phenomenon has been studied closely in respect to preferences, where Jon Elster has analysed various different ways in which the formation or modification of an agent's preferences might rightly be thought unsatisfactory due to an element of adaptation to circumstances.[13] In particular, adaptive preferences are those formed in response to the unavailability of certain options.

One of Elster's concerns about such cases is that they pose a problem for an agent's autonomy, because they involve a distortion of one's preferences by 'irrelevant causal processes.'[14] This reveals why adaptation—as a process analogous to the one that Elster describes but which might influence the development of value commitments—poses a problem for autonomy on my view, too. Suppose that an agent comes to value the things that she does through adaptation of the sort described by Elster. The mechanism by which she does this is one of which she is not aware, because the way things seem to her is determined by the availability of options in a manner that is opaque to her. To the extent that her judgments are adaptive, they are determined by what options she does not have, rather than by the nature of the possible options themselves. She lacks independence in respect of how she comes to see things the way she does. Hence, factors that prompt adaptation also violate the Independence Condition.[15]

Finally, there is a third source of danger to the Independence Condition, exemplified by coercion. In some ways, coercion is a paradigmatic threat to autonomy. However, it threatens it in various different ways. Drawing out what is distinctive about coercion requires examining them separately.

First, repeated coercion can be part of a causal process that leads an agent to take certain options to be disvaluable. This might work as a process of adaptation. If a child is repeatedly divested by bullies of her lunch money, she might over time come to regard as disvaluable those things which that money might allow her to do (to eat lunch, for example). Or, it might be a technique of conditioning. When it features in such processes, coercion clearly undermines autonomy, because it vitiates the Independence Condition, for the reasons given before in my discussion of conditioning more generally.

Secondly, particular instances of coercion can threaten autonomy in a way that does *not* undermine the Independence Condition. Suppose that I get mugged, and hand over my wallet. My motivations here are not opaque to me—I want to avoid getting stabbed—and my judgment is not content-insensitive, since my decision to surrender my wallet is the result of my being very sensitive to a new feature of the content of one of my options (namely that holding onto my money now involves a severe risk of injury). The problem is rather that being mugged makes it more difficult for me to live a life in which I pursue what I decide is valuable. I discuss this aspect of coercion—which it shares with various other situations we might find ourselves in—at greater length in Chapter 4.

Coercion also threatens autonomy in a third way, which is distinct from those considered so far, and *does* undermine independence. Coercion necessarily involves the subjection of one's will to that of someone else, in a relation of dominance: the explanation for one's action or choice is rooted in the will of the coercer, rather than oneself.[16] As Hayek says,

> Coercion . . . eliminates an individual as a thinking and valuing person and makes him a bare tool in the achievement of the ends of another.[17]

In most circumstances, the aim of the coercion will be an act, rather than a judgment about what is valuable. As I have noted, a mugger is not trying to alter my judgments, but rather to use them to make me give him my wallet. However, the relation of domination involved in coercion is itself something that undermines autonomy: judgments that we come to under such conditions are not independent, because the explanation of our judgments can be explained just by reference to the will of the person coercing us.[18] This relation of domination is clearly akin to conditioning and adaptation in the sense that the agent's will is being bypassed; hence, I suggest that it too is sufficient to undermine the Independence Condition.

So far, I have considered three things that are sufficient for our commitments to fail the Independence Condition. What is shared by all these things is that, albeit in different ways, an agent's will is bypassed in respect of her judgments about what is valuable. There is something peculiarly problematic about cases in which another agent dominates an individual's decisions about what is valuable, as is the case with coercion, and about situations in which an individual *in principle* could not be fully aware of the mechanism by which their commitments are formed, either because there is a psychological barrier to her being so (as there is in the case of conditioning) or because her commitments are formed in a way which requires her being unaware of the real reason (as there is in adaptation). It is those circumstances which tend to remove an individual's commitments from her own control, and hence violate the ideal of self-governance which lies at the root of conceptions of autonomy.

There may be other situations which are not easily conceived of as belonging to the categories I have described, but which also have the same effect: my list is not supposed to be exhaustive. If there are any such situations, they too will count as undermining the Independence Condition. So, if such factors as these do *not* obtain, then the Independence Condition seems to be met: and an agent decides for herself what is valuable if she satisfies the Endorsement Condition stated before.

This discussion is, perhaps, a little too abstract to give a fully fleshed-out idea of what the ideal of autonomy involves. In Section 2.3, I consider a number of imaginary lives, and discuss the extent to which they embody the value of autonomy. In so doing, I hope to make it clearer what are the different ways in which one might be said to have decided for oneself what is valuable.

2.2 LIVING AN AUTONOMOUS LIFE

So far, I have concentrated on what it means for people to decide for themselves what is considered to be a valuable life. The second aspect of autonomy on my conception is that an autonomous life must be active, in the following sense: autonomy does not just consist in deciding what is valuable, but also in pursuing those decisions. One must be able to make one's decision effective (though, in the case of easy satisfied or sedentary goals, living in accordance with what one things valuable *may* require little in the way of activity). So, how autonomous we are depends not just on satisfying the Endorsement and Independence Conditions. It also requires that our lives go in the way that we decide is valuable.

To repeat: autonomy is a global condition, which depends upon the extent to which we successfully pursue those things that we ourselves decide are valuable. Again, the rationale for this can be demonstrated by what it excludes. Someone living in a prison cell, or possessed by an uncontrollable phobia, might perfectly well be able to decide for themselves what they value but be unable to put that decision into effect. My formulation of the value of autonomy deliberately excludes such lives.

So, our lives going in accordance with values that we decide upon is necessary for them to be autonomous. It is not, however, sufficient. A life must also be *self-directed*. I take that to mean two things: first, the reason that my life goes that way must be that I made it so, and also I must bear the consequences of the way I choose to live it.

These rather vague conditions can be more precisely captured in terms of *responsibility* for our lives. In particular, we must be responsible in two senses, distinguished by Thomas Scanlon. First, our lives must be *attributable* to us: it must be recognisably our choices and actions that make our lives the way they are. And secondly, we must be *substantively responsible* for the way our lives go. That is, part of being the author of a life is being liable for the consequences of the things that are attributable to us.[19]

Precisely what this requires a difficult question, and I cannot here devote much time or space to the different accounts that have been given of responsibility. Matters are simplified somewhat by the fact that substantive responsibility implies attributability, so that we can focus our concern on providing the conditions necessary for the former. So, throughout the rest of this book, when I talk about 'responsibility', I will mean 'substantive responsibility'. And, concerning *that*, I shall just for the moment suggest the following as a necessary condition: at the very least, our choices must be voluntary if we are to be responsible for them. I derive this suggestion from the work of Serena Olsaretti, who gives the following definition of voluntariness: an action is voluntary if not non-voluntary, and it is non-voluntary if it is chosen because there are no acceptable alternatives.[20] Precisely what counts as an acceptable choice might, in practice, be filled in by various different theories. In Section 4.1.3 I suggest what should be our position on the matter, but neither my argument here nor my proposal there depends crucially on any particular understanding, so long as one has *some* explanation or other of what counts as acceptable.

Olsaretti suggests that voluntary choice is only necessary, and not sufficient for responsibility.[21] So, there may be other things that are needed if we are to be responsible for how our lives go. I defer my discussion of other conditions for responsibility until Section 4.4, since they do not become visible until we consider the distinctively political question of how to distribute autonomy-promoting effort between different people. So, for the moment, let us just say this: an autonomous life is one which is lived in accordance with values than agent decides upon (in the sense elucidated in the previous section), and where the agent is responsible for their life going in accordance with those values.

2.3 EXAMPLES

Defining autonomy as I do means I cannot give a full description of what an autonomous life must look like, because that will depend upon the individual concerned: so long as we can say that the individual lives the life they do having decided what is valuable, the content of the life is irrelevant to the question of whether they are autonomous or not. In this, I take myself to be following once more in the footsteps of the thinkers discussed in Section 1.3. As I have noted, Humboldt insisted that there is 'no pursuit whatever that many not be ennobling and give to human nature some worthy and determinate form',[22] and Raz says that autonomy can (and must) be 'described without commitment to the substance of the valuable forms of life with which it is bound up.'[23] By way of illustration, I here present a miscellaneous collection of imaginary biographies, to show some of the different ways in which people might succeed, or fail, in living autonomous lives.

Amanda

Amanda was brought up in frequent contact with many different adults, who disagreed amongst themselves about how to live a valuable life. Consequently, as she grew older she was aware that there is such disagreement, and worried about how her life ought to go. She had various talents—musical, and apt at sciences—but had no clear vocation, nor strong beliefs about what she ought to do with her life. She drifted into a moderately good university course and got a moderately good mark, and then tried to decide on a job. Reflecting on what she enjoyed, she thought that perhaps she would try to make a career out of a hobby (cartography) and applied to work with the Ordnance Survey. She has subsequently had a long and successful career making maps of the United Kingdom. Occasionally she wonders whether she would have done better doing something else—developing her talent for the violin, perhaps, or trying to retrain as a physicist to help ease the shortage of science teachers—but she always concludes that being a mapmaker has been enjoyable and is useful to other people.

Amanda was not driven to decide as she did by any overriding vision of what is valuable, but she did nevertheless reflect on what she ought do with her life, and acted in light of that reflection. By deciding to pursue cartography as a career, she made the successful production of maps valuable to her, and in that sense decided upon what was valuable. Moreover, she has remained open to reappraisal of her decisions. She does not very frequently worry about whether she is doing the right thing, but the thought does occur to her, and each time she reaffirms her original judgment. That she does so is not, I must emphasise, a necessary condition for her being autonomous. However, it *does* give us reason to think that, even when she is concentrating on her work and thus not being especially reflective, she has the disposition to judge that cartography is something valuable that she wants to spend her life pursuing. Her life has also been active in the pursuit of that value, in the sense that she has made effective her judgment of what would be a valuable life. She had the educational opportunities needed to be able to go into the profession, and has been successful in that profession. So, on my theory, Amanda lives a reasonably autonomous life.

Brian

Brian was raised by a Roman Catholic and an atheist, neither of whom imparted any particular religious beliefs to him. As it happened, though, he was always interested in religion as a child, and as he grew up and discussed such matters with his peers and teachers he came more and more strongly to believe the tenets of the Catholic Church. As an adult, Brian tried hard to live a life of charity and piety, in accordance with his best understanding of religious doctrine, and on several occasions seriously considered entering a monastery, wondering whether that is the best way to live a valuable Catholic life. As it is, he teaches at a university, and frequently argues with less religious colleagues about matters ethical and metaphysical. He takes seriously their worries about his faith, and shares many of the concerns they express about the church as an institution, but through all his serious self-questioning, he finds that his core beliefs about the right way to life his life remain constant.

To Brian, it does not seem that he chooses his values: he merely became more and more aware of what was demanded of him by his religious beliefs. He came to that realisation by himself: while his religious vision was shaped by discussions with parents, teachers and peers, none of those people enforced on him the views that he has come to endorse. His faith seems firm and unshakeable to him, but he does reflect on it quite frequently in response to questioning from his friends and colleagues. Contemplation of fallacies that have previously been endorsed for religious reasons persuades him that he *might* be in error, much as he does not believe that he is. He lives his life actively in pursuit of his religious values, and wonders about how best to make his life embody the ideal he endorses. For these reasons, on my theory, Brian lives an autonomous life.

Caradoc

Caradoc had an upbringing much like Brian's; surrounded by people with a range of views on what is valuable in life, he came to believe in a particular set of religious doctrines, and attempts to live his life in accordance with those doctrines. Unlike Brian, Caradoc decided to move to a deeply religious town, and pursue a career in which he would not be forced often to reassess his commitments; and so he has continued living his life in pursuit of what he considers valuable, without at any point reflecting on what he is doing.[24]

Caradoc's life illustrates what it means for the Endorsement Condition to require just a disposition. Let us stipulate that as a matter of fact Caradoc has the disposition such that, if he were to reflect on his values, he would still endorse them, and that he is not in circumstances which vitiate the Independence Condition (so, for example, his commitments do not derive from adaptation to the community in which he lives). This means that he is just as autonomous as Brian, on my concept of autonomy. This might worry people. Dispositions are to a great extent hidden from outside view, especially when (as in the present case) they are never as a matter of fact exercised. So, it might be objected that my theory makes Caradoc's autonomy opaque to us. In reality, if we were to look at a life like Caradoc's, we would not know how autonomous it is. The most we would be able to say is that it is *possible* that Caradoc's life is autonomous, not that it actually *is* autonomous. In Section 2.4 I argue that this does not matter, given the political nature of the project we are engaged in.

Denise

Denise was brought up in much the same way as Amanda: there was no strong religious influence on her as a child, and she grew up without any strong beliefs that she was obliged to live her life one way rather than another. So, she decided to pursue a life that interested her—one in which she combined a family life with a reasonably successful career as a local journalist. However, at a certain point in her adult life she came to believe that all she had thought previously was wrong. As a result of contemplating looming middle age, and the death of people dear to her, she had a religious conversion to a particular faith, and consequently felt the way she had been living her life had been thoroughly lacking value. Her conversion was painful and awkward, but she succeeded in changing course: by engaging in a religious community, and pursuing different projects and goals. Currently she is able to pursue what she thinks to be a valuable life. As it happens, she never now thinks about whether her new life is valuable. That is, like Caradoc, she never exercises the disposition required by the Endorsement Condition. Nevertheless, she does have that disposition. Were we to ask her, she would tell us that her new life certainly is valuable.

Denise's life also embodies the ideal of autonomy. Before her conversion, her life was much like Amanda's: she decided to pursue various projects in tandem, and successfully lived her life in pursuit of those projects. Her conversion posed a potential problem for her autonomy. The particular things she had been doing previously, and which had contributed to her autonomy (given her previous commitments) would no longer be appropriate. If after her conversion she had continued with her journalistic career (perhaps for fear of not being able to feed her children) despite sincerely believing that to be valueless, her autonomy would have been impaired. As it is, however, she has been able to alter her way of life in accordance with the alteration in values. Her present way of life contributes to her autonomy as much as her previous way of life did, for she still possesses the disposition to endorse her way of life, though she tends not now to exercise that disposition.

Denise's case illustrates two important points about autonomy. First, it shows that autonomy does not consist in a life having unity, in the sense that an entire life lived in pursuit of a single set of values might have unity. An agent can live an autonomous life that involves great changes in commitments and judgments on what is valuable. Whether an individual's life is autonomous or not depends upon the relationship between how their life goes and what they, at particular times, take to be valuable. It is just that if their commitments change, then so must their activities, if they are successfully to pursue the things that they now take to be important.

Secondly, and for precisely this reason, ascriptions of autonomy over a life diverge from how an agent feels, at a particular time, about how her life is going. Since her conversion, Denise retrospectively believes that her years as a journalist were at best wasted: she now believes that the things she did then were disvaluable. Conversely, if we were to show the younger Denise a vision of her future self, and to explain to her that she would come to have strong religious beliefs and to live in a devoutly religious community, she would probably be aghast, and consider that she would be making a terrible mistake later in life. At each point in her life Denise judges that half of her life has gone (or will go) very badly. In terms of autonomy, however, the crucial thing is whether at a given time Denise successfully pursues those things that, at that time, she decides are valuable: and this she has always done.[25]

Edmund

Edmund's life has been close in many respects to Denise's. Like her, he spent the earlier part of his life without any strong religious convictions, but underwent a conversion, and subsequently lives in a way dictated strictly by the tenets of his new religion. The difference lies in the way that the conversion took place. At a fragile moment in his life, Edmund joined what seemed like a useful support group, but which turned out to be a religious cult: his conversion came about as the result of brainwashing techniques applied to him by leaders of that cult, whereby his allegiance to the values of the cult was secured by severe psychological pressure.

Up to his conversion, the way Edmund lived contributed to his autonomy, but his conversion is problematic. He came to have the commitments he now has due to conditioning and manipulation practised by the leaders of the cult, and, as previously discussed, these are things that violate the Independence Condition. Hence, Edmund's commitments and behaviour now detract from, rather than contributing to, the autonomy of his life as a whole. Of course, there is a separate question of what the autonomy-minded state ought to do in light of this: I address *that* question later.

Fatima

Fatima lives an unfortunate life: at an early point she was thrown into a prison cell, and has languished there ever since. She lives listlessly from day to day, and never contemplates what might constitute a valuable life. Nor does she have the disposition such that, if she were to reflect, she would come to endorse anything.

Fatima's life is plainly not autonomous, on my statement of the ideal: she neither decides for herself what is valuable, nor does she live her life in accordance with any such decision. The interest of Fatima's case derives from considering a possible variation on her story. Suppose that, instead of living listlessly, Fatima *does* think about what might be a valuable life, and comes—in a manner that satisfies the Independence Condition—to think valuable a way of life that cannot be lived from within a prison cell: she thinks that mountain climbing is valuable, or acting as a missionary, or being a politician. On my theory of autonomy, Fatima's life is made no more autonomous by her coming to those judgments, for she is unable to live her life in accordance with those decisions.

Geraldine

Geraldine was brought up as a devout adherent of a culture that requires a strict and repressive upbringing, with as little exposure to other ways of life as possible. Her parents and teachers took care that Geraldine never felt as though she was able to decide for herself how her life ought to go. As an adult Geraldine is fully committed to the way of life that she lives: both to the practices it requires of her now, and the personal history that it involved. Having been brought up in the 'right way' is a central part of what makes her life valuable in her eyes. As a young adult, Geraldine is aware that other people disagree with her. We might also imagine that she possesses the disposition such that if she reflects on her life, she continues to believe, despite recognising the genesis of her commitments, that she is right, and she lives her life as best she can in keeping with those convictions.

Geraldine's life, on my view, can perfectly well be autonomous, for the same reasons as Caradoc's: she possesses the disposition to endorse her values if she reflects upon them, and she does so in a situation which ensures her independence. Her commitments have a causal history that usually vitiates autonomy, but that is compatible nevertheless with us being able to say later on that she satisfies the conditions needed for us to say that she has decided upon her values for herself.

The preceding sketches are not supposed to be an exhaustive catalogue of the ways in which people's lives might or might not be autonomous. However, they do serve to illustrate the ideal of autonomy I have developed in this section, by showing something of the variety of particular forms of life that it allows, and by making plain some of the places where endorsing the ideal might clash with our intuitions.

2.4 AUTONOMY IN POLITICAL PHILOSOPHY

Thus far, I have considered autonomy mostly as it applies to individual lives. In the rest of this book my concern is with autonomy in the context of political philosophy. My central contention will be that the liberal state should be autonomy-minded: it should aim to promote and protect the autonomy of its citizens. Considering the value of autonomy in *this* role, rather than simply as a moral standard to assess people's lives, brings different aspects of the value into prominence, and different problems. So, before I conclude this chapter, I shall say something about some distinctively political aspects of my ideal of autonomy.

First, if our primary focus is on autonomy as an aim of state action, some of the problems noted before disappear, or become less intractable. For example, in discussing Caradoc's life, I pointed out that we might have great difficulty in deciding whether someone actually lives an autonomous life. That question depends partially on whether or not they have a disposition, on reflection, to judge that the things they are pursuing are indeed valuable. Whether or not someone has a disposition can be a very difficult question in circumstances where it is not overtly exercised. I suggest that this ought not to trouble us, for it makes a false assumption about what political philosophy needs to provide. We do not need a practical set of criteria for working out how autonomous people's lives actually are. Rather, we seek a way of designing our political morality and institutions in the best way we can, from the point of view of wanting people to be as autonomous as possible. So, our question is not 'How do we know when X has the disposition to endorse her values?', but rather 'How do we design our institutions so as to best ensure that X (and each of her co-citizens) has that disposition?'. A practically useful answer to the former question is not needed to give a successful answer to the latter.

Secondly, some new problems emerge once our focus shifts to the political sphere. Recall, for example, Edmund, who joins a cult and comes to have the commitments he does through brainwashing. What do we *do* about someone who wishes to live their life a particular way, but has the wishes they do as the result of a vitiation of their independence at some earlier point, by coercion or manipulation by others? One possibility is that we might remove him from the cult and attempt to make him reassess his values, under conditions that do not violate his independence. Another is that we take Edmund's claims at face value: we might be suspicious of the reasons for his making the claims about the good life that he does, but refuse to second-guess his motivations.

I suggest that the autonomy-minded state would take the latter course. The epistemic problems mentioned in respect of Caradoc—that is, the difficulty of knowing why someone holds the values that they do, and whether they hold the disposition to endorse those values as required by the Endorsement Condition—apply here too. In practice, it will be hard for someone to know whether Edmund's express convictions are such that his autonomy is impaired. Given that uncertainty, we should err on the side of inaction: it is better (mistakenly) to take Edmund's express convictions at face value than (mistakenly) to override them. This does not mean that autonomy-minded liberalism is forced into inaction in respect of situations like Edmund's. Recognising the value of autonomy demands that we do the best we can to avoid such circumstances arising. In Chapter 4, I discuss what policies we might put in place to do this.

A third distinctively political aspect is that asking whether autonomy should be promoted by a political system might reveal features of my conception of autonomy not apparent if we consider it only in the context of assessing individual lives. Taking that value to inform the whole political system might reveal unpalatable consequences. If either of these were to be the case, it would suggest that the project of promoting autonomy is either undesirable, or impossible.

One popular argument along these lines runs as follows:[26] State promotion of autonomy requires (so the argument goes) that we make people value autonomy, and organise society to this end. This will make it more difficult for people to live their lives if they don't value autonomy: it will impose costs on them, or might even make certain goals impossible if their pursuit is incompatible with valuing autonomy. A liberal theory ought not to do this, however: it ought to accommodate those ways of life which do not involve valuing autonomy. Hence, autonomy-minded liberalism must be a bad liberal political theory.[27]

This is unsound as an argument against autonomy-minded liberalism based on the value of autonomy I have described. One feature of my formulation of autonomy that bears emphasis is the fact that an individual does not need to value autonomy in order to live an autonomous life: she can be perfectly autonomous without ever having that as a conscious aim. Indeed, she can be autonomous without ever entertaining the question of whether she is autonomous or not.[28] So long as she decides for herself what is valuable, and lives her life in accordance with that decision, her life is autonomous whether or not she herself takes autonomy to be valuable.

So, the argument previously described fails: since valuing autonomy is not necessary for an autonomous life, the autonomy-minded state is not obligated to make people value autonomy, or to make life difficult for those who do not. Indeed, we might worry that on my definition there would be something empty about an agent deciding to devote themselves to a life of autonomy and nothing else: what would it be to live one's life pursuing the value of deciding for oneself what is valuable, without having any particular value that one decides upon? This is not to say that autonomy-minded liberalism is entirely tolerant, but it is more ecumenical than the initial objection suggests. Someone need not value autonomy to live an autonomous life, on my view.

At this point, however, it might sound suspiciously as though I am claiming that the commitment to autonomy has no serious costs: the tenor of the previous discussion might be to suggest that an autonomy-minded liberal need not take a negative attitude to any ways of life, and the only commitment that a liberal state has is to enabling people to live the lives they wish to lead (though this commitment is in no sense minimal or trivial in terms of state action and resources, as we will see in Chapter 4). Plainly, this is not true. Autonomy does require that individual decide what is valuable in life. Hence, the autonomy-minded state must also try to ensure that people can make those decisions. Amongst other things, this entails that the state must put in place a compulsory system of education designed to promote autonomy. Such a system need not instill a belief that autonomy is valuable, for the reasons explained previously. However, it does seem to require some other definite measures, such as making children aware of a variety of possible ways of life, and offering them the conceptual wherewithal to choose between them.[29]

If the critic seeks a painful limit to the neutrality allowed by autonomy-minded liberalism, this is where they must look. The autonomy-minded liberal is committed to saying that there are certain ways of life that are beyond the pale, because they cannot survive the education process that autonomy-minded liberalism requires. The critic can then point out that, this notwithstanding, some people consider ways of life like these valuable. Recall Geraldine, who was brought up in a strict and repressive way, designed by her parents and teachers to foreclose the possibility that she might live any way of life other than the one that in fact she comes to live. As an adult, Geraldine is fully committed to that way of life—and, recall, I noted that if she both possesses the disposition to endorse her values when she reflects and *now* satisfies the Independence Condition, then the life she lives in accordance with her commitment is autonomous, despite the fact that her being so is tremendously unlikely given the history of her commitments. For these reasons, the autonomy-minded liberal will tend to endorse non-interference. Respecting Geraldine's autonomy means both preventing her from being unfairly penalised for living her life in the way she sees fit, and also refraining from attempts to impose on her a different lifestyle.

However, remember also that a central part of what Geraldine values is having been brought up in the right way, as she sees it. A particular personal history is central to her view of a valuable life: her life would not be as valuable to her as it is if she hadn't been brought up in the strict and autonomy-threatening way that she was. This presents us with a difficulty: for while autonomy-minded liberalism does not say that we should prevent Geraldine from living the life she considers valuable—quite the opposite, in fact—it *does* say that hers is a way of life which cannot develop under the liberal state. This is because the education (or lack thereof) required to ensure that someone grows up to live Geraldine's way of life is incompatible with the sort of education required by autonomy-minded liberalism.[30] Since her way of life requires an upbringing that impedes the capacity for autonomy rather than developing it, her life could not arise from an autonomy-minded education. So, Geraldine's way of life is one that the autonomy-minded liberal must be strongly biased against. This is not because such a life cannot be autonomous: it can. However, it is extremely *unlikely* that it will be autonomous: the conditions required for its formation will be ones that usually vitiate autonomy. *This* is why it cannot arise under the institutions of education to which such a liberal is committed. This rejection comes about as an indirect consequence of another commitment that the autonomy-minded liberal has, but is no less a rejection for that. The fact that people might find such a life valuable—and, indeed, that such a life might be autonomous—makes this commitment an uncomfortable one. Should it motivate us to reject the claim that the state should promote autonomy?

I suggest not, for the following reason. The crucial feature of Geraldine's way of life is that she lives it from the inside, and may indeed live it autonomously. The liberal will want to take her complaint seriously for that reason. Geraldine herself, of course, does *not* take that to be the reason why her commitment merits being taken seriously, and why people ought to be able to live her way of life. She sincerely believes that it is the only good way of life, and that people who don't have such an upbringing live tragically flawed lives as a result. But let us assume that Geraldine's reasons are not ones that the liberal will be inclined towards. Acting in a particular way because it agrees with Geraldine's claims about her way of life being the only good way to live would surely put any state uncontroversially beyond the liberal pale.

We might still feel the force of Geraldine's criticism, despite not sharing her particular commitments, for the following reason: we think that her claims about her way of life give us some reasons for action, not because we think them true, but because they are *hers*. If this is right, our discomfort stems from a belief that such a state should take seriously people's claims about the way they want their life to go, and because we believe that it is valuable for people to live autonomous lives. If we didn't believe something of that sort, then we would surely not be so unhappy about making it impossible for people to live the sort of life Geraldine considers valuable.[31] Therefore, the criticism—insofar as it will be taken seriously not just by those who themselves endorse the particular ways of life in question—is itself motivated by the view that the state should pay heed to autonomy.

So, our question is: what political system should we advocate if we want to take that underlying motivation seriously? The answer is this: the only way that we *could* respect the motivations that urge us to take Geraldine's demands seriously is by advocating that political system which best takes autonomy seriously. That is, the reason to be uncomfortable about a restriction on the development of ways of life like Geraldine's is at the same time a reason to endorse the political system which imposes that restriction. Hence, it seems as though the uncomfortable bias in autonomy-minded liberalism, if it is an evil at all, might be a necessary evil. Recognising this should comfort those who feel the force of Geraldine's criticism. We do not accede to her demands, but that is because we are committed generally to a political system which embodies the very same concern for everyone's autonomy as her argument relies on demanding for herself.

This argument will not please all those who feel the force of the worry. People who share Geraldine's values might say that it is a wilful misunderstanding of the situation: we should allow such ways of life because they are right, not because of some content-independent respect for those who might live those lives. My argument has little to say to such people. Those who start within a broadly liberal framework, however, should feel the force of it: if we *do* have some reason to take seriously the fact that people value a given way of life, and that reason is *not* dependent upon our also agreeing with the particular values intrinsic within that way of life, then my argument holds. Being committed to autonomy might mean being committed to some uncomfortable political conclusions: but unless we want to abandon the idea entirely that autonomy is something that the state should heed, that is the best we can do.

CONCLUSION

This chapter has been concerned with explaining in more detail what my concept of autonomy amounts to. I have explained what I mean by someone being autonomous; and I have tried to deal with various concerns that might be raised about the value that I sketch. Also, by painting a picture of autonomy as I see it—and by drawing the contrast with other less attractive conceptions, as I have done here and in Chapter 1—I have also attempted to give credence to the thought that autonomy (on my conception) is something that we might want to promote. If I have succeeded in that task, then that is good: the rest of this book can make plain what else one must accept if one is tempted to take autonomy to be valuable. However, there will be many who will not so far have been persuaded. It is to them—and especially to those of them who take themselves to be part of the broad church of liberal political philosophy—that I turn next.

3 Autonomy and Anti-Perfectionism

In this chapter, I outline an important argument, which serves both to offer a basis for criticising other positions that might be called 'liberal', and to offer further reasons to endorse autonomy-minded liberalism, my own position.

To start with, consider the position that the state ought not in its action to promote any value. By 'promotion' here, I mean intentional promotion: that is, putting into practice a policy with the intention of thereby increasing the extent to which a value or putative value is instantiated. So, for example, someone who agreed with the claim stated above would deem it unacceptable to aim to increase piety by giving tax incentives to attend a place of worship. There is another sense in which we might talk about a state which promotes values, on which a state promotes a value if it performs any action which has the effect of increasing the extent to which that putative value is instantiated, without *that* necessarily being what justifies the action. This, however, is not the sense of 'promotion' I will be concerned with here. Aside from anything else, there seems no way of avoiding promotion in this sense: any state action that is at all effective will change states of affairs to some extent, and any change will result in an improvement with respect to some putative value. Some anarchists may take this to be a very good reason to think all state action illegitimate, but I assume here that there is a sense in which we might object to the state promoting values which falls short of full-blown anarchism. The focus on avoiding *intentional* promotion allows us to capture this.[1]

The position I have just sketched is what I shall call 'anti-perfectionism', and it lies at the heart of my argument in this chapter. Let us consider it side by side with another claim:

The Autonomy Claim: The state ought to promote autonomy.
Anti-perfectionism: The state ought not in its action (intentionally) to promote any value.

The central claim of this chapter is that on my understanding of autonomy—as the value of people deciding for themselves what is valuable and living their lives in accordance with that decision—each of those claims implies the other. That is to say, the following is true:

> **The Equivalence Claim:** The state ought to promote autonomy if and only if anti-perfectionism is true.

This provides a problem for the two main alternative theories of liberalism, namely neutrality-minded (or 'political') liberalism, and perfectionistic liberalism. Defenders of the former are committed to anti-perfectionism, and claim that the state ought not to promote autonomy.[2] The main body of perfectionistic liberalism, conversely, affirms the Autonomy Claim, and denies anti-perfectionism.[3] Each of these positions endorses only one part of the biconditional Equivalence Claim and denies the other. Therefore, those positions are self-contradictory. Commitment to anti-perfectionism is inconsistent with denying that the state ought to promote the value of autonomy, and *vice versa*. Neutrality-minded and perfectionistic liberals must either accept the half of the biconditional that they deny, or they must abandon their positions altogether.

This conclusion depends, of course, upon their understanding autonomy in the way I suggest. In Chapter 1 I explained why I think that it is fair to see autonomy-promoting perfectionistic liberals as using the same conception of autonomy as me, and hence why they would endorse the Autonomy Claim understood as I suggest. The same is true of some neutrality-minded liberals too, for whom the antecedent commitment to anti-perfectionism will be precisely what rules out the promotion of the conception of autonomy I described in Chapter 2. So, for example, Larmore says that the promotion of autonomy in any sense—including the ideal defended by Mill—is a betrayal of the 'liberal spirit', because it fails to be anti-perfectionistic.[4] Now, this may not be true of all neutrality-minded liberals. In particular, my discussion in Section 3.3.3 suggests that some (especially Rawls) will have in mind a different conception of autonomy to mine, and that they might well endorse the Autonomy Claim on my conception. The argument here will not then prove such people wrong. It will, however, show just how close the connection is between autonomy and anti-perfectionism, and give reasons for such philosophers to conceive of neutrality as a much less important part of their own positions, and to give the explicit promotion of autonomy a greater prominence in their accounts of their own theories.

As well as threatening the perfectionistic and neutrality-minded liberals, the Equivalence Claim should also help to motivate the thought that autonomy (on my conception) is valuable. In Section 3.1, I explain why this seems to me the most promising strategy to employ. I then go on to perform an important clarificatory task. On the face of it, the Equivalence Claim appears to be self-contradictory. Surely if anti-perfectionism is true, then the state ought not to promote autonomy, since autonomy is a value? If this were to be so, then my argument would fail, since the Equivalence Claim would then be analytically false. In Section 3.2, I show that this is not the case. Talk about anti-perfectionism *simpliciter* involves an equivocation, because it fails to recognise that there are two types of value with respect to which one can be a perfectionist or an anti-perfectionist. I will argue that autonomy is a second-order value, and that anti-perfectionism should be understood in these contexts in its first-order form. Hence, it is consistent both to endorse anti-perfectionism, and to say that the state ought to promote the value of autonomy. Once this has been established, in Section 3.3 I argue for the Equivalence Claim, and hence demonstrate that both neutrality-minded liberalism and perfectionistic liberalism are self-contradictory.

3.1 ARGUING FOR THE VALUE OF AUTONOMY

In the sections that follow, I take myself to be giving reasons for people to think that autonomy is valuable, and hence that there is a reason to endorse autonomy-minded liberalism. This is because the Equivalence Claim locates autonomy within a nexus of connected ideas, and shows that it is inextricably linked to positions that are commonly held, especially amongst self-described liberals. This does mean that the argument for autonomy is a conditional one: only if one accepts the starting assumptions does it force one to accept that autonomy is valuable. So, if someone were prepared to reject the other positions I will link with the value of autonomy—anti-perfectionism principally, but also some varieties of relativism and pluralism—then the following argument will have very little to say to them. This is a shame, but it is doubtful whether any argument in political philosophy can aspire to much greater certainty. By linking autonomy to anti-perfectionism, I hope at least to raise the theoretical costs of rejecting autonomy: such a rejection would mean jettisoning other claims which we might feel we have good reason still to endorse.

In case my lack of ambition seems deplorable, it will be worth briefly explaining why this seems to me the most promising way of proceeding. So, I shall briefly discuss why we should consider the other types of arguments that might be advanced inadequate.

3.1.1 Bandying Intuitions

There are various ways that one might go about arguing that autonomy is valuable. One is simply to point to bare intuitions. For example, Steven Wall says that the best way to argue for the value of autonomy is 'to appeal to intuitions about particular cases and then show that the intuitions are best explained by the truth of the claim that autonomy is intrinsically valuable.'[5] I do not follow this approach here, for two reasons.

First, it seems methodologically unpalatable. By using an inference to the best explanation in this way, Wall brings a host of difficulties upon his argument. We might ask: Is such abduction a valid form of reasoning? If it is, what are the rules governing when it may and may not be used? How do we decide what is the best explanation for phenomena, since we plainly cannot appeal to some aspect of the phenomena themselves? Is it appropriate to use abduction in ethical arguments? What sorts of things count as explanations of moral intuitions? How authoritative ought we to take intuitions to be, anyway? Philosophical work has, of course, been done on all these questions, and I don't mean to suggest that the correct answers to any of them would necessarily vitiate a project like Wall's. However, it seems as though using an argument for the value of autonomy based on an abductive move *without* making any attempt to answer these questions is methodologically unsound, and Wall's unreflective use of the argument form is a weakness in his theory. I do not want to tackle the questions mentioned above, and so I must refrain from using these sorts of arguments.

Secondly, even if we were confident that moral abduction is an acceptable form of argument, any case for the value of autonomy that relied solely upon abduction would lack argumentative force. It relies on people sharing the same intuitions, to start with. The first case that Wall describes, as a way of provoking the intuitions which he intends to use, is as follows:

> Suppose I know that you are wise and that you have an excellent understanding of what is good for me. You know my talents, temperament and vulnerabilities and you know what types of project would best suit my nature. Further suppose I know that you are a person of good will who cares about my well-being. Given these facts, we can ask: Would my life go better if I let you take control of it? [6]

Wall takes it that almost everyone would give a resounding 'No!', but—absent any evidence—that is pure speculation. It may be that a bit of real sociological research would give a very different answer—certainly, a morning spent by the author asking people Wall's question gave a very mixed set of responses. More importantly, the people whose intuitions differ from his with respect to this case will be precisely the people that he needs to persuade. The same point could be made about the abduction itself: unless one is already inclined to think that autonomy is valuable, there is little reason to think that the best explanation for our intuitions is going to be a value of autonomy.

Perhaps this is not a big problem for Wall. If it turns out that there is a large enough consensus that autonomy is valuable, he will be able to justify an autonomy-valuing political system to the members of that consensus. In that case, though, the argument is impoverished in its ambitions. Such an argument could never provide an external justification for an autonomy-based political system.[7]

So, I have methodological reasons to eschew arguments based on abduction from intuitions. Instead, as I have said, I will rely on establishing the claim that anti-perfectionism both implies and is implied by the Autonomy Claim; hence, if one is an anti-perfectionist, one ought also to believe that we should promote autonomy. The inspiration for the argument comes from some comments made in passing by Raz, as I shall explain.

Before giving the detail of the argument, though, one might worry that I will be relying on the selfsame strategy I have just condemned. If my argument for the value of autonomy relies upon people's intuitive support for other positions such as anti-perfectionism, is not it just as weak as Wall's? I believe not. My main problem with Wall's argument is not its reliance upon intuition *per se*, but its abductive form. My argument is not an abduction over intuitions: I will not argue that the value of autonomy is the best explanation for anti-perfectionistic intuitions which I take uncritically to be true. My argument is instead about what sets of commitments one might have. In particular, one cannot endorse anti-perfectionism without thereby being committed also to the Autonomy Claim, on pain of inconsistency. This is a much weaker conclusion to draw, but it is strong enough for my purposes.

Why do I consider this the best we can do? Raz himself didn't think so. He never says, outright, that a good reason to believe that autonomy is valuable is that it is implied by anti-perfectionism, and the argument crucial to his own case is expounded much later in Chapter 14 of *The Morality of Freedom*. This has subsequently become known as the Social Forms argument, in which Raz argues that autonomy is constitutively valuable in modern Western societies: because of the social forms of such societies, the only way to achieve well-being in them (where by well-being he means the wholehearted and successful pursuit of valuable goals) is to be autonomous.[8] In addition to the importance he places upon it, this argument has also generally been taken to be Raz's most significant argument for the value of autonomy, both by his defenders[9] and detractors.[10] So, it will be useful to say something about why I believe that Raz's Social Forms argument does not work, in order to motivate my focus upon the anti-perfectionism argument.

3.1.2 The Social Forms Argument

Raz's Social Forms argument for the value of autonomy runs as follows. We have reason to value that which promotes our well-being, which is (according to Raz) mostly a matter of the successful and wholehearted pursuit of valuable goals.[11] What goals we can have is dependent on the pursuits and activities actually prevalent within our society, which Raz calls 'existing social forms.'[12] Moreover, he asserts, the social forms of modern Western societies make them 'autonomy-enhancing': they favour flexibility in familial arrangements, adaptability in one's work and geographical mobility, all of which require some level of autonomy, or at least make it advantageous. Hence, goals open to pursuit by individuals in such societies will mostly be ones for the satisfaction of which autonomy is useful or necessary.[13] Autonomy will therefore contribute to well-being in such a society, and is derivatively valuable for that reason.

There are various problems with this argument. Why, for example, should we think that the comprehensive goals someone might adopt must be dependent upon existent forms of behaviour? One is not committed to thinking that one can form projects in a vacuum to think that people can develop radically new forms of life, after all. Also, Raz's argument for the value of autonomy depends upon his account of well-being, but we might question both whether well-being is the correct notion upon which to ground our political system, and if his theory of well-being is itself plausible. I will not develop these objections here, as they have been discussed at length elsewhere,[14] and the answer is irrelevant here, for *even if* the Social Forms argument is sound, it fails to establish that autonomy has the sort of value that is needed for it to justify liberalism as a political creed.[15] This is because the crucial question I take myself to be answering is why we ought to have an autonomy-fostering society. So, any purported argument must tell us why we have a reason to arrange our political institutions to promote it. Since Raz's premises take for granted that we already have an autonomy-fostering society, there is danger of circularity. Wall takes it to be a virtue of an account that it leaves it 'an open matter whether, and to what extent, this political morality is binding on other societies.'[16] There is a grain of truth in this thought: maybe we *do* want to leave open the possibility that there are sound political philosophies other than autonomy-minded liberalism. That is, though, still consistent with saying that autonomy-minded liberalism is itself a sound and attractive position, for reasons that don't depend on an autonomy-fostering society already existing. Since I am concerned with that more ambitious claim, I shall avoid reliance on the Social Forms argument.

3.1.3 Reflections on Anti-perfectionism

Rather earlier in *The Morality of Freedom* than the Social Forms argument, there appears a passage in which Raz suggests that a commitment to anti-perfectionism in some way implies a commitment to the Autonomy Claim. In the rest of this chapter, I develop an argument for a stronger version of this; namely the Equivalence Claim. Before doing so, however, it is worth seeing precisely what Raz says on the matter, and what is the problem with it.

In preparation for his arguments in favour of perfectionism, Raz ruminates on the motivations people might have for rejecting that position. 'The spring from which anti-perfectionism flows', he says,

> is the feeling that foisting one's conception of the good on people offends their dignity and does not treat them with respect.[17]

Later, he identifies one of the intuitions underlying it as 'the thought that anti-perfectionism is necessary to prevent people from imposing their favoured style of life on others.'[18] Both these statements hint that anti-perfectionism is in some way based upon a (perhaps tacit) commitment to autonomy. The connection is made more explicit in his introduction to Part II, when he says that anti-perfectionism is

> inspired by the thought that people are autonomous moral agents who are to decide for themselves how to conduct their own lives and that governments are not moral judges with authority to force on them their conception of right and wrong. That is why anti-perfectionism is often regarded as being a doctrine of political freedom.[19]

Frustratingly, these hints never turn into a more explicit argument at any point. They do suggest, though, that Raz might endorse an informal argument somewhat along these lines:

> "Consider what it is to be an anti-perfectionist. In practice, it means believing that the state may not promote values through its organisation, or its operation, if doing so means that individuals are forced either to promote values with which they don't agree, or suffer in some way if they resist the actions of the state guided by such values. Why, though, do we think that is wrong? A deep intuition is that it offends people's dignity as autonomous agents, and shows inadequate respect for their autonomy. But if that is the intuition which motivates anti-perfectionism, the anti-perfectionist is committed to the value of autonomy; in which case, why should they resist the thought that the state ought to promote *that*?"

Insofar as Raz might endorse this argument, he would extend it a step further, as a *reductio ad absurdum*. If anti-perfectionism is based on a commitment to autonomy that looks distinctly perfectionistic, then it is self-refuting. He says something that supports such a reading at the very end of the relevant section:

> The sources of the appeal of anti-perfectionism are sound. It stems from concern for the dignity and integrity of individuals ... These concerns are real and important. They do not, however, justify anti-perfectionism.[20]

This, though, is not the conclusion I wish to draw from Raz's hints, for I do not wish to argue against anti-perfectionism: my aim is to show that anti-perfectionism and the Autonomy Claim are equivalent, each implying the other. So, let us rest one step prior to the *reductio*, with the conclusion that the anti-perfectionist is covertly committed to there being a value of autonomy. What might we say about this argument?

Our initial reaction must be that there is a clear problem: it seems as though the argument cannot possibly be valid, because it contains anti-perfectionism as a premiss and perfectionism about autonomy as a conclusion (precisely the feature, indeed, which makes it plausible to interpret Raz's argument as a *reductio ad absurdum*). So, on the face of it, as an argument for the Autonomy Claim, it looks unpromising.

There are two ways that we might try to repair the argument to avoid this problem. One is to read Raz a different way: the premiss he relies upon is not a statement of anti-perfectionism, but rather the intuitions about particular cases which (he says) underwrite anti-perfectionism (the feeling that perfectionistic political action offends against people's dignity and shows them a lack of respect, and so on). But in that case we return to simple abduction, and I rejected this form of argument for methodological reasons in Section 3.1.1.

So, in my argument for the Equivalence Claim, I need to show how we can avoid the apparent contradiction: that is, to show that it is not inconsistent to assert anti-perfectionism at the same time as saying that autonomy is perfectionistically valuable. It is with this task that the next section will be concerned.

3.2 FIRST- AND SECOND-ORDER VALUES

Contrary to appearances, the Equivalence Claim—that the state ought to promote autonomy if and only if anti-perfectionism is true—is not self-contradictory, for it involves an equivocation between two types of value: what I shall call 'first-' and 'second-order' values. I argue that we can sensibly talk about two types of perfectionism corresponding to these two types of value, and those types of perfectionism can come apart (that is, one makes very different claims depending upon which sort of perfectionism one rejects or endorses). Also, I shall show that autonomy on my conception is a second-order value. This means that when the Equivalence Claim is clarified, it loses the appearance of contradiction, since we can claim that *first-order* anti-perfectionism is true if and only if the state ought to promote the *second-order* value of autonomy.

Before drawing the distinction between first- and second-order values, it will be useful to discuss a different (though related) distinction much more familiar in the literature, namely the difference between content-specific and content-neutral values. This will be instructive for two reasons. First, it will make clear that the first-/second-order distinction, while it is *related* to the content-specific/content-neutral distinction, is not the same. Secondly, I characterise the first-/second-order distinction using the notion of a *variable in the specification of a value*, a notion easier to introduce in the context of an already familiar distinction.

3.2.1 Content-specific and Content-neutral Values

This section examines a familiar distinction between content-specific values and content-neutral values, and argues that the distinction is best thought of as structural: content-neutral values are characterised as those values which contain what I shall call 'ineliminable variables' in their specifications.

Suppose that I am trying to find out how to live the good life—that is, trying to find out what makes a life valuable for the individual living that life. I therefore ask two people about their conceptions of the good life, and receive the following answers:

> **Harriet** says: 'All that is valuable in life is to be able to play Bach's Cello Suites flawlessly.'
> **Imogen** says: 'What is valuable in life is satisfaction of desire.'

Suppose also that Harriet's statement is to be taken at face value—that she believes Bach's Cello Suites to be intrinsically and non-derivatively valuable (rather, for example, than thinking that playing the cello is the best way of being happy, where happiness is what really counts). The distinction I want to draw is between two different types of non-derivative value, which Harriet's and Imogen's different responses illustrate.

This distinction can clearly be seen in what I would have to do to pursue the values specified. To follow Harriet's advice my course of action is, in one sense, rather simple. I must acquire a cello, and also a good cello teacher. I must be able to keep body and soul together during the long years of practice that my task will entail—and, of course, I must hope that I am sufficiently musical to be able to play Bach's Cello Suites, and to play them flawlessly. Harriet's advice does not specify an undemanding value, but it *does* say everything there is to be said about that value. I do not need any further non-practical information to identify states of affairs I ought to be promoting in order to ensure that, by her lights, my life goes well: I just need practical information about *how* to promote those states of affairs. Moreover, Harriet's advice allows me to look at anyone else and see whether they are also living the good life. If they are giving recitals of the Cello Suites in the Wigmore Hall I will know that they are, and not otherwise.

Imogen's advice, by contrast, requires us to find more information about the value itself to know whether it is instantiated in specific cases. To use it to guide my own life, I must know what my desires are, and what will satisfy them. To use it to assess other people's lives, I likewise must know what their desires are: without knowing this, I can have no idea whether their life is going well. The value is, in this sense, without full content.

Suppose, for example, that I note of two people that they are both living the lives of concert cellists, frequently performing the Cello Suites in the Wigmore Hall. Suppose also that one has always wanted to be a concert cellist and play to an audience in this way, whereas the other has had this activity forced upon her by over-zealous parents. This would mean that, by Imogen's specification of the good life, the life of the first is dramatically better than that of the second—but unless I know about their desires, I can't tell simply by looking at the facts about the way they live their lives.

Accounts of well-being that fully specify what constitutes the good life (like Harriet's) are called *content-specific*, while those (like Imogen's) which don't are called *content-neutral*. The specifications of content-specific values are in some sense complete, whereas content-neutral ones are incomplete, generally because they are sensitive to individual attitudes, such as beliefs or preferences.

The characteristic feature of content-neutral values is that this incompleteness is ineliminable—we cannot get rid of it by substituting a more specific and definite specification of the ideal of the good life (as I will shortly show). Crucially, though, this incompleteness is not a flaw in a proposed definition of a value. Imogen's sentence by itself will fail to guide me, but not because Imogen has been negligent, or failed to communicate everything she could have: there is something intrinsic to the sort of claim she makes that cannot give me a completely informative set of instructions, as Harriet could.

To demonstrate that the incompleteness in Imogen's claim is ineliminable, consider what happens when I try to eliminate it. An elimination would consist in a translation, whereby I try to replace the term involving the incompleteness ('desire-satisfaction') with something that fully specifies what is valuable. Presumably, this will be what I desire: if whisky is what I desire at the moment, I could simply say 'What is valuable in life is to drink whisky'. However, this would miss an important feature of Imogen's advice: it refers to what I desire *de dicto*, rather than *de re*. What is valuable in life is the satisfaction of desires, whatever they happen to be: it just happens, for me at present, to be whisky that will do. We might compare this with yet another piece of advice:

> **Jessica** says 'Well, I think you've been brought up well, and you tend to desire all the right things. So, if you satisfy your desires, you will be doing what is valuable.'

Jessica's advice refers to what I desire *de re*: she informs me that a particular thing is valuable, and that it is what I desire, and therefore that my best way of pursuing it is to use the latter to find out what it is. The satisfaction of my desires functions, in Jessica's advice, just as a useful way of tracking value: the ideal of the good life that underlies her claim is ultimately of the same content-specific form as Harriet's.

This means that the substitution of 'drinking whisky' for 'desire-satisfaction' in Imogen's advice would be incorrect for two reasons. First, the grammatical form of the two is identical, thereby giving a misleading impression of universal application and stability: Imogen might say, in response, 'That's wrong! It's true of everyone that desire-satisfaction is what is valuable in life, but it's certainly *not* true for everyone that whisky is valuable: not everyone desires whisky.' A translation that changes the truth value of a claim is hardly an acceptable one. Nor would it be any good to respond to Imogen's worry by taking there to be an implicit clause relativising the second claim so that it applies just to me: '*What is valuable for Ben is* drinking whisky'. Insofar as 'drinking whisky' is being suggested as a substitution for 'desire-satisfaction', the translation is flawed if it turns a statement that refers to everyone into a statement that refers only to me. Moreover, we lose something important by moving away from Imogen's formulation. According to her, desire-satisfaction *really is* valuable, and whisky is only derivatively valuable insofar as it is what satisfies my desire. To put it the other way round would be to place priority on the wrong thing.

For these reasons, the incompleteness in Imogen's advice is ineliminable. This distinguishes the value she specifies from Harriet's, which contains no such incompleteness. It is the presence of an ineliminable incompleteness like this that characterises a content-neutral as opposed to a content-specific value. For the sake of simplicity, let us define a *variable* as that space in a value's specification which corresponds to an ineliminable incompleteness. In different contexts, different things will be substituted for the variable. For a desire-satisfaction theorist, it will be that which satisfies a particular agent's desires. For a hedonist; that which brings a particular individual pleasure. However, the variable cannot be eliminated (that is, permanently replaced with something specific) without changing the truth value, or the meaning, by losing generality.

Before going on to discuss the related distinction between first- and second-order values, it is worth asking what significance the distinction between content-specificity and content-neutrality has for the theory of autonomy, as doing so will allow me to repudiate one line of attack often used by those who argue that autonomy is *not* valuable.

We now have a more systematic way of distinguishing between the different conceptions of autonomy discussed in Chapter 1. As I said, some writers on autonomy take it to be an ideal of a particular way of life: most frequently one of relentless Socratic questioning, perpetual reassessing of motives and desires, and careful, rational action.[21] By contrast, most writers that I located in the same family of conceptions as myself tend to say that autonomy is characterised by *not* specifying any particular way of life needed for an individual to be autonomous. This seems to be what lies behind Hurka's claim that to be autonomous 'is to direct oneself where different directions are possible', and Raz's insistence that autonomy is an ideal of self-creation.[22]

In light of the distinction between content-neutral and content-specific values, we can now see that these two ways of talking about autonomy differ in referring to two different types of value. The first refers to a content-specific value: there is a particular set of things that one must do in order to be autonomous. The understanding on which the autonomous life is one of Socratic self-questioning is one such interpretation. The second refers to a content-neutral value; some conditions are specified, but there is an ineliminable variable which stands for an individual living the sort of life that she deems valuable. The notion of autonomy that I suggest—deciding for oneself what is valuable and living one's life in accordance with that decision—is of this second sort.

Both content-neutral and content-specific understandings can stake a plausible historical claim to the word 'autonomy'. However, for our purposes it will be important to distinguish them. Since I am going to argue that we should take a form of content-neutral autonomy to be valuable, I will reserve the term 'autonomy' for that alone. Content-specific ideals of autonomy I will henceforth call 'autarchy', and none of what follows should be taken as a defence of autarchy as a value.[23] Any argument against the value of autonomy which is actually directed against autarchy will fail, on account of not noticing that there are two different notions at work here.[24]

To conclude, here is the first of our distinctions. Some values are content-specific: their specification contains no variables, by which I mean ineliminable incompletenesses. Other values are content-neutral: their formulation includes such a variable. Autonomy, as I take it, is a content-neutral value, and should be distinguished from a content-specific value (autarchy).

3.2.2 First-and Second-order Values

Having discussed content-neutrality and content-specificity, I will now characterise a second distinction between first- and second-order values, using the notion of a variable in a value's specification. Second-order values contain variables which can themselves contain nested variables. First-order values, on the other hand, *cannot* contain nested variables. This can be for one of two reasons: either they are content-specific, in which case they contain no variables at all; or they are content-neutral but contain only variables incapable of having nested variables. Before giving a more formal specification, though, let us draw the distinction informally by looking at more examples.

Suppose that I continue my quest to find out how to live the good life, and receive the following advice:

> **Kerensa** says 'What is valuable in life is to do what your parents value.'

By this, Kerensa means that I should act in accordance with my parents' judgments about what is valuable, whatever they in fact are: her reference to my parents' values is *de dicto*.

Since it contains a *de dicto* reference, Kerensa's answer is rather like Imogen's (that desire-satisfaction is what is valuable). Both posit content-neutral values, containing ineliminable incompletenesses. Above, I showed that Imogen refers to the things that satisfy our desires *de dicto*, and so any attempt simply to substitute a description of those things will result in a loss of meaning. The same is true of Kerensa's sentence: the reference to my parents' values is *de dicto* because, according to Kerensa, I should follow my parents' values just because they are my parents' values. Again, it might be fruitful to contrast Kerensa's advice with a *de re* reference to my parents' values:

Luke says: 'Your parents know what is valuable; to pursue a valuable life, do what your parents think is valuable.'

The incompleteness in Luke's specification *is* eliminable, since he refers to my parents' values *de re*, as a way of tracking value. If I were to ask my parents what they consider to be valuable, then I could substitute their specification into Luke's advice without a change of meaning. By contrast, the incompleteness is not eliminable in Kerensa's specification.

Although Imogen and Kerensa both posit content-neutral rather than content-specific values, there is an important difference between them. If I seek to know what I should pursue to achieve the values they describe, I will be looking for different things. In Imogen's statement, I will need to find descriptions of states of affairs: in particular, those which satisfy my desires. I cannot ever substitute a description of a state of affairs (or a conjunction or disjunction of such descriptions) for the variable, but it is over such descriptions that the variable ranges. Kerensa's statement, on the other hand, tracks other statements of value. To complete her statement, I need something which is itself a specification of a value. When she says 'What is valuable in life is to do what your parents value', her specification of value refers to another such specification, rather than a state of affairs. *That* claim about values (i.e. the specification that my parents give me) is what will determine which states of affairs I should pursue (if I am trying to live the good life myself) or look for (if I am trying to assess how good other people's lives are).

Informally, then, here is our distinction. Some values are specified in such a way as to refer *de dicto* to other specifications of values. Others do not: either they attach value to states of affairs *de re* (and are content-specific), or they refer to states of affairs *de dicto* (and are content-neutral).

This can be put more precisely. What distinguishes Kerensa's from Imogen's statement is the nature of the variables contained in each specification of value. The variable in Imogen's specification ranges over (that is, tracks) states of affairs which satisfy my desires; the variable in Kerensa's ranges over other specifications of values. Let us call variables which range over states of affairs *first-order variables*, and those which range over specifications of value *second-order variables*.[25]

Second-order variables, by their nature, are capable of containing another (first-order) variable nested within themselves. The point can be made by once again comparing Kerensa's *de dicto* reference to what my parents value with Luke's *de re* reference to the same.

Suppose that, as it happens, my parents believe that desire-satisfaction is valuable. Now, because Luke's reference to what my parents value is *de re*, I can without loss of meaning substitute 'pursue desire-satisfaction' for 'what your parents value' in his advice. Once I have done this, I have gone as far as I can—as I argued earlier, the value posited by desire-satisfaction theorists is content-neutral because it contains a variable standing for what specific states of affairs satisfy the desires of each individual. So, in pursuing Luke's advice in a situation where my parents believe in desire-satisfaction, I encounter an ineliminable variable in the same place as I do with Imogen's advice.

With Kerensa's advice, I encounter a variable a stage further back in my deliberations. Because her reference to my parents' values is *de dicto*, I cannot simply substitute 'pursue desire-satisfaction' for 'what your parents value' without encountering the same problems I observed in Section 3.2.2: to do so would be to turn a universal claim into one relative to a single agent at a single time, saying nothing about anything else. So, with Kerensa's advice, it is impermissible to go even so far as the ineliminable variable associated with the desire-satisfaction theory.

Ex hypothesi, though, my parents are desire-satisfaction theorists. Therefore, their specification of value itself contains a variable. Since this specification is what the second-order variable in Kerensa's specification refers to, that specification contains *two* variables: one ranging over specifications of value, the other over states of affairs. Moreover, they are nested—the second sits within the scope of the first.

So, second-order variables have a structural feature which distinguishes them from first-order variables: they can contain first-order variables nested within them. However, it seems that they need not do so: containing a nested first-order variable is sufficient but not necessary for a variable to be second-order. For consider an alternative scenario to the one just described, in which my parents instead believe in some content-specific value (like Harriet's, for example). In that case, Kerensa's advice would not have a second variable, since the specification to which it refers would not itself contain a variable to sit nested inside Kerensa's. Nevertheless, because the structure of Kerensa's claim cannot not be dependent upon what her parents happen to believe, the variable in her specification is still at a higher level than that involved in the specification of the desire-satisfaction theory.

Here, then, is how we might more formally define the distinction between first- and second-order values. In the specification of some values, there are second-order variables which range over (or track) other specifications of value. Let us call 'second-order' any value which *can* include a second-order variable. Other values *cannot* contain such a variable: either they specify particular states of affairs, or they contain first-order variables, which range only over states of affairs. Let us call values of this sort, both of the content-specific and content-neutral kind, 'first-order'.

This distinction having been established, we can see that autonomy (understood as an agent deciding for themselves what is valuable and being able to live their life in accordance with that decision) is distinctively a second-order value, for it refers to other judgments about what is valuable; namely, those which an individual might take as guidance in their life. Moreover, it makes that reference *de dicto*: in the same way that I described previously in discussing content-neutral values, to take the reference to be *de re* (and therefore to allow us to substitute into the specification of autonomy sentences expressing our actual judgments about value) would be to mislocate what is valuable. Therefore, our specification of autonomy must be able to contain a second-order variable, and autonomy (as opposed to autarchy) must be a second-order value.

It should now be clear how the appearance of contradiction in the Equivalence Claim can be dispelled. There is an equivocation in talking about perfectionism (or anti-perfectionism) *simpliciter*. In saying that one is a perfectionist, one might be endorsing perfectionism about first- or second-order values, or both.

As it appears in the Equivalence Claim, let us understand 'anti-perfectionism' to mean 'first-order anti-perfectionism'. That is a fair reading, since most people who endorse anti-perfectionism have the state promotion of first-order values (of both content-specific and content-neutral varieties) as their target.[26] Since autonomy is a second-order value, it is consistent both to endorse anti-perfectionism (so understood) and to say that the state should promote autonomy.

3.3 THE EQUIVALENCE CLAIM

At the beginning of this chapter I identified the Equivalence Claim: anti-perfectionism implies that the state ought to promote autonomy, and *vice versa*. We can now see more clearly how that claim ought to be interpreted: autonomy is a second-order value, and anti-perfectionism, in this case, should be understood as first-order anti-perfectionism.[27] This allows the Equivalence Claim to avoid the whiff of paradox noted earlier, and allows us to consider the substantive argument in its favour.

The argument runs as follows:

1. If anti-perfectionism is true, it must be justified.
2. If the state ought to promote autonomy, then anti-perfectionism is true.
3. Any justification for anti-perfectionism implies that the state ought to promote autonomy.

4. (From 1 and 3): If anti-perfectionism is true, then the state ought to promote autonomy.
5. (From 2 and 4): The state ought to promote autonomy if and only if anti-perfectionism is true.

The argument is valid. Its soundness therefore depends upon the truth of the premisses: that is, claims 1, 2, and 3. I argue for each of them in the remainder of this chapter.

3.3.1 Must Anti-perfectionism be Justified?

Premiss 1 states that anti-perfectionism, if it is true, must be justified. I take it that this is a plausible assumption. Not all true claims require external justification (consider, for example, analytic truths, or claims about sense data). However, practical prescriptions about state action (such as the claim of anti-perfectionism) surely *do* require some justification, whether that be in the form of an independent and more foundational position which implies that prescription, or in the form of a coherent network of beliefs in reflective equilibrium which support it.

This is not a conclusive argument for Premiss 1, but the cost of rejecting it would be high. In particular, it would mean committing to one of three positions about the truth of anti-perfectionism: that it is analytic, that it is given directly in sense-data, or that it is neither of these, but given in some sort of moral intuition that guarantees its truth without reference to any other justification. I take it that the former two are absurd. The third position is possible, but unattractive; and it is notable that no defender of anti-perfectionism about state action defends it on these grounds (indeed, the thought would be presumably be anathema to defenders of anti-perfectionism like Rawls). So, while it is possible that someone might disagree with Premiss 1 by taking this line, the position is sufficiently unpalatable that nobody will in fact adopt it.

3.3.2 From Autonomy to Anti-perfectionism

In this section, I argue that holding that the state should promote autonomy implies anti-perfectionism, and thereby justify Premiss 2 in the argument given above.[28]

The anti-perfectionist believes that the state should not promote perfection amongst its citizens by aiming to make them manifest first-order values. One reason one might hold such a view is because one believes that such values are, in some informal sense, under the control of individuals. Recall Harriet, who believes that it is non-derivatively valuable to play Bach's Cello Suites consummately well. We might imagine (all other things being equal) that her life goes better if it manifests this value. Nevertheless, the anti-perfectionist says that the state ought not to promote cello playing, and gives two reasons. Cello playing is valuable only for those, like Harriet, who consider it valuable; and is valuable for Harriet only because she so considers it: she must endorse cello playing for it to be valuable for her. These facts show, the anti-perfectionist might continue, that such values must be decided by the individual: the state has no business deciding for them.[29] One clear reason to hold such a position is that one endorses autonomy: it is *valuable* that an agent decides for themselves what is (first-order) valuable, and is able to live their lives accordingly. If the state should recognise the value of autonomy in this sense, then it *must* leave questions of first-order value up to individuals, and so anti-perfectionism is true.

At this point, it might be objected that the conclusion I have reached—valuing autonomy means allowing agents to decide for themselves what is valuable—is not sufficient for anti-perfectionism. In addition to saying that the state shouldn't decide what is of value, the anti-perfectionist must also say that the state shouldn't promote particular first-order values even if it does not decide them. *That* injunction does not necessarily follow from what I have written above. For example, we might think that as long as it is true that Harriet has decided for herself that playing the Cello Suites is valuable, the state can promote cello playing for her without violating the first injunction, for it will not thereby be determining what is valuable. If the commitment to autonomy is really a justification for anti-perfectionism, then it must also account for this second aspect.

Two considerations show that the commitment to autonomy can indeed do this. One consideration is practical, the other more principled.

First, the practical point. Any autonomy-minded state (by which I mean one concerned with promoting the second-order value of autonomy) wanting to promote first-order values would have to bear in mind the restrictions upon the scope of those values. In particular, to promote a first-order value that is not endorsed by *all* citizens would be to make some citizens live their lives according to a value which they didn't recognise—contrary to the demands of autonomy that an agent be able to decide what is valuable and live their lives according to that decision. Moreover, an agent's idea of what is valuable can change over time. Forcing an agent at a given time to live according to a value which they do not endorse at that time is likewise contrary to the demands of autonomy, even if they have at another time endorsed that value. So, an autonomy-minded state that wanted to promote first-order values would have to be aware of what every single one of its citizens valued at all times, so as to avoid violating its commitment to autonomy. The inefficiency of this process, and the drastic violations of privacy it would inevitably involve, give a strong reason for someone commitment to autonomy likewise to endorse the whole of anti-perfectionism. Strictly speaking, we should say that the value of autonomy justifies *either* full anti-perfectionism *or* holding that an autonomy-minded state can promote first-order values so long as it does not decide those values. The costs, however, of making promotion of first-order values consistent with respecting individual decision concerning those values would be sufficiently extreme as to make the latter disjunct prohibitively unattractive.

There is a second way in which the commitment to autonomy implies that the state shouldn't promote particular first-order values, which I take to be somewhat more important: doing so would be ruled out as illegitimate by our reasons for caring about autonomy in the first place. These reasons are encoded in the fact that autonomy is a second-, rather than a first-order value.

Recall the argument I gave in Section 3.2.2 for the ineliminability of the second-order incompleteness in such a value. In the specification of a second-order value, any reference to a first-order specification of value is *de dicto*. Therefore, there is no way of substituting a first-order specification for the second-order incompleteness without an illegitimate shift in meaning: at best we turn an unrestricted generalization into a value claim that is indexed to a particular individual at a particular time, and at worst we will translate a true sentence into one that is false. I also noted that these translation problems indicate that attempting to eliminate the variable misidentifies what is of value. This is clearest in examples where the variable is a first-order one: even if I am a desire-satisfaction theorist who desires whisky, the sentence 'Desire-satisfaction is valuable' cannot be translated into 'Whisky is valuable' *precisely because* trying to do so locates the value in the wrong place. Desire-satisfaction is what is valuable, and insofar as whisky has any value it has it only derivatively as that which satisfies my desire. The same point can be made with respect to second-order values.

An autonomy-minded state, if it acted so as to promote some first-order value, and justified that by pointing to the second-order value of autonomy, would be making an error of this sort. Either they would simply be violating the demands of autonomy, or they would be mistranslating the claim that autonomy is valuable by eliminating the second-order variable. And that latter mistake would not *simply* be a matter of semantics (though the semantic problem identifies where the deeper mistake lies). It would be a usurpation by the state of an authority to decide on the deep questions of value in individuals' lives which properly belongs only to them.

Therefore, a commitment to autonomy would entail *both* parts of anti-perfectionism. If it is impermissible to eliminate the second-order variable in the value of autonomy, a state must neither decide on nor promote any particular first-order value. Hence, Premiss 2 of the argument for the Equivalence Claim is true.

3.3.3 From Anti-Perfectionism to Autonomy

To establish Premiss 3—that anti-perfectionism implies that the state should promote autonomy—I must show that there is no other justification for anti-perfectionism than the appeal to autonomy. That is, I must show that there is no claim that is true, implies anti-perfectionism, and does not imply that the state ought to promote autonomy. In what follows, I show that the main alternative potential justifications for anti-perfectionism all fail this test. Each of them is either implausible, fails to justify anti-perfectionism, or justifies anti-perfectionism only if it is supplemented with the claim that the state ought to promote autonomy.

Such a strategy is inconclusive: a case-by-case refutation of possible counter-examples cannot of itself show that there could not be a possible motivation for anti-perfectionism that has not been considered. So, what follows is not a proof of Premiss 3. However, it will support the premiss by giving inductive reasons to suppose that any purported motivation save the Autonomy Claim will suffer one of the three fates mentioned before. This shifts the burden of proof to those who would seek to deny the premiss, and also gives a method which might be used to attack other putative counter-examples not examined here for reasons of space.

Relativism

One possible motivation for anti-perfectionism is that one endorses relativism in some form. Relativism is frequently taken to undercut the claims of states to promote values by casting doubt on the idea that there are any non-relative values for them to promote.

There are various forms of relativism. The most radical—that all truth itself is relative—I take to be sufficiently implausible that I need not argue about it here.[30] I will deal, however, with a weaker form of relativism, limited to value claims. Relativism, so understood, is the theory that values are relative to individuals. That is, we cannot make sense of the claim that something is valuable *simpliciter*: instead we must always talk about things being valuable for (or to) an individual. So, when one says 'piano playing is valuable', that claim should be understood as containing an implicit relativising clause: 'Piano playing is valuable *to x*', where *x* is an individual. According to value-relativism, value claims can be true, so long as they are either explicitly or implicitly relativised to individuals. In what follows, I argue that this claim either fails to justify anti-perfectionism, or is equivalent to the claim that autonomy is valuable: in which case, my major claim (that anti-perfectionism implies that autonomy is valuable) remains intact.

Understood crudely, the claim that value-relativism supports anti-perfectionism is self-contradictory. This is because anti-perfectionism is a substantial normative position, that the state ought not to promote any first-order values. The normative claim made is *not* relative to individuals: it is taken to be a general injunction. Hence, the sincere value-relativist will either fail to understand what it means, or is forced to reject it for the same reason that he rejects any unrelativised claim about what it is right to do.[31]

How else might we understand the claim of value-relativism? Another possibility is that what is valuable is relative to facts about individuals' needs and situations. So, for example, I could say 'artificial insulin is valuable'.

Someone else might disagree with me, and say 'But artificial insulin can do dreadful damage to people if they are not diabetic, or if it is taken in inappropriate doses at the wrong time by people who are.' I could respond by making explicit a relativising clause, indicating an implicit restriction upon my first claim: 'Artificial insulin is valuable for A, on account of her diabetes, so long as it is taken only twice a day when her blood sugar is above a certain level.'

There are two problems with supposing that such a position could support anti-perfectionism. First, a properly relativised moral claim, on this view, is one that applies universally: the relativised claim 'artificial insulin is valuable for people in such-and-such circumstances' differs from the unrelativised claim 'artificial insulin is valuable' only insofar as it gives a tighter criterion of applicability. However, it is true of all people that if they are in the relevant circumstances, artificial insulin is valuable: in which case, a relativist of this stripe seems to have no principled reason to rule out a state applying that rule. Hence, value-relativism of this sort does not fully motivate anti-perfectionism.[32]

A third way of understanding value-relativism is to see it as the claim that values are relative to individuals in the sense that they depend upon individuals' attitudes about what is valuable. In that case, using it as support for anti-perfectionism would mean being committed to saying that the state oughtn't to promote first-order values because individuals determine for themselves what is valuable, and hence they should decide for themselves.

This, though, is so close as to be indistinguishable from the claim that autonomy is valuable (which on my conception is the claim that agents should be able to decide for themselves what is valuable, and live their lives according to those values). So, value-relativism does not serve as a distinct motivation for anti-perfectionism: it only does so if one holds also that autonomy is valuable. But this is precisely what I set out to prove: relying upon value-relativism to motivate anti-perfectionism would still imply that autonomy is valuable. Hence, relativism is no counterexample to Premiss 3.

Pluralism

A position frequently held in conjunction with anti-perfectionism is pluralism about values: that is, some version of the claim that there are various valuable ends one may pursue, where their value cannot be accounted for by reference to a single value. Pluralism comes in a Weak form, which states simply that there are diverse possible values worth pursuing; and a Strong form, which adds that those values cannot all be instantiated at once.[33] Contrary to appearances, neither can act as a counterexample to Premiss 3: only if held in conjunction with the claim that autonomy is valuable does any form of pluralism support anti-perfectionism.

Weak Pluralism states that there are at least two distinct first-order values, neither of which can be reduced to (or shown to depend on) the other. Imagine we have a state which is considering promoting one of those first-order values (call it 'A'). If Weak Pluralism were to support anti-perfectionism, we would have to think that promoting A is wrong because there is an alternative (call it 'B'). That is implausible, though. Showing that there is an alternative does not imply that it is impermissible for the state to promote A. It just shows that, if we are minded to promote things that are of first-order value, there are different options, namely A or B. When reasoning about choices generally we don't think that the presence of alternatives to a given option can by itself make that option unacceptable: if we are to accept such reasoning with respect to values, we need something extra to explain what makes the difference. So, by itself Weak Pluralism fails to motivate anti-perfectionism.

If Strong Pluralism is true, then there is an additional factor which one might consider salient, namely that the promotion of A necessarily involves decreasing the extent that B is instantiated: the state has a choice between promoting A at the expense of B or *vice versa*. By promoting things which are valuable with respect to A, a state would fail to promote things which are valuable with respect to B, or even promote disvalue with respect to B. This might represent a stronger argument than the one based on Weak Pluralism, for we might be able to say that there is a reason to avoid disvalue with respect to B, and hence to not promote A. From this, a simple generalization would imply that such reasons would exist for any value, and Strong Pluralism would imply anti-perfectionism.

Such a reason, though, could not be compatible with anti-perfectionism. One way of understanding anti-perfectionism is as saying that the state should not act on reasons which appeal to particular first-order values. These sorts of reasons can come in both positive and negative forms. So, taking Bach's Cello Suites to be valuable might generate positive reasons for things that promote that value (sending children to music school, for example), and negative reasons to avoid things that promote the corresponding disvalue (preventing the loss of the last cello factory, perhaps). Both positive and negative reasons necessarily appeal to the relevant first-order value. So, on pain of inconsistency, the anti-perfectionist cannot appeal to *either* in justifying their anti-perfectionism. This, however, is exactly what they would be doing if they followed the argument from Strong Pluralism given above. Hence, Strong Pluralism is in no better a position than Weak Pluralism. It too fails to offer a reason, compatible with anti-perfectionism, for thinking that the promotion of a given value is impermissible because there are other values that might also be promoted.

Offering such a reason is strictly unnecessary for my purposes here. However, considering what it *could* be is instructive. Neither pluralist can appeal to first-order values, and the prospects for an explanation based on an appeal to *no* values seems dim: moving in that direction tends rather towards indifference than either perfectionism or anti-perfectionism. So, the most fruitful course would be to appeal to a second-order value. This brings us back to the value of autonomy. If we think that *individuals*, rather than the state, ought to decide between different first-order values, then the argument becomes sound: given a plurality of first-order values, the state has no business promoting any one of them, because it is (second-order) valuable that individuals should decide which are worth promoting for themselves. If *this* is how the anti-perfectionist would use either Weak or Strong Pluralism as a motivation, they would do so only by presupposing that the state should pay heed to autonomy. Hence, pluralism provides no counterexample to Premiss 3.

Scepticism

A third potential counterexample to Premiss 3 relies on an epistemic argument. We can never know (so the argument goes) what is valuable with sufficient certainty for the state to be justified in using its powers to promote putative values. Hence, we should be anti-perfectionists about state action on the basis of scepticism.[34]

As it stands, the argument is incomplete: it gives no reason why these epistemic problems should make state promotion of a putative value unacceptable. In what follows, three possible hidden premisses will be considered, each of which might seem to plug the gap. In examining them, a familiar pattern will re-emerge. On one interpretation the argument collapses, on the second it fails to support anti-perfectionism, and on the third it does support anti-perfectionism, but relies on an implicit appeal to autonomy.

One possible hidden premiss is as follows: scepticism demands caution because a state promoting a putative value could thereby unwittingly be undermining value with respect to (or at least failing to promote) some other value which these epistemic difficulties keep hidden. If this is the hidden premiss, then the argument from scepticism collapses. The other values about which we are supposed to worry are not being explicitly identified, but they are still, on this view, providing reasons for state action. As noted in the previous discussion of pluralism, appealing to negative reasons grounded in a value is incompatible with anti-perfectionism, just as appealing to positive reasons would be. So, the argument from scepticism on this understanding is unsound: the hidden premiss contradicts the conclusion.

A second possibility is that a state promoting a putative value is mistaken not because (as in the previous argument) there may be something else that it ought to be promoting or protecting, but rather because we should be sceptical about there being any values to be promoted at all. If this is the hidden premiss, then it is at least consistent with anti-perfectionism. However, the argument, so understood, fails to establish its conclusion. On this view, there is nothing morally at stake when the state (mistakenly) promotes a putative value. Why then should we consider such action forbidden, even if it is a mistake? As noted before in respect of pluralism, taking this route leads us to indifference between perfectionism and anti-perfectionism rather than justifying the latter. So, once again, the argument from scepticism fails to justify anti-perfectionism.

A third possibility is this: the danger posed by the epistemic problems mentioned is that the perfectionistic state might promote a value which is not endorsed by the people who are affected by that state action, and *that* is the source of the injunction against such action. This, though, is precisely the same line of thought pursued previously, where it was argued that the difficulty of knowing what individuals value at each moment is one of the things that commits the autonomy-minded liberal to anti-perfectionism. That argument is sound, and does justify anti-perfectionism, but only if the Autonomy Claim is presupposed.

There may be other ways that one might think that the epistemic problem should constrain state promotion of values, and hence justify anti-perfectionism in a way that does not imply that the state should be concerned with autonomy. However, the failure of the three attempts discussed here—and the manner of that failure, echoing the points made before in respect of relativism and pluralism—should give us inductive grounds to doubt that the argument from scepticism can be made successful. Hence, we should reject it as a possible counterexample to Premiss 3.

Neutrality

A fourth and final possible counterexample to to Premiss 3 is based upon an appeal to neutrality: that is, to the claim that state action must presuppose no particular comprehensive conception of value.[35] The argument goes roughly like this: if it is to be legitimate, a state must be neutral, and if it is to be neutral, it must be anti-perfectionistic.[36] My argument will concentrate on the later work of Rawls, since the argument is most influentially formulated there; but in course of this general points about *any* appeal to neutrality will emerge.

In the book of the same name, Rawls argues for the thesis of Political Liberalism: for a state to be legitimately stable, it must be neutral, in the sense that it is based on principles of justice which presuppose no particular conception of the valuable life.[37] So, while Political Liberalism implies more than just anti-perfectionism, it does at least imply that perfectionistic state action is ruled out by the need to be neutral. I argue that Rawls' argument cannot provide an alternative justification for anti-perfectionism: even assuming its soundness, the argument relies on a tacit appeal to autonomy.[38] So, whether his argument succeeds or fails, it cannot threaten Premiss 3.

Rawls' theory concerns how a stable society can be achieved, and achieved legitimately. It is the latter constraint that concerns us here. His concern was that, in the face of reasonable disagreement about 'religious, philosophical, and moral doctrines', state action based on any particular comprehensive doctrines involves citizens being governed by principles that they might not affirm.[39] That, said Rawls, would vitiate legitimacy. This implies—though Rawls didn't put it in these terms himself—that the political liberal state must be anti-perfectionistic, since perfectionistic state action aiming to promote a particular value would have to be premissed upon a comprehensive doctrine in which that value is affirmed.[40]

As it stands, though, this argument is incomplete: it does not justify the moral injunction against state action premised on a comprehensive doctrine with which some people disagree. Though he didn't explicitly say so, Rawls seemed to take this constraint to arise because the state must treat us as persons free and equal in respect of possessing two fundamental moral powers: a sense of justice (that is, a willingness to 'act in relation to others on terms that they also can publicly endorse') and 'the capacity to form, to revise, and rationally to pursue a conception of one's rational advantage or good.'[41] These moral powers are part of citizens' essential nature, according to Rawls, and their exercise is an important good.[42] It is respect for these moral powers which grounds the demand that putative state actions be justifiable to the individuals who possess and exercise them.[43]

Notice, though, that Rawls' second moral power is the same as the capacity for autonomy as I define it; namely an agent deciding for herself what is of value (or, equivalently, what is good) and living her life in pursuit of that value. If the exercise of the moral powers is an important good, then *autonomy itself* must be important. And this is what bridges the gap in Rawls' argument. To be legitimate a state must be anti-perfectionistic because its actions must be justifiable to citizens as free and equal possessors of the two moral powers: which is to say, *inter alia*, as people whose autonomy is valuable and demands recognition. Without this appeal to concern for autonomy lying at the roots of Rawls' theory, there would be no justification in *Political Liberalism* for his claim that legitimacy demands that we not ride roughshod over people's reasonable disagreement with putative value-promoting state action. To buy into Rawls' argument, we must *already* be committed to the Autonomy Claim.

This discussion has concentrated on Rawls, but the points made also apply more generally to those who consider that a state must be neutral to be legitimate, and anti-perfectionistic to be neutral. It is implausible to claim that the demand for neutrality needs no justification, for the same reasons that I gave in Section 3.3.1 above when rejecting the parallel claim for anti-perfectionism itself. Hence, we must ask why neutrality is needed, and why its lack is taken to undermine legitimacy. The preceding discussion of Rawls strongly suggests that at that point some explicit or implicit appeal to the value of autonomy is necessary. Therefore, a concern for neutrality cannot threaten my Premiss 3. Justifying anti-perfectionism by claiming that the state must be neutral between comprehensive conceptions of the good already presupposes that the state ought to act in such a way as to secure its citizens' autonomy.

Premiss 3 of the argument for the Equivalence Claim states roughly that any true justification for anti-perfectionism implies that the state should promote autonomy. I have shown that this is true of four putative justifications, namely appeals to relativism, pluralism, scepticism, and neutrality. In each case, the claim being appealed to is false, or does not provide support for anti-perfectionism unless held in conjunction with the claim that the state should promote autonomy.

It is again important to note that this is not a conclusive argument: the fact that four potential counterexamples can be defused does not indicate that there can be no such counterexample. But their failure does give inductive support to Premiss 3, which by itself would be sufficient for my purposes. In addition, it has revealed two interesting and important points. First, there is a pattern in the failure of each of the putative alternative justifications. For each, there was some way of understanding the claim being made which *does* support anti-perfectionism—but only if the state's business in promoting autonomy is presupposed. The form of value-relativism that can justify anti-perfectionism claims that values are relative to individuals' attitudes about what is valuable. Pluralism justifies anti-perfectionism so long as one feels that it should be the business of individuals themselves to decide which of a variety of contrasting and conflicting values to pursue. Scepticism justifies anti-perfectionism only if we are concerned about the possibility of state action promoting values which the individuals within the scope of that state action have not themselves endorsed. The need for principles of justice to be neutral between comprehensive conceptions of the good in order to be legitimate depends upon the assumption that there is something illegitimate about people being forced to pursue values which they would not decide upon for themselves. Each time, a concern for autonomy seems to lurk behind its potential rivals. This strengthens the inductive argument. Not only do these potential counterexamples to Premiss 3 fail, but they fail in the same way: each ends up presupposing the Autonomy Claim in order to justify anti-perfectionism. This gives us reason to anticipate the same thing happening to other putative counterexamples.

Secondly, this argument has shifted the burden of proof to my opponents. Having shown in Section 3.3.2 that the Autonomy Claim can serve as a motivation for anti-perfectionism, and shown in this section that the other extant contenders cannot serve, the onus is now upon those who disagree with my contention to provide a new alternative. In the absence of that, it is now reasonable to take Premiss 3 to be sufficiently well-established that it ought to be accepted. This is all that is required if my argument for the Equivalence Claim is to be sound.

CONCLUSION

As I argued in Section 3.1, the Equivalence Claim (which is that the state ought to promote autonomy if and only if anti-perfectionism is true) seems to me the most promising way to motivate the claim that autonomy, on my understanding, should be promoted. This is because it ties autonomy so understood into a nexus of interconnected commitments—such as anti-perfectionism, certain types of value-relativism, pluralism and neutrality—that are commonly held amongst self-described liberals. The argument is still a conditional one: one might still reject the Autonomy Claim if one were prepared to reject anti-perfectionism and all that hangs on it. I have shown, though, that the theoretical costs of rejecting the Autonomy Claim are much higher than might previously have been thought. In particular, those costs include abandoning the very claims that most liberal opponents of the Autonomy Claim take to be constitutive of their own positions.

The Equivalence Claim creates problems for the two main alternative theories of liberalism to autonomy-minded liberalism. Perfectionist liberal writers such as Hurka, Raz and Wall endorse the claim that the state ought to promote autonomy, but deny anti-perfectionism. Neutrality-minded liberals such as Larmore endorse anti-perfectionism and deny that the state ought to promote autonomy, even on my understanding. It should be clear that the Equivalence Claim makes both positions untenable. And there are other neutrality-minded liberals—most notably Rawls, as I showed in Section 3.3.3—who are shown by this argument to lie more decisively in the territory of autonomy-minded liberalism than it might have seemed at first sight. In general, my argument has shown that there are two parts of the philosophical terrain—those which each deny one half of the Equivalence Claim—which cannot be occupied.

This leaves open one alternative to my autonomy-minded position, for I have said nothing about the prospects for an anti-autonomy perfectionistic theory. This negligence is intentional: I go on in Chapter 5 to discuss such theories, but doing so requires that I first elaborate upon the political morality and theory of institutions associated with the liberalism I endorse. For the moment, then, the question of whether mine is the *only* consistent form of liberalism must be left hanging.

4   Autonomy-Minded Liberalism

In this chapter, I outline the political morality of a liberalism based on the commitment to the value of autonomy described and justified in the previous chapters. The 'political morality' of a theory is the account of what values ought to inform political action (which, for convenience, I shall take to mean actions performed by states or other institutions with power) and provide a standard in respect of which those actions should be assessed. Political morality (in this sense) is often contrasted with a theory of institutions, which takes our political morality, and explains what institutions are required (or recommended) to promote that morality, or prohibited to protect it.[1] I shall here deal only occasionally with the theory of institutions, but my conclusions have sufficient practical bite that they might be used to develop such a theory in greater depth.

Much of the previous chapter was a discussion of political morality, since it was an attempt to justify and clarify what I take to be the prime political value (autonomy). There is, however, more to say. In particular, two questions must be asked about the *manner* in which we should promote autonomy. First, what is the relationship between autonomy and freedom? Freedom has often been taken to be the quintessential liberal value; and has also often been conflated with autonomy. It is in Section 4.1 that I consider this relationship, and explain the connections between the values of freedom and autonomy. In Section 4.2 I go on to explain how far the autonomy-based liberal ought to endorse the value of freedom, and state the conditions and limitations this conclusion places upon when and how the autonomy-minded state should promote freedom.

Secondly, there is a question of how we ought to balance different people's autonomy claims. Autonomy, as I describe it, is predicated of individuals' lives. So, the claim that autonomy is valuable does not by itself give us any guide to how autonomy-minded state action should respond to the autonomy claims of different individuals: that is, how autonomy-promoting effort should be distributed. In Sections 4.3 and 4.4 I argue that the autonomy-minded state must show equal concern for autonomy, by providing equal access to autonomy for all. Finally, in Section 4.5 I explain something of what this implies for the policies of the autonomy-minded state.

4.1 AUTONOMY AND FREEDOM

Freedom, or negative liberty, has historically played a central role in the theory of liberalism. This is freedom understood as a lack of constraint: an agent is free with respect to a particular action, if there does not exist some external preventing condition upon their performing that action.[2] This definition of freedom relativises it to particular actions, but can be generalized in the following way. Let us say that an *option* is an action that I am free to perform, and that my *choice-set* at any given time is the set of all my options. Then, a generalized definition of freedom might be as follows: an agent is more or less free as their choice-set contains a greater or lesser number of options.

My focus on freedom understood in *this* way is somewhat at variance with some other writers who have also taken autonomy to be central to liberalism. Considering negative liberty, however, seems to me appropriate for two reasons. First, it is freedom thus understood which underlies much of the historical liberal tradition and provides the context for questions about the nature of liberalism.[3] Historically, it is therefore the more interesting notion. Secondly, those who understand freedom as positive liberty tend to make the question of its relationship with autonomy uninteresting. Raz, for example, says that (positive) freedom is defined just as the possession of the necessary capacities for autonomy.[4] On such an understanding, it is trivially true that promoting freedom must promote autonomy. Raz's conclusion that freedom is 'intrinsically valuable because it is an essential ingredient and a necessary condition of the autonomous life' turns out to be inevitable and unilluminating.[5]

My task here is to elucidate the relationship between autonomy and freedom (understood as negative liberty). In Sections 4.1.1 and 4.1.2 I argue that some increases in an individual's freedom do not increase their autonomy, and some threaten or diminish it. I go on in Section 4.1.3 to suggest as a reason for this that for our choices to contribute to our autonomy, we must make them *voluntarily*, not just freely. This allows me in Section 4.2 to explain what this means for the policies of an autonomy-minded state. Such a state generally has good reason to promote the freedom of its citizens, but only when this promotes opportunities for voluntary action.

4.1.1 ILL-INFORMED FREEDOM

It might be assumed that more freedom will always be conducive to autonomy, but in this section I show that this is not so: there are knowledge conditions that must be fulfilled if our autonomy is to be promoted by increasing the number of options we are free to choose from. At the very least, we must be aware of the existence of an option and minimally well-informed about it, if it is to promote our autonomy. It is possible, however, to increase an agent's freedom by adding options to their choice set without that agent being either aware or sufficiently well-informed of the additional options. In such cases, increased freedom would not promote autonomy; so, there is be no autonomy-based reason for the state to promote freedom without *also* either providing information, or the opportunity for people to acquire it.[6]

Suppose that, one day, a rich philanthropist decides to pay for a holiday for any political philosopher who approaches him and asks for it. In so doing, he increases my freedom. In addition to the options I had before his decision, I now have an additional one: to go on a holiday he pays for. However, I am unaware of this option, due to lack of advertisement. There is no way that it can contribute to my autonomy: since I am unaware of it, it will be unable to feature in my pursuit of what I deem to be a valuable life. Nevertheless, I am free to take the holiday—there is no external preventing condition upon my doing so. So, adding options of which we are unaware will increase our freedom, but not promote our autonomy.

In addition to being aware of the bare existence of an option, we must also be to some extent well-informed about them if they are to promote our autonomy (where by 'well-informed' I mean that an agent has enough information to make a reasonable assessment of their value). Being well-informed, however, incurs costs of time and resources. Gerald Dworkin makes the point with respect to consumer choice: 'the proliferation of products, services, and so forth . . . brings with it the need to know more and more to make intelligent choices'. Dworkin points out that when Henry Ford offered his customers only black model-T cars, he gave them less freedom than he would if he offered a wide range of models and colours. However, having a wider range from which to choose would mean that his customers would have to answer questions such as 'Which is safest?', 'Which colour will be most fashionable in five years?' and so on, which would make their decisions more lengthy and expensive to make in a way that leaves them satisfied. Dworkin suggests that similar considerations apply to more serious decisions, such as which universities to apply to, or which is the best route across a mountain range.[7]

In general, for an increase in freedom to promote autonomy, we must be able to take advantage of that increase. However, to take advantage of any particular option, we must (amongst other things) be well-informed about it, and that has costs.[8] Increasing the number of options in an agent's choice-set therefore also increases the costs of being able to make a well-informed decision about each of them. Since we have neither infinite time nor infinite resources, there will be some increases in freedom for which we won't be able to pay the cost of being well-informed. These are increases in freedom of which we cannot take advantage, and in such cases the increase in freedom will not result in an increase in autonomy.

So, here is a first conclusion. Some increases in freedom do not promote autonomy; namely, those increases which involve additional options about which we are insufficiently well-informed, and where the cost of being well-informed is too high. Therefore, the autonomy-minded state would have no autonomy-based reason to promote freedom *unless* it is sure that its citizens can be aware of the options available to them and they are able to make an informed choice about those options.

4.1.2 DANGEROUS FREEDOM

In this section, I consider the possibility that increased freedom can impair autonomy. It is possible that an individual can adopt a valuable goal which involves their freedom being restricted; in such cases, their autonomy is promoted by that restriction—since it allows them better to determine the way in which their life goes—and increasing their freedom would involve a concomitant impairment of their autonomy.[9]

The point is easiest to demonstrate by discussing the famous case of Odysseus and the Sirens.[10] On his long journey home to Ithaca, Odysseus' ship passed close to the island of the Sirens. Circe had told Odysseus of the remarkable beauty of the Sirens' song, and that it inspired an unconquerable desire to swim ashore and stay there until the hearer died of starvation. Odysseus nevertheless wanted to hear the song, on the grounds that such a beautiful experience would give great value to his life. Therefore, he instructed his crew to tie him to the mast, so that he would be prevented from following his desire to jump into the sea. This allowed him to listen to the song in safety, for (though he struggled against the bonds) he was unable to move, and so his plan worked.

Odysseus' freedom was curtailed, because he was prevented from jumping into the sea.[11] However, this curtailment promoted his autonomy: it meant that his life as a whole involved success in following a valuable pursuit upon which he had decided. Odysseus' case is therefore one in which autonomy is promoted by a decrease in freedom.[12]

Moreover, if we consider variations upon Odysseus' story, it becomes clear that this is a case in which an increase in freedom would hinder autonomy. Suppose, for example, that Odysseus' shipmates refused, out of respect for his freedom, to tie him up—or that, when he struggled to escape from his bonds during the Sirens' song, they decided to increase his freedom by untying him. In so doing, they would hinder Odysseus' attempt to live an autonomous life. Because they would make it impossible for him to resist the desire to jump into the sea, he would have either to abandon his pursuit of hearing the Sirens' song, or die in the process. So, the increase in freedom would detract from his autonomy.

One might argue that this is mistaken. Autonomy, the argument might go, is at least partially an ideal of self-control: it is about deciding what is valuable in life *and pursuing it with nothing but one's own resources.* Our life being ordered so that we pursue what we consider valuable does not constitute autonomy unless it is the result of our own actions and decisions. Consider, for example, an agent who has benign guardians, who gently force them into acting in accordance with the agent's values. Such a life, it might be argued, is not autonomous, since it requires restraint by others, rather than self-control. Likewise, perhaps, if Odysseus does not rely on his own resources to pursue what he considers valuable, then his doing so cannot promote his autonomy, in which case his shipmates' refusal to restrict his freedom would not affect his autonomy adversely (since he would not have been acting autonomously anyway). The properly autonomous man would be some alternative Odysseus—call him Odysseus Two—who is able to resist the Sirens' song simply by gritting his teeth and exerting his will-power. For such an Odysseus Two, any restriction in freedom *would* be a restriction of autonomy.

This argument relies on an implausibly austere claim about the role self-control should play in an autonomous life. As argued in the previous chapter, it is important to draw a distinction between the second-order notion of autonomy I am using, and the notion of autarchy, which values lives which are self-sufficient and independent. If one valued autarchy, one might place importance on self-control in this manner: certainly, Odysseus One (who relies on other people to make his attempt to listen to the sirens a success) is less autarchic than Odysseus Two. However, someone committed to autonomy is not thereby committed to saying that either autarchy *or* self-control is valuable. Hence, the objection relies upon an error about the nature of the value of autonomy, and there is nothing to rule out external constraint as a legitimate autonomy-promoting tactic. The point still stands that cases like Odysseus' demonstrate that increasing freedom could threaten autonomy.

It is important to note that only *some* restrictions of freedom count, in this way, as autonomy-promoting. We must have control over the restriction for it to have this effect: it must (to anticipate my argument in the next section) be a restriction *voluntarily entered into*. To make the point, let us consider Odysseus Three. Like One and Two, he wants to hear the Sirens' song without jumping into the sea. Three believes that he has titanic will-power, like Two, and so expects to resist by clenching his jaw alone. However, his shipmates are aware that his will-power is not titanic, and that he will not be able to resist the song. So, they bind him to the mast. They row past, he listens to the song, and (on account of the bindings) he does not jump. However, in this case it is not nearly as clear that Three's autonomy has been promoted by the restraint. The crucial difference between his situation and that of Odysseus One is that One's restriction was voluntary, whereas Three's was not. His shipmates acted so as to allow him successfully to pursue something he considered valuable, but they did so in a way the rendered that pursuit out of his control, and beyond his responsibility. Hence (for the reasons I gave in Section 2.2) that pursuit *cannot* contribute to his autonomy.

In this section, I have made two points. First, I have argued that there are cases in which promoting freedom can damage or endanger an individual's autonomy. Therefore, the autonomy-minded liberal cannot always be taken to have a reason to promote freedom, even if that freedom is mini-mally well-informed in the way I described in Section 4.1.1. This might be thought to raise the ugly spectre of paternalism: it might seem I am in dan-ger of leaving open the possibility that an individual's autonomy might be better promoted by coercion than by their freedom. If I were to be commit-ted to that, it would be a serious problem, since it seems a quintessentially illiberal position to hold. Thankfully, I am not so committed. My second point was to observe that a restriction of freedom that is not voluntary does not promote autonomy in the same way as a voluntary restriction of freedom. This suggests a way in which we might explain the relationship between freedom and autonomy by using a third notion: voluntariness.

4.1.3 Voluntariness, Freedom and Autonomy

In Section 2.2, I introduced Olsaretti's concept of voluntariness, on which an action is non-voluntary if and only if it is performed because there are no acceptable alternatives, and voluntary if it is not non-voluntary.[13] There, I noted that the importance of an agent having responsibility for the way her life goes gives great importance to voluntariness for an account of auton-omy: an agent is responsible for shaping her life according to values she decides on *to the extent that* it is shaped by her voluntary choices.[14]

Olsaretti's concept is introduced in the context of her work on the dis-tinction between voluntariness and freedom.[15] She argues that freedom and voluntariness are orthogonal: an increase in one need not correspond to an increase in the other.

This explains the peculiarities of the relationship between freedom and autonomy. As I wrote in Section 2.2, if the choices we make as we live our lives are to promote our autonomy, then they must contribute to our responsibility for our lives, which is to say that they must be voluntary. The opportunity for voluntary choice is generally, but not always, widened by increasing freedom. Therefore, increasing freedom will generally, but not always, promote autonomy. That voluntariness *is* the notion that mediates between autonomy and freedom is supported by the cases considered in Sections 4.1.1 and 4.1.2, in which increased freedom either fails to promote autonomy or actively impedes it: there, the ability of the agents in question to act voluntarily is likewise either unimproved or affected adversely.

If one is unaware of an option, then it cannot be something that is chosen voluntarily: hence, if one is unaware of alternatives to an option, then those alternatives cannot appear in any motivational reason for picking that option. Therefore, the presence of unknown alternatives cannot affect whether we act voluntarily or not. So, when increased freedom fails to promote auton-omy due to ill-informedness, it *also* fails to give us additional options that we might choose voluntarily (and will not affect whether or not we can volun-tarily take the options we already had). Conversely, an increase in freedom which *does* consist in additional options that we can choose voluntarily *will* have a beneficial effect upon autonomy, since it will give more scope for an agent to choose and pursue what they decide is valuable.[16]

Similar considerations apply to the Odysseus case. In that, a voluntary restriction on freedom seemed to promote his autonomy, whilst refusing to bind Odysseus to the mast—that is, refusing to restrict his freedom— would impair it. He would be forced into a situation where (against his will) he would have to refuse to listen to the Sirens, because all alternatives would lead to his death. In other words, increasing his freedom like this would decrease his opportunity to choose voluntarily, and thereby diminish his autonomy.[17] Again, a good explanation for the case is that voluntary choice is necessary for autonomy.

Taking this to be so indicates why some increased freedoms will harm autonomy, but it also shows how limited the scope will be for restrictions of freedom justified by autonomy. I have noted that Odysseus Three's nonvoluntary restriction of freedom does not obviously have the same autonomy-promoting character as One's voluntary restriction. No restriction of freedom can promote autonomy unless it is voluntary, and so unchosen freedom-restriction can never be justified, even in cases where that coercion might make someone more successfully pursue something they consider valuable.

Since increasing an agent's freedom will under normal circumstances increase their opportunity to make voluntary choices, an autonomy-minded state will have good—but conditional and defeasible—reason to promote freedom. This allows us to retain intact the intuition that liberalism is committed to promoting freedom, but it also shows that we cannot *simply* promote freedom: there are other conditions necessary for autonomy that must also be satisfied. I discuss these in the next section.

4.2 FREEDOM IN THE LIBERAL STATE

To recap: the autonomy-minded liberal must believe that we are committed to increasing freedom only insofar as it means increasing the opportunity of its citizens to make voluntary choices. He should try to ensure that any increases in freedom do increase that opportunity; and should be neutral with respect to any increase in freedom which cannot increase that opportunity. Furthermore, he should oppose an increase in freedom which delivers a larger choice-set at the cost of a voluntariness-impairing decrease in the quality of the options available. In this section, I describe in more detail what is required for voluntary choice; and, in so doing, give the conditions under which the autonomy-minded liberal should endorse the value of freedom.

Olsaretti suggests that we adopt an objective criterion for what counts as unacceptable: an option is unacceptable if it involves violating some objective standard of well-being.[18] In suggesting an objective standard for acceptability, Olsaretti eschews a familiar but subjective standard, on which something is acceptable just in case I consider it acceptable. This is because using a subjective standard would, given the structure of the theory, lead to the unattractive conclusion that whether we act voluntarily would be likewise subjective.[19]

However, whether an act is voluntary or not also depends upon the reasons for which an agent acts. In asking whether someone acts in such-and-such a way *because* the other alternatives are unacceptable, then we are not just asking about the nature of those alternatives: we are asking for the motivating reason for their action. This means that an agent's beliefs about their options—even if incorrect—are centrally important to the question of whether they act voluntarily or not. An agent can *in fact* have several acceptable alternatives to an action, but it might nevertheless be non-voluntary due to their ill-informedness about those alternatives.

This means that there are three factors which can affect how far an individual can make voluntary choices. In addition to considering how free an agent is—that is, how many options there are in her choice-set—we must also consider whether enough of those options are acceptable, and how well-informed she is about them.

In general, as I argued earlier, being well-informed promotes our ability to make voluntary choices, because if an agent is completely unaware of options other than that which she in fact performs, or if she is insufficiently informed about the alternatives that she cannot assess them properly, then it is unlikely that she will be able to act voluntarily. Admittedly, well-informedness is not a necessary condition for voluntary action, for the same reason that freedom is not necessary for voluntary action. Olsaretti gives an example of a woman called Wendy who lives in a city surrounded by a wire fence, but who sufficiently enjoys her life in the city that she has no desire to leave: Wendy is unfree to go away from the city, but her staying is not because she has no acceptable alternatives.[20] By extension, being aware of alternative options is not necessary if one happens to hold the correct attitude towards the one option of which one is aware.

So, since being well-informed is not necessary for voluntary choice, and it plainly is not sufficient, can we say *anything* general about the connection between the two, and (by extension) about the relationship between freedom and autonomy? I suggest that we can, as is shown when we consider in more detail those cases where action can be voluntary (and so, can be autonomous) but unfree. Let us consider Wendy's situation once more. Clearly, hers is a rather unusual situation, since her preferences happen (happily for her!) precisely to align with the one option that she is free to take. If she wanted to do anything other than live in the city, her staying *would* be non-voluntary, since then she would be forced to do so by being unfree. Relying on luck, though, is unacceptable. All other things being equal, such a fortunate conjunction is improbable. If we take the set of an individual's preferences and beliefs about what is valuable, and then consider it against choice-sets of varying sizes, then the smaller the choice-set (and so the less free the individual is) the less likely it is that there will be an option which our individual will be able to choose voluntarily. So, since voluntary choice is necessary for autonomy, an autonomy-minded state will have a reason to promote freedom, not because this will necessarily promote autonomy, but because it will probably do so.

Of course, it may be that it is not just luck: perhaps Wendy is happy to stay in the wired city as a result of her preferences being adapted to her circumstances. However, as I discussed in Section 2.1.2, adaptation undermines the Independence Condition. Hence, the autonomy-minded state is forbidden from relying on adaptation to ensure that people can make voluntary choices, not because choices made on the basis of adaptation aren't voluntary, but because they could not be autonomy-promoting.

So, relying on luck or adaptation would be unacceptable; luck because it is unreliable, and adaptation because it is ruled out by the concern for autonomy which motivates our interest in voluntariness in the first place. Therefore, imperfect though it is, the autonomy minded-state should promote freedom, since that is generally the best way to encourage voluntary choices, and therefore to foster autonomy.

This pragmatic argument has so far been concerned only with freedom, and not with well-informedness. However, *mutatis mutandis*, the same considerations can be applied to that. Those cases in which remarkably ill-informed people can make voluntary choices must also be attributed either to luck or to manipulation; and since neither is an acceptable basis on which to decide a course of political action, we must conclude that there is also reason for the autonomy-minded state to want to promote not just freedom, but well-informed freedom.

This section has been concerned with describing the attitude that the autonomy-minded liberal ought to take towards freedom. I have argued that attitude should be one of qualified approval. Greater freedom will generally mean greater autonomy, but only if that freedom means more opportunities for voluntary action. That means that increases in freedom must consist of options that are of good enough quality that agents could choose them voluntarily, and must also be accompanied by action ensuring people are sufficiently well-informed about their additional options. This emphasis on information hints at the importance education would have in the autonomy-minded theory of institutions; though I will not go into the details of such a theory here, it should be clear that the education system will play a pivotal role in delivering the commitments of the autonomy-minded liberal in respect of freedom.

4.3 AUTONOMY AND EQUAL CONCERN

How should the state distribute its autonomy-promoting effort? Commitment to promoting a value might involve simply maximising the presence of that value within a society without paying heed to how it is distributed amongst persons. On the other hand, it may be as important to distribute something valuable in a particular way. In what follows, I argue that autonomy is a value of the latter sort, and that considerations of common humanity—that is, noting that we are all equal in the sense that we are all humans—dictate that *if* we show concern for *anyone's* autonomy, then we should show equal concern for *everyone's* autonomy.

My argument to this end, which I give in Section 4.3.2, is a negative one. It rests on shifting the burden of proof to those who would favour an unequal distribution of a good, arguing that they must show that there is some respect in which people differ relevant to how the good ought to be distributed. If we recognise that the respects in which humans differ are not relevant to how valuable we should consider their autonomy, we must take the autonomy of each individual to be equally valuable. Hence, autonomy-promoting policies must show equal concern for everyone's autonomy.

Before I give my own argument it will be worth explaining why I do not endorse another argument from common humanity that one might try to make. Rather than relying on shifting the burden, could we not give a positive argument for the state promoting autonomy equally by showing that all humans are similar in some respect that demands equal treatment? In Section 4.3.1 I examine one such argument, and show that it is either unsound or inconclusive. I also suggest that the reason for this will generalise to any attempt to provide a positive argument—hence the motivation for the more modest argument I go on to develop myself.

4.3.1 The Desire for Autonomy

Bernard Williams hints at a positive argument for guaranteeing equal autonomy for all humans.[21] Williams claims that there is a property which all humans share, namely 'a desire for self-respect', by which he means

> a certain human desire to be identified with what one is doing, to be able to realise purposes of one's own, and not to be the instrument of another's will unless one has willingly accepted such a role.[22]

Williams never explicitly uses the term 'autonomy', but this passage seems clearly to describe the sort of life that instantiates the ideal of autonomy I have sketched (that is, an agent deciding for themselves what is valuable and being able to pursue it). Williams' argument can therefore be interpreted in the following way: *if* we consider that the state ought to satisfy the desire for autonomy for anyone, then it ought to do so for everyone, and everyone equally, since they share that desire equally. This is only a conditional claim, but in conjunction with some other argument to show that the desire for autonomy should be satisfied, it would imply the stronger conclusion: the state should aim to promote everyone's autonomy equally.

The problem for this argument is that a cursory look at some of the philosophical literature shows the descriptive claim—everyone desires autonomy—is simply not true. For example, William Galston and Chandran Kukathas both suggest that desire for autonomy is a preoccupation geographically and historically peculiar to the modern West,[23] and Bhikhu Parekh doubts whether it is especially widespread even in that limited context.[24] These criticisms often involve conflating the distinct notions of autonomy and autarchy. If by 'autonomy' Galston, Kukathas and Parekh mean the latter (that is, a putative first-order content-specific value incorporating elements of self-sufficiency, rational self-questioning and so on) then we might be able to show that their skepticism does not bear on the question of whether Williams' claim is correct. Nevertheless, their voices give us *prima facie* reason to doubt that claim, and highlight the difficulty of proving such a strong empirical assertion.

We might instead say that everyone desires autonomy *implicitly*. One way of doing this is, as I have said, to show that those who claim not to desire autonomy would be better understood as claiming not to desire autarchy. For example, consider the Native Americans who made the Longest Walk in protest (amongst other things) at the general presumption in American society in favour of a life of self-sufficiency and individualism over one of communal interdependence.[25] As I have shown, one need not value these (autarchic) goods in order to be autonomous, and denying that they are valuable is not sufficient to reject the value of autonomy. Moreover, in their manifesto the Longest Walkers ask 'How do we convince the U.S. government to simply leave us alone to live according to our ways of life?' This sounds like an implicit demand that their autonomy be respected: they should be allowed to decide for themselves what is valuable, and to live their lives in pursuit of those values.[26] Hence, they implicitly rely on—even if they explicitly deny this—the claim that it is important for people to be left to live their lives as they see fit. Unless that were so, they could not take themselves to be giving persuasive reasons for the U.S. government to do as they ask, since the government does not (and cannot) share the substantive commitments that motivate *them*.

Suppose we grant, for the sake of argument, that this particular hermeneutical story is plausible. That might then give us reason to think that similar accounts might be given of other cases where people explicitly deny that they value autonomy. Perhaps the general account would be this: insofar as people claim that their judgments of what is valuable should be taken as authoritative concerning how they should live their own lives, they are implicitly relying on a demand that their autonomy be respected, even if the denial of that claim is precisely the content of the judgment they make. If this were so, then Williams' claim that we all value autonomy would look a lot stronger.

Now, this may be true: I certainly don't deny it here. However, it is hard to see how it might ever be established with any degree of certainty. One would have to be sure not only that a hermeneutical account could be given of each actual case where people refuse to value autonomy, but that an account could be given of any possible such refusal. Attempting to argue for this is such a daunting prospect that I suggest the autonomy-minded liberal ought to eschew it.

I do not propose complete pessimism about finding a positive argument of this sort. Indeed, Chapter 3 could be taken as part of such a project: I showed there that many people who do not explicitly value autonomy nevertheless either rely on its value in their arguments, or are committed to it in virtue of their other commitments. So, the hermeneutical project I describe is not impossible. I merely suggest that, for present purposes, we take a less difficult path.

4.3.2 The Norm of Non-discrimination

The main reason for the failure of the argument in the previous section was its ambition: a positive argument, based on positing a property which is shared by all humans, and justifying equal treatment by reference to that property. I only examined one putative property there—the desire for autonomy—but we can see that, in respect of their ambitiousness at least, *any* positive argument is likely to run into similar problems.[27] Therefore, I conclude with a negative argument, based on showing not that we are all the same in some relevant respect, but that the respects in which we are *not* the same are not relevant. The thought is this: considerations of common humanity support a norm of non-discrimination, when we are considering the sorts of values—like autonomy—which are non-aggregative.[28] A government policy aiming to promote some such value should aim for that property to be shared equally amongst people *unless* it can point to some relevant difference between them. I then argue that, since there is no difference between people which could be relevant to the value of autonomy, the government should show equal concern for everyone's autonomy.

Relying on this negative argument should not be taken to indicate that I believe there could be no successful positive argument. What I say is quite consistent with there existing some property, equally shared by all people, which might ground the claim that autonomy-promoting action should show equal concern for everyone's autonomy. The reason for pursuing the argument that follows is just that we needn't identify such a property to reach the same conclusion.

Williams, in his discussion, notes that the claim that we are all equally human has some practical bite, despite its apparent weakness. One sometimes finds policies which are objectionable precisely because they treat different groups within society differently despite being justified with respect to properties shared by all members of society.[29] Since we are all equal insofar as we are all human, however, differential policies must be justified with respect to some relevant difference between us. This allows us to shift the burden to someone proposing an unequal distribution, for it establishes a norm of non-discrimination: unless one can point to a relevant difference, we should presume that state action designed to promote a given value should show equal concern for everyone possessing that value.

As both Williams and his critics note, this is a weak conclusion. It is, for example, compatible with very unequal distributions indeed, if one were to have a generous notion of what counted as a relevant difference in respect of a given value. So, it could appear consistent with the norm to endorse discriminatory policies of apartheid, just as long as one took racial differences to be relevant to the proper distribution of opportunities and resources.[30] It is also consistent with very inegalitarian outcomes if the rule being considered for application were discriminatory. So, for example, suppose that we have a rule according to which people get resources in proportion to their merit: the very meritorious get lots of resources and those without merit get none. This rule could then be applied consistently with the norm of non-discrimination: it is true of everyone, without discrimination, that they will get lots of resources if meritorious and no resources if not. However, that could (probably would) produce a very unequal outcome.

This suggests that the norm of non-discrimination is so weak that almost anyone ought to accept it. It is, however, sufficient to establish the following claim: the autonomy-minded state should promote autonomy in a way that shows equal concern for everyone's autonomy, unless there is some property in respect of which people differ and which is relevant to our judgment of how valuable their autonomy is.

It should be clear that there is no such criterion. One of the things that distinguishes autonomy from autarchy is, as argued in Chapter 3, that the former refrains from attaching intrinsic value to the possession or exercise of particular cognitive capacities and processes. Admittedly, for the autonomy-minded liberal, processes of self-questioning and rational reflection might be instrumentally or constitutively valuable insofar as they are means to decide upon one's values. Those skills are not, however, valuable *in themselves*, just as *means* to an autonomous life. Nor does the fact that people possess them to differing degrees affect how valuable we consider their autonomy to be. Why would it? People do indeed differ in their capacity to live autonomously, but that is irrelevant to the question of whether it is valuable for a given individual to do so. It is not the *capacity* for autonomy that is intrinsically valuable, it is *actually living* an autonomous life: only if the former were intrinsically valuable could we justify treating people unequally due to their unequal possession of those capacities. As it is, people do indeed differ in respect of ability to judge between values, and power to promote them, but that does not mean that they differ in respect of the value in their being able so to do.

This allows us to make two related points. First, as I've said, it shows that there is no relevant difference that could justify a state promoting autonomy in a way that treats people with unequal concern. Secondly, it tells us something more about the content of the injunction to promote autonomy. As previously noted, it is possible for the norm of non-discrimination to be satisfied by a very unequal distribution, even if one thinks there are no relevant differences between people, if the rule being applied is of a particular sort. My prior example was distribution according to merit. The reason this is compatible with an unequal outcome is because the rule of merit has a particular structure: it is the conjunction of several conditional clauses which link properties (namely the descriptive indicators of merit) with different outcomes.

When we consider the injunction to promote autonomy, though, it clearly cannot have this differentially conditional structure, because (as previously argued) there is no property of individuals which might act as the antecent of a conditional clause. Hence, the norm of non-discrimination implies that autonomy-minded political action must take everyone's autonomy into account equally, by demonstrating equal concern.

4.4 EQUAL ACCESS TO AUTONOMY

The conclusion of the previous section establishes that the autonomy-minded state must show equal concern for everyone's autonomy. By itself, though, that is not enough to give us a positive account of such action which obeys that constraint and gives practical distributive guidance. In what follows, I first show that such an account would be useful, due to the lack of serious attempts to uncover the connections between autonomy and distribution in the literature. I then provide such an account myself, by arguing that to show equal concern we must aim for equal access to autonomy. That is, we should aim for the only inequalities in the actual autonomy of individuals' lives to be those for which they themselves are responsible.

4.4.1 The Need for an Account

The position I defend in what follows draws heavily on the work of egalitarian philosophers who do not themselves focus on autonomy. This is because—surprisingly—very little has been done by those who are (like me) committed to the state promotion of autonomy to address distributive aspects of that commitment. To take two examples discussed earlier: Steven Wall (who defends a theory of perfectionism about autonomy understood in a very similar way to mine) takes some care to reject the claim that we should aim to maximise autonomy, but gives no positive account of the distributive implications of his commitment to autonomy in respect of autonomy-promoting effort.[31] Joseph Raz (who likewise thinks that the state should be in the business of promoting autonomy understood as an ideal of self-authorship) discusses egalitarianism in general, and rejects it as a basis for political morality, but his reasons for doing so are not based on his theory of autonomy, and he never gives any indication of what the conclusions of rejecting egalitarianism are for questions concerning how autonomy is to be promoted.[32]

Thomas Hurka is a seeming exception to the general silence on the relationship between autonomy and distribution. Hurka defends a broad perfectionism, including a commitment to state promotion of autonomy; and he argues that his theory's 'broad thrust is egalitarian', by which he means that it gives good reason to aim for material equality (though he does not make clear what sort of material equality he has in mind).[33] Unfortunately, Hurka's position is not fully worked out, and therefore at best it provides a promissory note for a full theory. Also (as we will see in what follows) what Hurka *does* say leads to problems, which is why I give my own account of the distributive commitments of autonomy-minded liberalism.

Hurka's argument for his rough egalitarianism has three premisses.[34] First, he says that everyone has roughly equal talents: if we consider abilities holistically, rather than focusing just on particular attributes (like mathematical ability or physical strength) then we will see that 'most people have some [talents] worth developing'.[35] Secondly, he says that resources devoted to perfection show diminishing marginal utility: a given block of resources will produce more perfection if given to someone who is rather low down on the scale of perfection than to someone who has already achieved a lot. Thirdly, he says that perfection is co-operative, rather than competitive. Many perfections (knowledge, for example) are such that my achieving them has no effect upon your doing so: they are not in that sense rival goods. Others—like friendship—really only obtain at all if they are shared equally.[36]

Hurka's principal concern in making this argument is to head off the charge that his perfectionism is elitist (in the sense that it requires allocating resources to the individuals in a society who can be most perfect). Using the three premisses already mentioned Hurka draws the contrary conclusion, which is that his position has 'a strong but defeasible tendency to favour material equality.'[37]

Here I am not concerned with whether Hurka's argument is valid. As it happens, it is very hard to perceive the steps by which he reaches his conclusion, given the premisses already stated, but that does not concern me, for I shall limit myself to pointing out some problems with those premisses, in particular the second and third.[38]

The second premiss (diminishing marginal utility) seems true enough. There is, however, a mismatch between that premiss and the third (achieving perfections, including autonomy, is not competitive): they seem to point to different conclusions, and taken together cannot establish the endorsement of rough material equality as Hurka claims.

The second premiss, since it is explicitly concerned with the allocation of resources, does indeed indicate the (rough) material equality Hurka takes himself to be arguing for. The same cannot be said of the third premiss, however, if we understand it in the same way—that is, as referring to the material resources that might be devoted to promoting perfections. There *is* competition between people for the material means to perfections, and that is true even when those perfections are co-operative. The fact Hurka adduces in support of his third premiss might very well be true (my achieving a perfection like knowledge or autonomy does not in itself conflict with others doing so too).[39] However, this ignores the fact that, in a situation of limited resources, we might have to compete for the material *means* to achieve those things. So, understood as referring to the material means to autonomy (and the other perfections), Hurka's third premiss is false, and his argument does not work for that reason.

There *is* a reading of the third premiss where there is not this problem: that is, if we understand the 'rough egalitarianism' that Hurka refers to as a claim that we should show roughly equal concern for everyone's autonomy. If that *is* what he has in mind, then the fact that the means to autonomy are rival goods is not a problem. But in that case, the third premiss cannot be used in an argument to establish the material egalitarianism Hurka says he is aiming for (and which the second premiss also indicates). So, at the very least he overstates his conclusion in saying that it justifies rough 'material equality'.

So, Hurka's theory—despite its ostensibly dealing with the questions I seek to examine here—gets us no further than the conclusions I reached in the previous section. For this reason, Hurka's discussion of the distribution of autonomy-promoting effort is of little use here. Since, as I have suggested, there is no serious discussion of the matter amongst other autonomy-minded liberals, we would do best to look elsewhere for an answer to the question of what we must do to show equal concern for autonomy.

4.4.2 Equal Access and Responsibility

I suggest that we understand equal concern to demand that we provide *equal access to autonomy*: that is, we should aim for the only inequalities in the actual autonomy of individuals' lives to be ones for which they themselves are responsible. That seems to me the only way of understanding an equal concern in sympathy with the reasons for endorsing autonomy-minded liberalism in the first place.

To start with, it retains an *ex post* focus upon outcomes, and in doing so is attractive for the same reasons as autonomy-minded liberalism more generally is (at least on the conception of autonomy I described in Chapter 2). What's important is people actually living autonomous lives: thinking that autonomy is important at all seems to commit one to thinking that it is important of everyone that their lives are as autonomous as possible. Ultimately, this means that our ideal should be one of full and equal autonomy for all.

However, I do not take aiming for *that* to be what is demanded by equal concern for autonomy. There are principled limitations on what we can do to promote individuals' autonomy, either fully or equally.[40] Those limitations are internal to the conception of autonomy I defend: the nature of the commitment to respecting autonomy implies restrictions on what we may do. As I will argue, they show that trying to promote full and equal autonomy by means of direct action upon individuals would be self-defeating, since it would end up vitiating their autonomy. So, the best we can do to help people to be fully and equally autonomous is to provide equal access to autonomy, by which I mean that we should ensure that the only inequalities in actual autonomy are ones for which individuals are themselves responsible. Hence, aiming for *that* is what equal concern demands.

The first limitation derives from the Independence Condition, which I argued for in Section 2.1.2. This states that an individual, if she is to count as deciding on her values for herself, must do so in a context where her independence is not undermined by factors such as coercion, adaptation or manipulation. This precludes certain types of paternalism (the restriction on someone's liberty, without their consent, on the grounds that it will be good for them). For example, we might think that one way to promote autonomy would be to find some outcome that is easy to provide equally, and then make everyone endorse that outcome as valuable: if we make everyone think that eating Pot Noodles is valuable, then it will be relatively easy and inexpensive to arrange things so that everyone lives their lives in accordance with what they value. Such interventions, however, will generally act through mechanisms such as those previously mentioned, which remove agents' decisions from their own control. (To make everyone value Pot Noodles, for example, we might have to hypnotise them, condition them through advertising, or something of that sort). Hence, they would undermine independence, and for that reason fail in their aim to promote autonomy (since people would not then be pursuing values *which they had decided for themselves*). So, paternalistic interference with the content of people's judgments with a view to making it possible to equalise autonomy is ruled out.[41]

The second limitation on autonomy-promoting state action is much more important. It derives from something I talked about in Section 2.2, and discussed in more depth in Section 4.1.3. That is, it is not sufficient for autonomy just that an agent's life goes in accordance with values that she decides upon. She must also be *responsible* for her life going that way, where (as I said in Section 2.2) the concept of responsibility I have in mind incorporates both attributability (that is, the reason for her life going that way being her actions and choices) and substantive responsibility (that is, bearing the costs of the way that life goes).

This has significant consequences which become clear when we turn to considering what is demanded by equal concern for autonomy. Most relevant here is that some forms of state intervention would vitiate an agent's autonomy because they would reduce the extent to which *she herself* is responsible for her life going according to what she considers valuable.

This means that there will be deficits in actual autonomy that the state should not aim to correct. It may be that we make choices—for which we are responsible—which result in our living less autonomous lives, because they make it harder for us to live in accordance with those values we have decided upon. A state that aimed always to correct for such inequalities, however, would be one that undermined people's responsibility for the way their lives go, and hence also vitiate their autonomy. So, such action would be interdict for the autonomy-minded state. A system aiming to promote autonomy would therefore have to respect agents' responsibility, even when as a matter of fact this leads to inequalities in actual autonomy.

In saying this, I echo Richard Arneson in his explanation of why he endorsed equality of opportunities for welfare, rather than equality of welfare *simpliciter*.[42] Though Arneson's concern is with welfare, the structure of his argument is similar to mine. Ultimately what we care about, in his view, is the achievement of actual welfare, which he understands as preference-satisfaction.[43] However, he *also* thinks that we must recognise the importance of individual responsibility and choice. He notes that it is possible for individuals to arrive at different levels of welfare because of choices they make 'for which they alone should be responsible', and says that 'It would be inappropriate to insist upon equality of welfare when welfare inequality arises through the voluntary choice of the person who gets lesser welfare.'[44] Hence, Arneson says that the focus of our egalitarian concern should be on providing equal opportunities, by which he means a distributive scheme such that 'if each [person] behaves as prudently as could reasonably be expected, all will attain the same level of welfare.'[45] This means that any differences in welfare will be ones for which it is right to hold the agent responsible, and hence which should not be corrected.

Arneson's argument suffers from the fact that he never states explicitly *why* insisting on equality of welfare would be inappropriate in cases where the inequalities arise through the voluntary choice of the people who get lesser welfare. The importance of responsibility is, for Arneson, an external constraint, for which he does not provide much motivation. My own position is somewhat different. As I have said, it is part of the ideal of autonomy that people should bear responsibility for how their lives go. So, insofar as respect for responsibility acts as a constraint on state action, it is internally generated by the ideal we are promoting in the first place. Hence, an analogous argument to Arneson's (mentioning autonomy rather than welfare) provides good reason to take equal concern to demand that we aim rather for equal opportunities for autonomy rather than equal autonomy itself. I will differ somewhat from Arneson's terminology, however, by describing my aim as equal *access*, rather than *opportunities*. This terminology derives from G.A. Cohen, who uses it to emphasise that we should be concerned not just with the external conditions for achieving some outcome (which is all he thinks 'opportunities' refers to), but also the internal capabilities required for the same. Since I share Cohen's dual concern, I follow his usage.[46]

4.4.3 The Conditions of Responsibility

As I have said, the principal reason for my focus on equal access rather than equal outcomes is a proper recognition of the importance of personal responsibility as part of the ideal of an autonomous life. How far does such responsibility extend? A full account of equal access to autonomy needs to say what deficits in autonomy we should (or can) properly be held responsible for, and hence how far inequalities in autonomy are consistent with equal concern as I understand it.

My answer is this: there are four necessary conditions for holding people responsible for deficits in their autonomy. Taken together, they are jointly sufficient. They are as follows:

- The deficits in autonomy must come about as a result of voluntary choices, on the definition of voluntariness that given in Section 2.2.
- People's decisions about what is valuable must satisfy the conditions laid down in Section 2.1, namely the Endorsement Condition and the Independence Condition.
- People must also make those decisions against a background of information about the differential costs and payoffs of those decisions.[47]
- Both people's decisions and their lives must take place against a background of institutions designed, so far as possible, to provide equally the minimal conditions (internal and external) for an autonomous life.

Each of these requires some further elucidation, so in what follows I say a little more about what they amount to, and also where taking this position places me by comparison to other responsibility-sensitive egalitarians in the literature.

I should also clarify that each of these conditions can be satisfied to different degrees. For ease of exposition I discuss them categorically, but the matter is not binary. People are responsible for how their lives go—and hence for deficits in their autonomy—to the extent that these conditions are satisfied. Hence, equal access to autonomy requires that we do no more than providing these conditions.

Living through voluntary choices

It is possible for people to live less autonomous lives than they could do as a result of the choices they make. So, I might decide to spend a lot of money on a holiday in Africa, and find on my return that I have little left over to pursue other things I might want to do. Or, to take another example, I might decide to study philosophy at university, but later come to think that I would rather have studied architecture: the expense of a second seven-years run in higher education would make it either impossible or very costly (in terms of other autonomy-promoting projects I might pursue) to change.

My position concerning such things is as follows. All other things being equal (which is to say, assuming that the other conditions are also met) we should hold people responsible for choices that reduce their autonomy if those choices are voluntary; or if the deficit in autonomy arises from something that they would choose voluntarily if the question arose (that is, we can take people to have chosen situations that they would not repudiate, even if that situation's obtaining was not the result of an actual choice by them). For deficits in autonomy that do not arise from voluntary choices (or which people would *not* choose voluntarily), we should offer compensation. So, for example, if I decide that being a physicist is valuable, but find myself in a situation where I have to work long hours at a tedious manual job just to stay alive and hence forego the option of being a physicist, I *am* owed compensation for the deficit in autonomy that would result. My life would be less autonomous because I am not doing what I think is valuable, and that is because of choices that were not voluntary.

Endorsement and independence of decisions

The second necessary condition for being held responsible for deficits in autonomy is that decisions about value on the basis of which we live must satisfy the Endorsement and Independence Conditions. To recap, that means that we must have the disposition such that, if we reflect (or were to reflect) upon what putative values we ought to pursue, we judge (or would judge) of some such things that they are valuable; and that we possess that disposition under conditions of independence. I discussed in detail both the motivation for these conditions and what they require in Section 2.1.

Being informed about the costs of decisions

A third necessary condition arises from a feature of our decisions about what is valuable that only really emerges when we consider them in the context of a discussion about how resources might be distributed. Different decisions have different costs and payoffs for the people who try to live their lives according to them. These costs can come from various different sources, both internal and external. Suppose, for example, that I decide that being a jeweller is important, and more particularly that my vocation is to create jewellery from some very costly rare metal like rhodium. My decision about what is valuable is then more expensive than the corresponding decision of someone who decides to be a silversmith (or a dry-stone waller) because of the external costs involved (namely the rarity of rhodium). On the other hand, suppose that (despite my sluggish metabolism) I decide that being an athlete is valuable. That decision will be more costly for me—because I will require more training and more exercise to keep me at my physical peak—than for someone with a more condign set of physical abilities, because of the internal costs involved.

The condition is this: we can have responsibility for the differential costs of our decisions, so long as we are, or should be, aware of them as we make those decisions (or while we possess the disposition to endorse the values concerned). So, we must be able to know about the natural scarcity of resources, our own talents, the demand for resources from other people, the pay on offer for different jobs that we might do, and so on. This imposes an information requirement stronger than what was implied by the condition that our choices must be voluntary. Section 4.2 showed that if we want people to be able to make voluntary choices, there is a strong but contingent reason to make sure they are well-informed about their choices. The condition now being considered shows that even having enough information for a choice to be voluntary may may not justify holding people responsible for deficits in autonomy: their decisions about what is valuable must also have been in the presence of information about different costs and payoffs that their decisions might have.[48]

This is, to repeat, just a necessary condition. The first and second conditions mentioned before must also hold, and as we will see, there are some costs we cannot reasonably be expected to bear even then. But it does seem reasonable that, all else being equal, there will be many costs for which it is appropriate to hold us responsible so long as we are aware of them, or in a position where we should be aware of them.

As I have noted both in this chapter and in Section 2.2, someone concerned with autonomy will want people to be responsible for the way that their life goes, for their being so responsible is part of the ideal of autonomy I defend. So, the autonomy-minded liberal will have good reason to put in place an institutional framework designed to foster such responsibility, by ensuring (as far as possible) that people are well-informed about the costs of the ambitions that they might adopt. It seems likely that this could best be done through an education system which makes such information available and ensures that people have the wherewithal to seek it out themselves. I discuss the autonomy-minded commitments in respect of education, so I shall not go into more detail here. My point here is that, against the background of a framework designed to make sure that people are aware of the costs of their ambitions, we would be justified in taking them to be responsible for deficits in autonomy traceable to those costs, just as long as the other conditions for responsibility are also met.

The minimal conditions for autonomy

The fourth and final necessary condition for being held responsible for deficits in autonomy is this: one's life must take place against a background which guarantees the minimal conditions required for one to be able to live an autonomous life. This has various implications. One is that the autonomy-minded state will have a double reason to ensure that they have the basic skills and knowledge required to be able to live autonomously. Such provision will both promote autonomy, and also provide the conditions for people being held responsible for such deficits in autonomy as still remain.

Another implication is that people with physical or mental disabilities leaving them effectively unable to live autonomous lives cannot be held responsible for that fact, even if they satisfy the other three conditions described before. So, someone committed to equal access to autonomy would be committed to neutralising the effects of such disabilities if it is possible, or to compensating if it is not.

A third and final implication becomes clear when we consider a special set of cases, where people at some point in their lives fall below this mini-mum level of access to autonomy through choices and decisions which are attributable to them. I shall conclude my discussion of the four conditions for (substantive) responsibility with a slightly more detailed discussion of this point, since it identifies an important element of my position, and helps to locate it within current thinking on egalitarianism.

It is possible for people—in a way that satisfies the three conditions just mentioned—to fall below the minimal conditions for autonomy, and so find themselves unable to live an autonomous life without assistance. For example, I might choose to spend all my money on a fast car, and therefore find myself (after a few exciting road trips) lacking the means to pursue any other things I might consider valuable, or indeed do anything more than merely subsist. Or, in a fit of enthusiasm for a recreational drug and the cosmological insights that it brings, I might damage my internal capaci-ties to the point where I am incapable of doing anything but drooling and talking about the smell of petroleum. Recalling my evocation of Scanlon's distinction between two types of responsibility earlier, we might say that I am responsible for my predicament in such cases, in the sense that my being so is attributable to me. However, I should *not* be held substantively responsible for my deficit in autonomy (that is, I should not bear the conse-quences). In these extreme cases (and in them alone) the autonomy-minded state would have a duty of rescue.

My reason for this is as follows. In Section 2.2, I said that being respon-sible (in both senses) for the way that our lives go is a necessary part of those lives being autonomous: only then can we say that it is we ourselves who make our lives go in accordance with what we decide is valuable, and who bear the consequences of it doing so. However, this is not to say that people who are responsible (again, in both senses) for their lives will thereby always be actually more autonomous than they would be otherwise. That would be a dubious sleight of hand, and ignore the fact that people can, as a result of choices they make, find themselves less able than otherwise to decide what is valuable, or to live their lives in accordance with such decisions. My point was that it would be impossible to promote people's autonomy in respect of such decisions: a state system which aimed to make them more autonomous by correcting for these sorts of things would fail to do so, precisely because it would undermine their responsibility (and their lives going in accordance with their decisions about what is valuable would not then contribute to their autonomy).

This point does not apply, however, to cases where someone no longer has the minimal conditions for living an autonomous life. In such cases, state action which ignores their attributive responsibility for being in that condition cannot threaten their ability to live an autonomous life (as it normally would), for *ex hypothesi* we are talking about cases where the chances of living autonomous lives are gone anyway. So, in such cases holding them substantively responsible for their plight could never support their autonomy.

Moreover, such action is *demanded* by autonomy in these cases where it is impossible to live autonomously without assistance. Since there can be no autonomy-based reason to respect responsibility here, it is better to offer assistance on the grounds that it is the only way someone in such a position might now have a chance of living an autonomous life at all. So long as we think that (after being helped in this way) someone can start taking responsibility for the *subsequent* course that their life takes, we will think that there is an autonomy-minded reason to provide such assistance, even though at the time of the assistance it will undermine the extent to which their life is attributable to them, and divest them of substantive responsibility for part of the costs of the way that their life have gone.[49]

For that reason, the autonomy-minded liberal would have good reason to design institutions that provide assistance for people who fall below the minimal capacities for living autonomously. I leave aside the question of where precisely this level lies, since I assume that it is plausible that there *is* such a level. I also leave aside the question of precisely what form these institutions would need to take. My discussion of education in what follows offers some thoughts; it seems that subsistence welfare and perhaps a guarantee of access to housing might also be justified on these grounds. But the details of those policies I can safely leave to another time.

To conclude, I note that this ability to incorporate a guarantee of assistance for non *ad hoc* reasons reveals one way in which my autonomy-minded theory is more resilient than other broadly egalitarian views that are sensitive to responsibility in this way. This is because I am able easily to avoid the charge (made by Elizabeth Anderson and others) against responsibility-sensitive egalitarians that their theories cannot incorporate such a safety net, and that this fact is indicative of a failure to show equal concern.[50] That charge may or may not be correct as it applies to Cohen and Arneson but, even so, the argument I have just given shows that it cannot be applied to me. My theory *does* incorporate concern for people that fall below the basic level needed to live autonomously, at the same time as it recognises that the importance of personal responsibility makes variations in autonomy above that level acceptable.

So, to recap: for the most part, equal concern for autonomy demands that we provide equal access to autonomy, ensuring that the only inequalities in actual autonomy are those people are responsible for. There are four conditions that must be guaranteed for this to be so. Individuals must be able to live their lives through voluntary choices; their decisions about what is valuable must satisfy the Endorsement and Independence Conditions that I laid down in Section 2.1; they must be informed about the different costs and payoffs of different decisions that might be made; and they must make their decisions and live their lives against the background of an institutional framework that secures equally for all—so far as is possible—the minimal conditions of an autonomous life.

4.4.4 Autonomy and Egalitarianism

Before I discuss the practical commitments entailed by the theory of equal access to autonomy, I shall point out some of the ways in which my position differs from a few main other egalitarians who incorporate a constraint of responsibility into their theories.

First, my position differs from Ronald Dworkin's. Dworkin says that people should be held responsible for their ambitions (that is, the things that they want to do and what they cost) but not for their endowments (which is to say their resources and the circumstances they find themselves in).[51] On my view, by contrast, people should be held responsible for their decisions about what is valuable (which I take to be roughly the same as what Dworkin means by 'ambitions') only when their decisions satisfy the Endorsement and Independence Conditions, and should be held responsible for the expensiveness of those decisions only when they are (or should be) aware of the differential costs and payoffs involved.

As I have said, the autonomy-minded liberal has reason to put in place institutions which ensure that those conditions are met. So, there may be a certain amount of practical convergence of my position with Dworkin's, for under the right conditions the autonomy-minded liberal will hold people to be responsible for almost all the things Dworkin does. However, the principled differences remain.

Secondly, my position differs from others who might broadly be called 'luck egalitarians', despite the fact that my emphasis on the importance of voluntary choice somewhat echoes what they say. Equal access to autonomy differs from these positions in various respects. First, in one respect it places more stringent conditions on responsibility: voluntary choice is only a necessary and not a sufficient condition for responsibility on my view, whereas Arneson's position (for example) is that we are responsible for all and only those things that we choose. Inequalities are acceptable if they reflect our choices, and unacceptable if (and to the extent that) they reflect anything else.[52] In other respects, my position allows greater scope for inequalities in autonomy to be justified by responsibility. Most responsibility-sensitive egalitarians say that—precisely *because* they reflect something other than our choice, we must compensate for all inequalities deriving from unequal bad brute luck.[53] I have had very little to say explicitly about the attitude I take to luck, but it should be clear that my position is different: I am *not* committed to neutralising the effects of all unequal bad brute luck. My third condition for responsibility allows that people can *take* responsibility for making their decisions about what is valuable in light of the costs of those decisions (so long as the other three conditions are met) *even if* those costs are a matter of unequal bad brute luck. So, this marks a major departure—at least in principled terms—from other views in the territory.[54]

In practical terms, this difference may be smaller than it sounds, for it may be that I recommend compensation for many of the same things as Cohen and Arneson, despite doing so for different reasons. In particular, many disadvantages which constitute unequal bad brute luck, and hence merit compensation on their views, will vitiate one of my four conditions of responsibility, and hence also merit compensation on mine. For example, there are certain expensive ambitions which my position is committed to compensating for, because their expensiveness derives from the individual's lack of the basic conditions for autonomy. Someone with a very low overall level of talents, for example, may need extra resources (in the form of education and other forms of support) to be able to pursue anything that she might decide is valuable. Any decision about what is valuable will be expensive for her to pursue. Cohen and Arneson would say that this is bad luck, and we should compensate accordingly. My position also says that we should compensate, but because the reason her tastes are expensive indicates that the fourth condition for responsibility is not being met: she is not making her decisions against a background guaranteeing her the basic conditions for autonomy. To the extent that such cases are common, my position will see some degree of practical convergence with luck-egalitarianism on Cohen and Arneson's lines.

I shall say no more to compare my position with those of other egalitarians now, but the next (and final) section of this chapter should make plain sufficient of the practical commitments of equal access to autonomy to allow the reader to compare autonomy-minded liberalism with other positions in the egalitarian literature.

4.5 EQUALITY IN THE LIBERAL STATE

My discussion of the theoretical connections between autonomy and freedom in Section 4.1 led to some specific practical implications explored in Section 4.2. In this section, I perform the same task for the conclusion of Sections 4.3 and 4.4, by considering what showing equal concern for everyone's autonomy by guaranteeing equal access to autonomy implies about the practical commitments of an autonomy-minded state.

Ensuring the four conditions that were laid out in the previous section requires various policies. For the sake of convenience, I divide those policies into two groups, concerned respectively with securing the internal capabilities and external conditions that equal access to autonomy demands.

4.5.1. Internal Conditions for Autonomy

Equal access to autonomy implies various practical commitments in terms of what we might call the 'internal' capacities for autonomy, which include both mental and physical abilities, and also the knowledge and skills that individuals need for various purposes. Providing these is important both because it promotes autonomy, and because it provides the conditions for people being held responsible for inequalities in autonomy that remain. Here, I explain what those commitments are.

To start with, consider the first condition required by equal access to autonomy: people must be able to live their lives through voluntary choices. In Section 4.2 I said something about what would be needed if we wanted to secure for everyone the opportunity to do this. To recap, if we want people to be able to make voluntary choices, then we have good reason to ensure they are well-informed about their options, by providing an education system which gives them the cognitive skills necessary to acquire such information. Since this coincides with much of the educational programme I will discuss next, I need not go into further details here.

The second condition—that people's decisions about what is valuable must satisfy the Endorsement Condition and the Independence Condition—commits the autonomy-minded state to guaranteeing that everyone has the necessary cognitive ability to reflect upon what is valuable in life, and what they ought to take to be worthy of their pursuit. This is not to say that it must guarantee that everyone *actually* reflects on such matters, but it must try to ensure, so far as possible, that the ability is there, even if it is not exercised. That is, we must try to ensure that it is possible that everyone could reflect fruitfully if their mind turned to it, and there must be no block—ignorance or conditioning, perhaps—to prevent their mind turning to it. People also need access to sources of inspiration about what might be thought valuable in their lives, and to knowledge that would allow them to see what is entailed by different choices they might make: their decisions must be informed. They must also have the ability to recognise (and to some degree to resist) possible dangers to their independence: a resilience to brainwashing, for example.

The third condition required by equal access to autonomy is that individuals must be in a position where they are able to be informed about the relative costs and payoffs about the decisions that they might make. This also requires that information is freely available about such matters, and that people have the cognitive skills to be able to seek out information that they do not have.

The fourth condition (that people's lives take place against a guaranteed set of minimal conditions for living an autonomous life) commits the autonomy-minded liberal to several different things. As I noted before, equal access to autonomy demands such support as is necessary to bring people with physical or mental disabilities up to the level where they are able to live a decently autonomous life. More generally, it implies that people must have what we might call skills of agency: the ability to recognise options, make choices, seek information if it is needed to make those choices, and act on the basis of those choices.

More specifically, given the decisions that people do in fact make, there will be various different things they need to make those decisions effective. Part of the minimal conditions for autonomy for a given individual will be possession of (or the real possibility of possessing) these things. Some will be physical skills: someone who decides that dry-stone walling is valuable will need a reasonable level of physical strength and proficiency, for example. Others will be mental skills: someone who decides that pursuing knot theory is valuable will need to excel in performing tasks of a mathematical bent.

The autonomy-minded state will therefore need to ensure that people have the basic mental and physical skills needed to engage in a wide range of pursuits (or, to be more precise, the generic skills that allow them to acquire the particular skills they need given the particular decisions they make). However, as I noted previously, this is not to say that the autonomy-minded state would have an obligation to ensure that everyone has all the skills needed for whatever they might want to do. Given an education system which encourages people to be aware of their strengths and limitations and make decisions in light of that awareness, we can reasonably expect some of an agent's talents to act as parameters upon their ambitions. So, as well as developing people's various skills, an autonomy-minded education would also need to encourage people to be aware of their limitations and strengths and to make their decisions accordingly.

In addition to having skills, making one's decisions about what is valuable effective requires knowledge. In some cases having certain knowledge is a constitutive part of what is considered valuable (as it seems to be in the case of knot theory, for example). In other cases, practical knowledge is required—to be a dry-stone waller, one must know how to fit stones together to stand up without the need for mortar. In yet other cases, theoretical knowledge is needed as a means to the ends sought: the knot theorist must know about other parts of mathematics to be able to learn knot theory, for example, and the dry-stone waller must know about the properties of stones.

Once again, equal access to autonomy demands that people have the real possibility of acquiring such knowledge, by ensuring that they have the basic knowledge required for a whole range of pursuits, and also what is needed to be able to seek out the particular knowledge relevant to the decisions they make.

So, to recap: if it is to provide equal access to autonomy, the autonomy-minded state has various practical commitments which concern what we might call people's internal capabilities for living autonomous lives. These include commitments to the ready availability of information, and to people's ability to acquire and understand it: this will support their opportunities to make voluntary choices, ensure that their decisions about what is valuable take place in a context where they can know about the costs and payoffs of their decisions, and be part of guaranteeing them the basic conditions required for an autonomous life. They also include commitments to ensuring possession of the cognitive abilities required to reflect on what is valuable, and the basic mental and physical abilities required to live an autonomous life.

At this point, it will be helpful to add a word on how this political morality might inform practical policies. The best means that a government has for ensuring that everyone has these internal conditions for autonomy is through a universal programme of education during childhood, in conjunction with lifelong support for those with mental and physical disabilities as discussed. This is for several reasons. First, because it is generally agreed that cognitive capacities are most easily and efficiently acquired during childhood. Second, childhood is also the time when in general (and regardless of their formal education) the capacities needed to function as adult humans are developed. Third, and finally, the constraints placed on us by respect for responsibility force our focus onto childhood, for with children there is *not* the constraint—as there is with adults—that we must respect their responsibility. As Brian Barry points out, one of the things that is distinctive about children is that it is inappropriate to take them to be responsible for their decisions, including decisions about education.[55]

I remain neutral for now on the details of the institutional form of such a programme. The best way to deliver the commitments that are described here might be through a state-owned and state-run system of schools, or it might be through a system whereby the state merely guarantees that everyone is educated to a certain level, leaving provision to private entities. My discussion here of the content of an autonomy-minded education does not presuppose any such arrangement, with the exception of two restrictions that follow from the commitment to equal access: I *am* committed to saying that the ability of parents to pay should not give a child a better education; and differing ability should not mean that children receive better or worse education in respect of the aims mentioned here (though that leaves open questions of selection by ability or comprehensive education being the best means to deliver the aims described in what follows).

The content of this education would need to include the following. First, children need to develop the ability to reflect upon what might be valuable, and to come to decisions about what values they endorse. This demands also that they have knowledge of differing ways of life that might be led, and of differences between people about what is valuable. It also requires that they know that they can decide on these things for themselves.

Secondly, the education system would need to guarantee for children what Joel Feinberg calls an 'open future': that is, they must be taught the skills and basic knowledge required for as broad a range of lives as possible.[56] This includes providing basic knowledge necessary for different lines of work: so (for example) literacy, numeracy, a basic knowledge of science and practical craft would all seem to be required. In addition the more general aptitudes needed to be a self-directed learner are needed; they would need to be able to identify the skills and knowledge they would need to pursue a chosen course, and be able to seek out those skills and knowledge. More specialised education would also have to be provided to allow them—with increasing self-direction as they grow older—to acquire the particular skills needed for the ways they decide to live their lives. Some of this will presumably continue to take place in a formal education system for the young, perhaps by offering the chance to take advanced qualifications in a narrower range of subjects studied more deeply than the, earlier, general curriculum.[57] The autonomy-minded education system would also have to introduce children to many more areas with less clear practical applications, and an awareness of how such areas of learning and human experience can enrich lives in ways unconnected with work.

The reasons previously adduced also give reasons to provide adult education so as to allow people (within the bounds of practicality) to decide later in their lives to retrain and pursue something new if they come to change their judgments about what is valuable. As I said before, in respect of adults the need to guarantee the minimal conditions needed for access to autonomy requires that we make available—though not force people to take up—such basic training as is required for them to enjoy those minimal conditions. Some of the content of this basic training can be specified generally: people always need to have the tools to reassess what they consider valuable, to reflect on matters of value, and to be aware of the different ways of life that might be valuable to them. Other parts will be specific to different societies at different times. In modern Britain, for example, basic numeracy and literacy might be minimal conditions in a way that they would not have been five hundred years ago.[58] This basic training must be available to adults irrespective of the means to pay for it, if it is act as a true safety net. Beyond that point, however, there is no obligation to provide adult education free. If we are to take seriously the fact that people sincerely change their views on what is valuable in life, then we will think it important for providing equal access to autonomy that adult education is available for retraining, or even just for introducing people to new areas of possible value. However, *given* the appropriate educational background for children, we are justified in taking people to be responsible for decisions they make in later life, and hence the autonomy-minded state would not be under an obligation to provide this non-basic adult education freely.

This discussion is necessarily sketchy. In particular, I have left two large areas untouched. The first concerns the details of an autonomy-minded education system. I have said enough to suggest conditions that the education system must fulfill if it is to satisfy the need to ensure equal access to autonomy, but no more than that. The details of how such an education system might be designed will have to wait for another time.[59]

Secondly, by focussing on education I have neglected upbringing more generally. Does autonomy-minded liberalism have anything to say, particularly, about the relationship between parents and children, concerning how rights to raise children should be distributed and delimited, and what parents are and are not allowed to do to their children? Given the significant effect family background has on people's lives, it is to be expected that the autonomy-minded liberal will have to take there to be some constraints upon the parental relationship. Indeed, what I have already said indicates some such constraints: the autonomy-minded state would be obliged to ensure each child has an education with the components mentioned before, even against the wishes of the parents. I say more about this in Chapter 5, where I show that this is indeed one of the central and distinctive claims of this form of liberalism. This leaves open the question of whether there are other respects in which the autonomy-minded state must constrain parents. I assume that there are: if there are parental practices we have good reason to think hinder the development of the capacities needed for a child to live an autonomous life, then the autonomy-minded state has a *prima facie* reason to prevent those practices.[60] However, I have no space now to discuss in detail what those interdict parental practices might be.[61]

4.5.2 External Opportunities for Autonomy

I have noted that in addition to internal conditions for living autonomously, there are also external factors that must be in place for an individual to live autonomously, and which must be secured if people are to be responsible for differences in the autonomy of their lives.

Securing the second condition of responsibility—that people decide what is valuable in a way that satisfies the Endorsement and Independence Conditions—requires that we ensure the absence of factors which tend to undermine the independence of agents' decisions. To repeat very briefly what I discussed in much more detail in Section 2.1.2, this would include coercion (which puts people under the domination of others), or manipulation and adaptation (which involve commitments being determined by causal mechanisms that are necessarily hidden from them).

Another external requirement becomes clear when we consider the first and fourth conditions of responsibility, which state respectively that people must be able to live their lives through voluntary choices and that their lives must take place against institutions securing, equally for all, the basic conditions for autonomy. These both imply that the autonomy-minded state needs to ensure the presence of (though not necessarily itself directly provide) a broad and equal range of opportunities for different ways of life, and the components thereof: that is, we should prefer (all other things being equal) that people have open to them many careers, leisure pursuits, charitable causes and so on, and we should insist that these things are open to all equally.[62]

It might be objected that, on my understanding of autonomy, it is *not* necessary to have broad opportunities available to everyone in order to provide equal access to autonomy. The argument might go as follows. Earlier in this chapter, while discussing freedom, I noted that an individual can live an autonomous life with no significant range of alternatives, so long as what she does is something she has independently decided is valuable. Suppose, for example, that an individual decides that being a teacher is valuable, and does not change their view at any time during life. This individual would be able to live an autonomous life even if being a teacher had been the only option open to them. Their having had more extensive opportunities (and the same as other people) would, in the end, have turned out to be immaterial to how autonomously their life went.[63] If that is so, it remains an open question whether equal access to autonomy *requires* that we provide a broad range of opportunities. Individuals have different capacities, and find different things valuable—hence, the argument might go, all that the autonomy-minded state need ensure is that each individual has access to some way of life which they find valuable, and it may be that more restricted opportunities will do this.

This argument can be addressed by returning to a point I have stressed various times. It may well be true that, if an individual decides that being a teacher (for example) is valuable, and does not change their view during their life, then they would be able to live an autonomous life if being a teacher had been the only option available. However, we might properly think that, as a matter of *political* decision-making, possibilities like the one just mentioned do not detract from the case for broad opportunities being available to everyone.

The reason for this is as follows: it is very rare for people to have single-minded vocations. That is, it is rare for an individual to decide at an early age on a single value which they deem worthy of pursuit and never change their mind for the rest of their life. Individuals frequently live lives in pursuit of various different things that are taken to be valuable; and often someone's views about what is important will change over the course of their life. On my conception, such lives are just as capable of being autonomous as the more single-minded type of life exemplified previously: I follow Raz in noting that autonomy is *not* the same as the putative ideal of giving unity to one's life.[64] Whilst it is strictly possible to live an autonomous life consistently with the sort of restricted opportunities present in the case described previously, it is improbable (and impossible to determine in advance) that any particular individual will be able to do so. This is sufficient to require the autonomy-minded state not to rely on such conditions obtaining, and instead to provide broad opportunities for everyone.

Why, however, insist upon opportunities being *equal*? The preceding argument is insufficient to justify *that*, for requiring broad opportunities for everyone is not the same as requiring that they have equal opportunities. The latter can however be shown to be required by reasoning similar to that I used in Section 3.3.2, where I argued that the commitment to autonomy entails that the state oughtn't to promote first-order values, for the practical reason that doing so consistently with concern for autonomy would involve very costly auxiliary commitments. In particular, such promotion could not be acceptable unless accompanied by a very widespread monitoring programme whereby the state could know what each individual at any time valued, so as to ensure that promotion of first-order values never conflicted with people's individual decisions.

A similar argument applies here. A set of institutions embodying an unequal distribution of opportunities could only be consistent with autonomy-minded liberalism if there were some mechanism that guarded against individuals' ranges of opportunities being unequal in respects that unequally affected their chances of living autonomously. Such a regime might be possible in principle: there is nothing contradictory in the notion of a government that is aware of each individual's assessment of what is valuable, and which does what is necessary to provide exactly what is necessary for them to live the way of life that best embodies that value. Under such a regime, providing a range of ways of life open to people would be otiose. However, such a regime would incur a cripplingly heavy burden of information gathering. Not only would it have to find out what each individual decides is valuable at a single time in their life, but it would have to be continually ensuring that those views of what is valuable weren't changing in such a way as to render autonomy-harming that course upon which they had originally been set.[65]

It might be objected that there is another possibility. Perhaps unequal opportunities might be consistent with equal access to autonomy if there were substantial statistical correlations which could allow us to determine whether giving an option to a particular individual (or group thereof) would really be likely to contribute to their autonomy. So, for example, we might find out that middle-aged men rarely go to music festivals, or that elderly women rarely take up the opportunity to learn to play a musical instrument if it is offered. Acquiring such statistical information would not entail the massive costs involved in the more precise investigations described before. So, mightn't we be able to use such information to provide equal access without requiring equal opportunities for different ways of life?

I suggest not. To use such information, we would have to have confidence in the mechanism whereby people are antecedently identified as not desiring or benefitting from certain options. In particular, we would have to ensure that it did not rely on processes of adaptation, or on lack of knowledge of those options, due perhaps to their having been generally unavailable for economic or cultural reasons. So, for example, perhaps people who earn the minimum wage currently show little sign of being interested in visiting the ballet. Given the likelihood of attitudes being substantially influenced by the fact that ballet tickets are expensive, however, it would be unacceptable for an autonomy-minded state to take that statistical correlation as a reason for not needing to provide opportunities for the poor to visit the ballet. Indeed, we might want to draw almost the opposite conclusion. Correlations between an individual's social and economic status (or indeed *any* properties that might be used as the basis for such a statistical study) and a lack of interest in a set of options should make us worry that judgments about what is valuable might be unduly influenced by circumstances in a way that undermines the independence of an individual's decisions about what is valuable in their life.

This suggests an argument similar to the one I used discussing when people should be taken to be responsible for their ambitions. There, I said that it is a necessary condition for taking people to be responsible that we have in place a framework of education. The same perhaps holds here: maybe the only way that we could *really* have faith in such statistics—and hence to think that we need *not* provide equal opportunities—would be if people made their decisions about what to do against a background of equality of opportunity. Hence, if we are to provide equally the external components of equal access to autonomy, we must provide both broad *and* equal opportunities for living a range of ways of life and the components thereof.

I conclude with a few remarks on the policy implications of this commitment. First, and at the very least, it requires that opportunities be open to people irrespective of factors for which they are not responsible, such as gender, age, and race. Secondly, the commitment to *broad* opportunities will mean substantial expenditure on the part of an autonomy-minded state, if keeping open a broad range of options for ways of life requires subsidising or providing options which would otherwise disappear. Thirdly, the commitment to *equal* opportunities could have yet more radical implications. It seems plausible that there are distributions of wealth and resources which may, even in the presence of equal legal opportunities and the presence of a broad range of options, result in unequal access to autonomy, due to the greater bargaining power of wealthier members of society. If that is so, then there will be an autonomy-minded reason to endorse a redistributive scheme for resources that goes beyond what I have hinted at here, to remove that inequality in access. Consideration of such a scheme, however, will have to wait for another time.

CONCLUSION

This chapter has consisted of a discussion of the political morality of a liberalism founded on the commitment to the value of autonomy I argued for in Chapter 3.

I have shown what the connection is between autonomy and freedom, and argued that the autonomy-minded state should hold an attitude of qualified approval towards freedom. For the most part, people with greater freedom have more chance of being autonomous. However, that attitude is qualified by recognition that freedom only aids autonomy insofar as it allows people to make voluntary choices. This, I suggested, means that the promotion of freedom must go hand-in-hand with ensuring that people are not forced to choose the way they do because all other options are unacceptable. It must also be accompanied by action that ensures people are sufficiently well-informed about their options.

I also argued that, if the state is to promote *anyone's* autonomy, it should demonstrate equal concern for *everyone's* autonomy. This commits the autonomy-minded liberal to ensuring equal access to autonomy, which is to say that we should aim that the differences between the extents to which individuals live autonomous lives should only be such as to reflect things for which those individuals are responsible. This implies, in turn, a further egalitarian commitment to broad and equal opportunities for people to live a range of different ways of life.

Two observations are appropriate before we move on. The first is that this is hardly an exhaustive account of the relationship between autonomy and other putative political values: there are many values (community, for example) that I have not yet touched upon. My focus in this chapter has been deliberately tight upon freedom and equality, because those two values have for a long time been taken to be those especially connected with the historical tradition of liberalism. Since my concern in general is with finding a defensible and attractive position within that tradition, examining these values first is appropriate. Also, as this chapter has shown, understanding autonomy the way I suggest implies distinctive positions in respect of both freedom and equality; hence, it has also served to locate my own position in the contemporary territory.

Secondly, the particular practical point has emerged several times (despite my deliberately resisting the temptation to develop a theory of institutions alongside my discussion of political morality) that education is central to my theory of autonomy-minded liberalism. Freedom, if it is to support autonomy, must be accompanied by information. This implies one role for the education system: children must be given information about the sort of choices they will face, so that they are able to be well-informed about their options, and they must be given the skills of information gathering that will allow them to continue to seek out the knowledge necessary for them to be able to make well-informed choices throughout their adult lives. The limited egalitarianism I have outlined prescribes an even more crucial role to the education system, for it is only against the background of a particular education framework that we would be justified in holding individuals responsible for various aspects of how their lives go, in a way that is necessary to make my theory of equal access to autonomy workable. Moreover, ensuring equal access to autonomy means that all children must be given the chance to develop the cognitive capacities and experience necessary for them to be able to reflect on matters of value and to decide for themselves the course they want their lives to take; a state (or state-guaranteed) education system clearly seems to be the principal means by which an autonomy-minded state might attempt to ensure this. And, given that such a state should not prejudge what ways of life people will consider valuable, that education system should aim to equip people with the basic knowledge and skills necessary for a whole range of potentially valuable careers, hobbies and pursuits.

These conclusions, though just hints, are sufficient for my purposes here. I now turn to the final task in this book, which is to argue against the positions that were not ruled out by the Equivalence Claim in Chapter 3 (that is, purportedly liberal positions that are both anti-autonomy *and* perfectionistic). The conclusions of this chapter concerning education will be crucial to the arguments that follow. As we shall see, it is in its commitment to these roles for education that autonomy-minded liberalism is most distinctive; and it is here that it appears strongest by comparison with its remaining competitors.

5 Multicultural Liberalism

In Chapter 3, I considered two possible positions: that the state ought to promote autonomy as I conceive it, and that it ought to be anti-perfectionistic. I argued that those two positions are equivalent, and hence that my own autonomy-minded liberal theory has anti-perfectionism as a centrally important strand. Their equivalence also showed that the two main competitors to my theory—neutrality-based and perfectionistic (autonomy-minded) liberalism—are each committed to claims which are contradictory.[1] Defenders of the former are committed to anti-perfectionism but deny that the state should promote autonomy. Defenders of the latter say that the state should promote autonomy but reject anti-perfectionism. My argument showed that neither position is tenable. However, in rejecting those theories I left open the possibility that a liberal might deny both that the state should promote autonomy and that it should be anti-perfectionistic. This chapter aims to address that final possibility.

Doing so is a daunting task, given the range of putative values that might be appealed to as the basis of an anti-autonomy, perfectionistic political theory: this area occupies far more theoretical space than any of the other three discussed thus far. I do not need to consider most of these theories, though. As I have said, my aim in this book is to argue that autonomy-minded liberalism is the most defensible and attractive theory that sits within a broadly liberal territory. Most of the theories under question here are simply not relevant as competitors, since they are not recognisably liberal at all. Some types of theocracies, and fascist states built on a commitment to a moralised notion of national allegiance, would fit here, but given the nature of the present project, we can ignore them.

Even if we restrict ourselves to anti-autonomy, perfectionistic and *liberal* theories, there is a lot of ground to cover: there are various different values that people might appeal to as an alternative to autonomy as a foundation for liberalism. To deal with this, I restrict my discussion in this chapter to the main contemporary manifestations of such theories, which all sit within a family that I shall call *multicultural liberalism*. I will give more detail about what characterises the positions in this family, but generally they take as foundational some value other than autonomy, and argue that societies containing a diversity of cultures are quintessentially liberal (and hence that the liberal state must preserve such diversity, even if some cultures involve practices that restrict the liberty of their adherents).

Since I do nothing to demonstrate that there are no other anti-autonomy, perfectionistic liberal positions that one might hold, my conclusions are conditional. However, multicultural liberals *are* the only serious contemporary defenders of positions in that area. So, by concentrating on them, I march towards the sound of gunfire, and am guilty only of ignoring terrain that is at present unoccupied. Furthermore, the arguments I use against multicultural liberalism can also be used as the basis for constructing similar arguments about other putative rival theories that might be adopted, even though I do not explicitly consider them now.

Multicultural liberalism comes in various forms, differentiated both by the values advocated as the proper basis for liberalism, and by practical commitments. To take three examples: William Galston argues for a state guided by respect for the value of diversity, manifested as the protection (and promotion) of freedom of association.[2] Chandran Kukathas takes freedom of association itself as the fundamental value of his multicultural liberalism, and draws dramatic conclusions about the extent to which this justifies toleration of illiberal group practices (for example allowing communities considerable licence to deny freedoms of speech and worship to their members).[3] Will Kymlicka uses a theory of minority rights to advocate a strongly tolerant, multicultural society with considerable rights of self-governance for national minorities within a state.[4] There are, of course, many more than just these three, and I shall mention more in what follows.

I am aware that I am treating philosophers as allies who would be surprised to discover themselves in each other's company, for the people just mentioned are often as eager to criticise each other as the sort of autonomy-minded theory I defend. However, they all fit the characterisation of multicultural liberalism I gave previously, and certainly each occupies the philosophical terrain that is my concern in this chapter (that is, perfectionistic anti-autonomy liberalism). Furthermore, each of them believes that autonomy-minded liberalism is wrong for much the same reason: a liberal state built on the basis of autonomy fails to recognise other values which ought instead to be foundational. At best it will fail in a duty to promote those values, and at worst it will violate them in the name of promoting something (namely autonomy) which it ought not to promote. According to all these philosophers, in wrongly identifying a commitment to autonomy as the foundation of liberalism, autonomy-minded liberals have mistaken their own theoretical commitments and misstepped in their practical policy decisions. Given these links between their positions—and the identity of their target, the position I defend—it is fair (for my purposes) to treat them as part of the same family.

My argument will be that multicultural liberalism occupies no distinctive and plausible ground. In most cases, its prescriptions coincide with those of autonomy-minded liberalism. And when they don't, they either make an implicit appeal to autonomy, or are considerably more unattractive than they might at first seem, once they are pushed to their logical conclusion. Of course, saying that the positions which are characteristic of a theory are extremely unattractive is a long way from giving a decisive argument against that theory. So, I do not take myself to offer a *refutation* of multicultural liberalism. However, in conjunction with the argument in Chapter 3, what follows will perform an important task: it will identify the positions that someone must take if they are to resist adopting the autonomy-minded theory that I advocate. At the very least, that makes clearer the nature of the options. And if I am right that those positions are unattractive, it will give us good reason to consider my autonomy-minded position vindicated.

5.1 EDUCATION AS A TEST CASE

Often, it is hard to assess political theories because they share too little common ground: their commitments and conclusions are so radically different that dialogue is difficult to get off the ground. Here, the problem is precisely the opposite. Despite their disagreement about fundamental principles, multicultural and autonomy-minded liberals agree about so many practical political policies that it is tricky to find clear water between them. For example, like the multicultural liberal who aims to preserve cultural diversity, the autonomy-minded liberal will generally say the state should not prevent adults from joining groups that indulge in restrictive social practices, because such a liberal believes in the value of people being able to live their lives according to what they have decided is valuable (even if that means deciding to submit to the authority of an abbot, a Grand Master freemason, or a fitness instructor). Autonomy-minded and multicultural liberals can both argue that the state should generally permit such practices, much as they say so for different reasons.

So, autonomy-minded and multicultural liberals tend to end up with converging practical recommendations, despite their differing deep commitments. This causes problems, for it makes it impossible to use a familiar form of argument in political philosophy, namely pointing to the practical consequences of certain commitments and then examining those consequences for consistency both with each other and with our pre-theoretical intuitions.[5] In cases where there is practical convergence, those arguments dissolve into infertile disputes about whether our intuitions are grounded in an implicit commitment to autonomy or an implicit recognition of some multicultural value. The case-based intuitions themselves cannot arbitrate in such a dispute insofar as they are being appealed to as support for one position or the other. So, to assess how plausible those positions really are, it will help if we concentrate on places where there is not a practical convergence.

Also, one of my aims here is to make plain what must be believed by someone who wants to reject my autonomy-minded theory by occupying the perfectionistic anti-autonomy part of the theoretical terrain. Doing this requires that I find some practical implications which follow from the rival theory but not from my own.

My suggestion is that we concentrate on education, for this is where there is a very clear difference between autonomy-minded and multicultural positions. When posed with the question 'Who should have ultimate authority over our children's education?' our two forms of liberalism give very different answers, and for very different reasons. Establishing this test case will therefore put us in a better position to judge between autonomy-minded and multicultural liberalism in the remainder of the chapter.

As I discussed in Chapter 4, one of the most distinctive features of autonomy-minded liberalism is the type of education that it requires children be guaranteed. Crucially, the autonomy-minded liberal believes that such an education is owed to children regardless of the wishes of parents. Hence, we should override parents concerning their children's education if acceding to their wishes would mean threatening children's ability to live autonomous lives later on.[6]

By contrast, multicultural liberals like Galston disagree. He says that it is illegitimate for an education system to aim at allowing people to question their own way of life (which must mean, in the present context, the way of life they inherit from their parents). Rather, proper respect for diversity (or group rights) requires that parents and communities have ultimate authority over the education of their children, regardless of whether that education fosters autonomy.[7]

So, on the one hand the autonomy-minded liberal thinks that the educational process should promote children's future autonomy, whereas the multicultural liberal believes this to be illegitimate because it violates the claims of diversity, freedom of association, or the rights of groups.

Given this, the court cases of *Wisconsin v. Yoder* and *Mozert v. Hawkins County Board Of Education* are particularly useful for our present purposes.[8] In the *Yoder* case, the Old Amish community in the state of Wisconsin argued that their children should be exempt from the legal requirement to attend school. Their appeal was to freedom of religion as enshrined in the Constitution, on the following grounds: the requirement was contrary to the free exercise of religion because exposing children to 'alternative lifestyles' would threaten the simplicity and detachedness needed to sustain their religious community.

A similar argument was made in *Mozert*: a group of parents objected to a reading programme in a primary school on the grounds that the material described various ways of life not supported by a strict reading of the Bible. They had demanded that these readings should be prefaced by a warning from the teacher that such activities—a boy making toast for a girl, for example—were unbiblical, and therefore liable to condemn people to damnation. The school board refused, and the parents therefore demanded to be able to withdraw their children from the reading programme. The argument was this: the reading programme contravened their right to freedom of religion, because it exposed children to a variety of points of view on what people should do with their lives, and this variety threatened their religion. The *Mozert* case, unlike that of *Yoder*, was decided against the parents. I shall mostly in what follows refer to *Yoder*, but the points I make apply *mutatis mutandis* to the other.

Now, neither set of parents based their arguments on an appeal to a value of diversity or anything of the sort. In the philosophical response to the two legal cases, however, many such arguments *are* made. There is a clear division between autonomy-minded and multicultural liberal positions: multicultural liberals have tended to endorse the court's decision in favour of *Yoder*, while their opponents have not. Moreover, it is clear that these are the only consistent positions for them to take. To be at all distinctive, the multicultural liberal *must* say that these are precisely those cases in which a proper attention to the value of diversity or group rights demands that cultural minorities be protected against the attempt to promote autonomy. On the other hand, from the point of view of the autonomy-minded liberal, such cases are where our obligation to provide an autonomy-promoting education is clearest. Taking cases like *Yoder* as the testing ground between multicultural and autonomy-minded liberals is therefore to examine the positions where they are both distinct and clear, and where their adherents take their arguments to be strongest.

Incidentally, most of the writers whom I have called 'multicultural liberals' have not advocated communities having absolute authority over the education of children, but only parents. I mention communities as well because it is important to see precisely what the multicultural liberal argues for. Once we give up on the idea that the autonomy-based interests of the child are the weightiest considerations in this area, there seems no principled way to prevent the sort of argument used for giving parents control from applying also to communities. This might be because one argues (as Kukathas does) that illiberal communities should not be interfered with in their internal practice: a community which allows groups as a whole to override the wishes of parents seems to be as apt for defence by such an argument as one which gives parents control. Or, as I argue later in this chapter, if Kymlicka is correct that preserving culture is important for preserving people's context of choice then communities as a whole might have a claim to control children's education because that might be necessary for the preservation of culture.[9] Again, on its own terms this argument would seem to hold against the wishes of parents. So, the arguments could be used to justify rather more radical—and perhaps unattractive—positions on control of education than most of their proponents make clear.

5.2 DIVERSITY AS AN INSTRUMENTAL VALUE

One line of argument pursued by multicultural liberals is to appeal to diversity, conceived of as instrumentally valuable. Here, I examine and reject three such positions, according to which diversity is worthy of state promotion because it promotes (or protects) truth, diversity or freedom respectively.

5.2.1 Diversity and Truth

In *On Liberty* Mill argued that there is a utility to diversity of opinions, because it will tend to aid humanity in the search for truth.[10] Mill said that, given that we are fallible, our best chance of coming to true beliefs resides in debate and discussion, and we should engage in a communal search for the opinions that best survive the tests argument and dispute can throw. Hence, we have a positive reason to protect diversity of opinion, and even to promote it.[11]

Let us suppose, for the sake of argument, that this argument is sound. Even then, it will not justify the position taken by multicultural liberals with respect to culture and the educational case. The sort of diversity protected by the policy advocated in *Yoder* is very different to that defended by Mill, because it is not diversity that will result in public discussion and pursuit of the truth. In the *Yoder* judgment, remember, the central question was whether parents have the right to educate their children in such a way as to guarantee (or at least try to guarantee) that the children will uphold the parents' cultural or religious way of life. The effect of the actions considered in *Yoder* is to ensure the children have the same opinions as their parents, without developing the ability or inclination to revise or question those opinions.

Admittedly, there is a sense in which this might promote diversity of opinion. If the effect of public education is to homogenise beliefs, that will reduce the range of differing opinions held within a society. Precisely this was the root of Mill's belief that the state *should* require that all children are educated, but *not* specify what the content of that education ought to be.[12] Amy Gutmann characterises the position thus:

> Better [says the Millean] let parents shield their children from different ways of life than let governments impose on all children a similar civic education . . . State-run education, on this view, is bound to create conformity rather than individuality.[13]

So, the thought runs, allowing parents to control education will mean that there is a greater diversity of opinions within a society.

However, even as she defends it, Gutmann's formulation reveals just how paradoxical such a position must be. It implies that the imposition of conformity on children by parents through education is justified to preserve the existence of a greater number of opinions in society as a whole. Merely having a large number of opinions being held by people will not make it possible for any individual to discover what is the best way to live, unless there is the possibility of debate and experimentation on the part of individuals. So, diversity for Mill would only be valuable in a society wherein people are encouraged to engage with other points of view and in public discussion.

For that reason, the diversity protected in *Yoder* is not the sort of diversity which can be argued for by appeal to Mill's argument. There would be no open discussion and debate in a community of closed minds: there would merely be a society full of people convinced of their own opinions and therefore little inclined to engage in a public search for truth.

To recap: the proposal was that a Millean argument might offer an argument for taking diversity to be instrumentally valuable, and provide a foundation for a multicultural liberalism that offers a distinct and plausible alternative to autonomy-minded liberalism. The present argument shows, however, that this argument fails. The sort of diversity that argument gives us reason to value is not the sort of diversity that the *Yoder* judgment promotes: indeed, the latter would hinder public discussion and debate, rather than promoting it. In that case Mill's argument for the instrumental value of diversity provides no ammunition for a diversity-minded defence of *Yoder*, and hence no support for a distinct form of liberalism to rival the autonomy-minded theory I defend.

5.2.2 Diversity and Tolerance

A second argument is based on the demands of liberal citizenship. Stephen Macedo advances this argument in his consideration of the *Yoder* and *Mozert* cases, asking 'How can tolerance be taught without exposing children to diversity and asking them to forebear from asserting the truth of their own particular convictions?'[14]

This argument, that diversity has an educative value, suggests that diversity teaches people tolerance and respect for differences in opinion and ways of life. As such, the argument rests upon two presuppositions. The first is empirical: that the existence of diversity in a society has the effect of teaching tolerance and respect. Investigating this adequately would require empirical work beyond the scope of my project; so, I focus instead on attacking the second: if diversity is to have instrumental value because it promotes tolerance and respect, it must be the case that tolerance and respect are themselves valuable (whether intrinsically or instrumentally). The question that needs answering is not so much whether we value tolerance, but whether we value it in such a way that it can provide the basis for a distinct alternative to autonomy-minded liberalism. When we start to reflect upon why we might take tolerance to be valuable, the strength of the argument diminishes.

Consider, for example, the thought that tolerance is intrinsically valuable for the following reason: being tolerant *just is* recognising the equal moral worth of all agents. Tolerance is valuable, we might say, because it is a recognition of the fact that opinions one disapproves of are worthy of respect in virtue of being held by an agent with moral standing. Such an argument, though, cannot be appealed to by the multicultural liberal (or at least, it cannot if multicultural liberalism is to be a distinct alternative to my position) because it makes an implicit appeal to one of the central tenets of autonomy-minded liberalism: the state should pay heed to the decisions people make about what is valuable, not because it endorses the content of their decisions, but because it should recognise people's own decisions about what is valuable for them as authoritative. But that is just to say it should be autonomy-minded—and if this argument for the value of tolerance depends upon an appeal to autonomy, it plainly cannot be the basis for a justification of the *Yoder* judgment, and hence for a rival diversity-minded theory of liberalism.

On the other hand, consider the thought that tolerance is instrumentally valuable. It is not contradictory (though a little baroque) to have a theory in which diversity is instrumentally valuable because it promotes tolerance, which is itself instrumentally valuable with respect to some further value. However, when considering which value tolerance is supposed to promote, several of the most obvious answers face us with a problem. One is that toleration is instrumentally valuable with respect to autonomy: a society in which people are tolerant is one in which people find it easier to decide what is valuable and will thus live their lives accordingly. That may well be true, but it once again involves appealing to autonomy, which is—as I said before—unacceptable if multicultural liberalism is to be a distinct alternative. On the other hand, if tolerance is good because it involves respecting freedom of association or group rights, it rather seems as though the real philosophical work is being done by those posited values. Since I consider (and reject) the possibility that *Yoder* can be defended on these grounds later, I only observe here that in appealing to them, the appeal to diversity as an instrumental value is a fruitless diversion.

5.2.3 Diversity and Choice

Will Kymlicka argues that cultural diversity within a society should be promoted by the state because it is good from the point of view of individual choice and autonomy. There are two variants of this position, only one of which Kymlicka himself defends. Kymlicka's own thesis is this: to have meaningful choices, we must be part of a particular cultural community, because such a community provides us with the 'social context of choice'.

Without such a context, we cannot make sense of our choices.[15] In what follows, I concentrate on this argument, but it will briefly be worth examining the other version first.

The other reason one might think that diversity is good from the point of view of choices is this: multiplicity of cultures gives a multiplicity of choices about how to live. That this argument is associated with Kymlicka is for the most part an uncharitable misapprehension on the part of his critics, but an interesting line of thought.[16] It suggests that one is more likely to be aware of alternative ways of life in a multicultural society than in a strictly homogeneous society, and so someone with a commitment to individual autonomy has a reason to prefer the diverse society, since it is there that people have more effective choices as to how they can live their lives.

This argument is flawed because it relies on a naïve view that cultures are options that people can choose between. That claim seems incorrect for various reasons. In practice, as (for example) Rawls observes, it is sufficiently difficult to shift to a completely different culture that it is not a plausible option for most people in respect of many cultures.[17] So, if the value of diversity were dependent on cultures being such options, the diversity thus justified would be of a very restricted sort, and certainly not of the sort to provide a justification for the *Yoder* judgment. Furthermore, if by diversity of cultures we mean what Galston says (that such diversity means 'differences among individuals and groups over such matters as the nature of the good life [and] sources of moral authority'[18]) then there is another problem. Someone's culture or way of life necessarily involves their holding particular beliefs and convictions. This makes a culture or a way of life very different to the sorts of things we normally talk about as potential choices, because—from the inside, at least—those beliefs and convictions are veridical. If (because I belong to a certain culture) I believe that this or that is the correct way to live my life, I generally cannot choose to believe something different, any more than if I believe that it is midday, I can by an act of will make myself believe that it is midnight.[19] If Kymlicka's argument that diversity is valuable for providing a context of choice were to rest on these mistakes, it would fail.

Admittedly, there are places where Kymlicka supports such a reading—as, for example, when he writes that 'the value of diversity within a culture is that it creates more options for each individual, and expands her range of options.'[20] However, he also has a more subtle thesis. Kymlicka says that it is the culture in which an individual is steeped that gives a vocabulary with which to identify different choices, for example saying that 'Whether or not a course of action has any significance for us depends on whether, and how, our language renders vivid to us the point of that activity' where by 'language' he means a broad concept including our traditions and conventions.[21] Quoting Ronald Dworkin, he says that our culture 'provides the spectacles through which we identify experiences as valuable'.[22] Insofar as we consider individual choice valuable, this gives us a reason to preserve people's cultures. Therefore (and assuming that there are already various cultures in a society, as I state in the following paragraphs), there is an argument for government policies that give groups legal rights to prevent assimilation into the general culture of a country—an argument, in other words, for taking diversity to be instrumentally valuable, and for enshrining the protection of diversity at the core of our liberal theory.[23]

Can this subtle approach provide us with a justification for the *Yoder* judgment? At first sight, it seems like it could: Kymlicka himself takes his arguments to justify giving groups control over the education of children, since giving them such control might be necessary for the preservation of their minority cultures.[24]

There are, however, various problems with attempting to use Kymlicka's theory in this way. In what follows, I consider four: two of which are inconclusive, two of which are more damaging. First (and most trivially), we might note that it focuses primarily upon the relationship between individual freedom and membership of a *particular* culture. To get a justification of diversity, we must add another premise: that there already exist several different cultures within a state, with different individuals having different allegiances. Only then would policies aiming at diversity be necessary on Kymlicka's grounds. In a situation where everyone in a particular society shared the same culture, everyone would still have meaningful choice—there would, in such a society, be no reason to promote diversity. The rarity of such situations makes Kymlicka's assumption a fair one for practical purposes, but it is worth making it explicit.

Secondly, the account depends upon our having a reason to take individual freedom of choice to be valuable. In Section 4.1 I gave an account of why the autonomy-minded liberal should think that freedom is valuable, but a multicultural liberal plainly cannot give the same account, since mine relies upon appealing to the value of autonomy. Moreover, in that section I discussed various situations in which it looks as though increasing someone's freedom is either valueless or actually disvaluable. At the very least, then, Kymlicka carries the burden of proof: in the absence of a reason to value freedom of choice that is not based on an appeal to autonomy, his argument is incomplete.[25]

Thirdly, it is not clear how Kymlicka's theory ought to apply to educational cases like the *Yoder* judgment. At the start of the educational process it is not clear what we should take a child's culture to be—the cultural allegiances they feel and ways of life to which they are committed will be partly determined by the process itself. In *Yoder*, the contention was that parents or communities should be able to determine their children's education so as to ensure that the child is brought up in their (meaning the parents' or community's) way of life. This seems to be more than is demanded by Kymlicka's theory, according to which all that is needed for meaningful choice is some culture or other.

Kymlicka does consider something like this objection, when he asks 'is individual choice tied to membership in one's own culture, or is it sufficient for people to have access to some culture or other?' He goes on to ask why we cannot simply ensure a culture for everyone (and therefore a context of meaningful choice for everyone) by teaching the majority language and history. The minority culture might disintegrate, but they will then have access to the majority culture, which is all that they need. Kymlicka's response to this objection is that this underestimates the difficulties of shifting cultural allegiances: moving from one culture to another is not like 'worker retraining programmes for employees of a dying industry'. Given this, says Kymlicka, we cannot avoid the need to protect minority cultures, since doing otherwise would damage the context of choice for their members, many of whom would find it too hard to adjust to the majority culture.[26]

Within its context, Kymlicka's point seems correct. He uses it specifically as an argument against Jeremy Waldron, who says that since people can shift cultures easily, 'one argument for the protection of minority cultures is undercut . . . [the minority] can no longer claim that [their distinctive culture] is something that they need'.[27] Kymlicka argues that Waldron 'vastly overestimates the extent to which people do in fact move between cultures' and that he uses an implausibly weak conception of culture.[28] That seems fair. When Kymlicka and Dworkin talk about culture as the context of meaningful choice, they mean something more all-embracing and essential than the sort of culture where it makes sense to say that (to use Kymlicka's example in criticism of Waldron) 'an Irish-American who eats Chinese food and reads her child *Grimms' Fairy-Tales*' is fully part of Irish, American, Chinese and German cultures.[29] Even if we do accept Kymlicka's point, though, his conclusion is limited by the number of conditional statements on which it depends. *Only if* there are a number of different minority cultures (in Kymlicka's strong sense) within a state, and *only if* it is indeed true that there are individuals for whom the cost of leaving their minority culture would be unacceptably high, will Kymlicka's argument gives us a *prima facie* reason to preserve their culture.

Given that his argument depends upon these conditions holding, using education as our test case highlights the weakness of Kymlicka's position as a support for *Yoder*. Children's cultural allegiances are much more malleable than those of adults, at least to start with, and this reduces the costs of moving from one culture to another. Since Kymlicka relies on those costs being unacceptably high, this should make us question his defence in the case at hand. Furthermore, one effect of the education system is to determine what the culture of the child will be: the autonomy-minded liberal could argue that it is simply wrong to conceive of the education system as a re-education from one culture into another. It is simply begging the question to assume that the culture of the parents is automatically to be the culture of their children.

The fourth and final problem for Kymlicka's theory echoes something mentioned previously. Kymlicka takes diversity to be instrumentally valuable because it helps to protect meaningful individual choice. However, the type of diversity protected by the *Yoder* judgment would not do this. As discussed in Section 5.2.1, that diversity would involve the presence of many ways of life within a society, but at the cost of closing down the range of choice that individuals would themselves have. So, even if Kymlicka's argument does give us a reason to think that diversity is instrumentally valuable, this would not be the sort of diversity the multicultural liberal must embrace if their theory is to be a distinctive alternative to autonomy-minded liberalism.

Kymlicka might respond at this point by arguing that there is still a reason to allow parents to educate their children within their culture, this reason being the defence of the *parents'* free choice, rather than the children's. If there are not enough children being brought up firmly tied to a given culture, it will gradually be restricted to an aging population, and wither away. Moreover, if an important constituent of the culture consists in different roles played by younger and older generations (or duties owed by one group to the other), those older generations could find that an important part of the culture has disappeared before their death, if the younger generations are no longer willing to play those roles.

So, the argument really boils down to the interests of those older generations: to preserve their context of meaningful choice, we must (according to Kymlicka) preserve their culture. In some cases, this cannot happen if children are not educated within the culture—those children's freedom of choice could be served equally well by growing up within the majority culture, but their parents' would not. This is where Kymlicka's position is distinctive and a clear rival to mine: on his view, the rights of parents gives a *prima facie* reason to give them control over their children's education in the manner of the *Yoder* judgment.[30]

However, even on Kymlicka's own terms, this argument is inconclusive as a justification of *Yoder* (and hence as the basis for defending a distinctive and plausible multicultural liberalism). It is not clear that any harm done to individuals who find that their culture is disappearing could not be compensated for; and, if the state is concerned with promoting freedom of choice, compensation would be preferable to a situation in which children are deprived of a great deal of the freedom of choice they might otherwise enjoy. In that case, Kymlicka's own theory might pull us away from the *Yoder* judgment, and end up offering practical recommendations much the same as those made by the autonomy-minded liberal.

Of course, it *may* be that the loss of freedom members of older generations are threatened with is not the sort of loss that could be compensated for by the state, either because the level of compensation would be too high, or because the loss could not be repaired at all. If that is so, then we *do* find a clear difference between Kymlicka's version of multicultural liberalism and my own theory. Such cases present us with a tragic dilemma, for whatever is done involves a loss of something important for some agents: the loss of part of the context of meaningful choice for adults, or the impairment of future autonomy for children. And here is our acid test for the rival to autonomy-minded liberalism: someone using Kymlicka's argument to ground an anti-autonomy, perfectionistic liberalism must say that we should decide this dilemma in favour of the adults. This is what is needed if the *Yoder* judgment is to be justified on these lines, and hence what is needed if we are to find a distinctive and plausible alternative to autonomy-minded liberalism.

I cannot give a decisive argument against grasping that horn of the dilemma. I can, however, predict that doing so would be uncomfortable for many. It would involve using the future allegiance of children as a means to the satisfaction of present interests of adults. If one thinks that unacceptable, then one must instead grasp the other horn of the dilemma, and say that the disservice done to adults is regrettably demanded of us. Perhaps we might say that this is needed if we are to treat their children—conceived of as future adults—with the same concern that we display for them. But that would remove any distinctive territory for multicultural liberalism to occupy here.

5.3 DIVERSITY AS AN INTRINSIC VALUE

As we have seen, appeals to the value of diversity as an instrumental value are problematic. Some simply don't work, others involve having to hold positions considerably less attractive than defenders of multicultural liberalism might think. In this section, I move on to examining the prospects for building a rival to autonomy-minded liberalism that is committed to diversity as *intrinsically* valuable. I argue that there is no plausible such account, and it cannot therefore form the basis either for a defence of the *Yoder* judgment nor a distinct form of liberalism.

What does it mean to say that diversity is intrinsically valuable? William Galston defines diversity as differences among individuals and groups over such matters as the nature of the good life, sources of moral authority, reason versus faith, and the like.[31] To say that such diversity is intrinsically valuable is to say that a society in which there is greater diversity is, for that reason, better in at least one respect than a society in which there is less diversity. Also, we have at least a *prima facie* reason both to prevent a society becoming less diverse, and to promote greater diversity within a society. It is still consistent with a commitment to the intrinsic value of diversity that one should believe that these *prima facie* reasons are often outweighed by other reasons: believing diversity is valuable does not commit one to saying it is of such supreme value that other considerations (such as equality or liberty) might not sometimes proscribe the preservation or promotion of diversity.

However, if someone claims that diversity has intrinsic value, they are at least committed to preferring a more diverse society to a less diverse one, all things being equal, and to the *prima facie* reasons for action stated before. If the claim that diversity is intrinsically valuable can be sustained, we can see how it might motivate a defence of *Yoder*: that judgment was correct, we might say, because it protected diversity, which is of intrinsic value.

The view that diversity is intrinsically valuable, while not as common as the view that it is instrumentally valuable, is still not uncommon. Iris Marion Young, for example, talks about a 'value of diversity', meaning an intrinsic value.[32] Bhikhu Parekh says that diversity is 'a positive value to be cherished and fostered.'[33] Galston also is committed to diversity as intrinsically valuable. He does not explicitly say as much, but does endorse a form of liberalism that rests on a commitment to the value of diversity, which he seems to think intrinsically and independently valuable. Talking about a view with which he does not agree, Galston says that a standard liberal view . . . is that these two principles [i.e. autonomy and diversity] go together and complement each other: the exercise of autonomy yields diversity, while the fact of diversity protects and nourishes autonomy. He then expresses pessimism about the plausibility of this view, saying that there are many conflicts between the two principles.[34] Phrasing it this way (rather than, for example, saying that it is a standard liberal hope that diversity always *promotes* autonomy) and talking about a conflict between two separate principles strongly implies that diversity is taken to have independent and intrinsic value.

It is, however, never said why we should take diversity to have value in this way. No argument is given by either Young, Parekh or Galston. Moreover, other than an appeal to our intuitions—and an argument that these are best explained by our having an implicit commitment to diversity as intrinsically valuable—it is hard to imagine what argument *could* be given. I therefore assume that an appeal to intuition is the form of argument that they would use, if asked to defend themselves. In Section 3.1.1 I explained my reasons for thinking this sort of argument inconclusive. Abduction from intuitions, I said, is methodologically dubious: it is fundamentally unclear that such reasoning is appropriate in the context of normative argument.

Even if we grant for the moment that abduction from intuitions is reasonable, however, we run into a problem I noted in Section 5.1, namely that our intuitions could in most cases be argued equally to support both positions.[35] In particular, the sort of intuitions that might be appealed to in defence of diversity having intrinsic value seem to be at least equally well explained by the autonomy-minded liberal. So, even on its own terms, an argument to the best explanation of our intuitions will fail to establish the multicultural liberal claim. It is with showing this that the remainder of this section is concerned.

I will focus on a famous example of a situation involving loss of cultural diversity, namely that of the Aran Islands, off the west coast of Ireland. The

Aran Islanders maintained, into the modern era, an ancient and unique way of life, long after the rest of Ireland. In the early 20th century, however, electricity and a stable (and cheap) food supply became available. It was complained at the time that this would lead to the loss of that distinct way of life: many of the cultural practices which made the Aran Islands distinct were intimately tied up with the mechanisms the islanders employed to cope with their tremendous deprivation, and people feared that, absent those conditions, the songs, rituals and traditions would wither away.[36] In due course, the 20th century broke over the islands, and the distinctive culture was indeed lost. People started to speak English, children became aware of the possibility of moving elsewhere in Ireland to pursue different lives, and something beautiful disappeared.

Now, suppose that we think there is at least *something* to regret in this tale. What might we be regretting? Someone who believes in the intrinsic value of diversity has a ready answer available: with the loss of a distinct culture, there is less cultural diversity in general. So, they take cases such as that of the Aran Islands to provide intuitive support for their position. Our intuitions here, they might say, show we implicitly think diversity is important.

However, our regret can be explained in different ways. Perhaps what we regret is not the loss of diversity involved in the loss of a distinct way of life, but the loss of the way of life itself. Why might we regret the loss of a way of life? One reason might be because it consisted of things which we consider valuable. In the same sense that works of art can be valuable, perhaps rich oral traditions are also valuable. Another, and possibly more important reason, is that the way of life was valuable for the islanders themselves: it was *their* way of life, which they cherished, felt pride in, and from which they derived comfort and a sense of belonging.

It is because the Aran Islanders' way of life was valuable *to them* in this second sense that the autonomy-minded liberal can also give an account of our regret. At that crucial time, we might say, the Aran Islanders had to choose between two incompatible things that both had value for them—the choice either to maintain a culture that they celebrated and took pride in, or to enjoy the conveniences of modern life and be free from the deprivation of their meagre subsistence. The autonomy-minded liberal is quite at liberty to say that there is something to be regretted about having to choose between two valuable but incompatible goods, as the Islanders did, for such a choice necessarily involved relinquishing something of importance to them.

This disrupts the abductive argument made by those who posit an intrinsic value to diversity. There are other accounts of our regret which do not involve deeming diversity to be intrinsically valuable. Which explanation is the best? It is unclear how we ought to answer that question, and on what grounds—but that means that the case for the value of diversity is not made by considering these sorts of cases: we are left in an impasse, without a conclusion in favour of one account or the other.

Another lesson we can draw from the Aran Islands case identifies a commitment that *must* be held if one is to take diversity to have intrinsic value. At the very least, this clarifies what one must believe in order to reject my autonomy-minded theory—and should also serve to show how unattractive the consequences of rejection might be.

The two accounts of our regret in the Aran Islands case explain our intuitions, but they differ in the substance of those explanations. There is also asymmetry in another respect: they differ in what the regret gives us reasons to do. If the diversity-minded account is correct (and diversity is intrinsically valuable) then it gives us at least a *pro tanto* reason to preserve the way of life of the Aran Islanders from disappearance, for by so doing we will be preserving diversity. For the advocate of diversity, this reason would obtain *regardless* of what the islanders themselves wanted to happen.[37] On the other hand, the autonomy-minded explanation implies that, though it is regrettable the way of life is lost, if the islanders *themselves* choose to give it up to secure a less painful existence, we have no reason to override their choice.

So, let us ask the question: what should the state have done when the islanders themselves wanted to give up their unique way of life for the conveniences of modern life? The autonomy-minded liberal will say that it should do nothing to hinder them. The reason for our regret is that something of value to them is being lost, but the fact that our regret comes from this source ensures that it cannot act as a reason to override their wishes. The advocate of diversity, on the other hand, must concede that there is a reason to preserve that way of life, even against their wishes.

Admittedly, the latter account is committed only to a *pro tanto*, rather than an overall reason. It would be a caricature to imply that the advocate of diversity will say that the Aran Islanders *must* be preserved in their way of life against their wishes. However, if they think that, it must be because there are countervailing *pro tanto* reasons that win out—not because there was no diversity-minded reason in the first place. They must believe that the *pro tanto* reason to preserve diversity has some bite.[38]

Here is where the diversity-minded position is distinctive: it *can* stand as an alternative to autonomy-minded liberalism, but only if it is conceded that there is a real possibility that we might be required to force people, against their will, to live a certain way of life so as to promote diversity. So, at the very least I have identified in more detail what it would mean to occupy one position in the philosophical terrain which avoids endorsing my autonomy-minded position.

Once again, though, I suggest that I have done more than this. Insofar as our intuitions tell us anything, they surely show that such a situation would be intolerable, and even the possibility of a reason to promote diversity under such circumstances undermines the plausibility of the diversity-minded position. If I am right about that (and I don't take myself to have proved that I am) then this gives us good reason to eschew diversity-minded liberalism, and hence to endorse my autonomy-minded alternative.

5.4 ALTERNATIVE FOUNDATIONS

Diversity-minded theories of the sort I have so far examined are the most prominent and well-developed examples of multicultural liberalism. Having shown what must be borne by the defenders of such theories if they are to represent a distinctive and plausible alternative to autonomy-minded liberalism, I take my main task in this chapter to be complete. However, there are other versions of multicultural liberalism that people have held, and though they are not so promising as the appeal to a value of diversity, they are worth examining. The rest of this chapter will be concerned with cleaning up these odds and ends.

5.4.1 Freedoms of Association and Religion

Chandran Kukathas defends a version of anti-autonomy, perfectionistic liberalism based on an appeal to freedom of association as its foundational value. He says that 'The fundamental principle describing a free society is the principle of freedom of association.'[39] He also says that this freedom is 'the individual's fundamental right . . . his only fundamental right'.[40]

Kukathas himself only talks about freedom of association, but there is clearly a closely related position based on freedom of religion. (That, after all, was the explicit basis on which the *Yoder* and *Mozert* parents made their arguments.) So, in what follows I consider the two possibilities together.

There are various problems with taking these specific freedoms as foundational for a theory of liberalism. The first is similar to one mentioned in Section 5.2.3 (while discussing Kymlicka). To recap, in Section 4.1 I noted various problems with taking freedom in general to be intrinsically valuable. In the present context, that argument serves to shift the burden of proof: the multicultural liberal must explain why we should take these particular freedoms to be valuable in the requisite way. Only if we have such an explanation will a multicultural liberalism on these grounds succeed in being *plausible*. And even then, it might fail to be *distinctive*, if the reason to think that freedom of association and freedom of religion are important is ultimately grounded in a appeal to autonomy (as I suggested was true of freedom in general in Section 4.1). Kukathas himself notes about Kymlicka that his freedom-based multicultural theory seems to rely upon such an appeal.[41] If we agree, then we might worry that the same thing afflicts a multicultural theory based on specific freedoms, such as Kukathas' own.

At this point, it might seem that we need to examine all the various possible reasons to consider freedoms of association and religion valuable. There is no such need, though, for *even if* we grant for the sake of argument that there is some such distinctive and plausible reason, it will not suffice to justify a distinctive multicultural position in respect of the *Yoder* judgment, the central test case.

To start with, talk of freedoms in this generalised sense is ambiguous. When considering cases like *Yoder*, there are at least two different ways that we might appeal to freedom: we might be talking about the freedom of children, or the freedom of parents.[42]

If we are talking about the freedom of children, the argument fails. One reason it fails is that it is not at all clear that these freedoms *should* be granted to children. Certainly if our account of the value of these freedoms depends on their role in enabling people to live autonomous lives, we might properly think that—in the interests of being able actively to live an autonomous life as an adult—it is appropriate for children *not* to have freedom to associate as they wish. Even if for the sake of argument we *do* grant that children might bear rights of this sort, we should surely (as I have said before) not take a child, at the start of the educational process (or at the start of upbringing more generally) to be a member of any particular religion, culture, or association. True, they are born into families and communities which have particular religious and cultural allegiances. But to take the child's allegiances to be identical to *those* is to beg the question. So, for these reasons, appealing to *childrens's* freedom of religion and association is not going to work.

In a sense, it ought to be obvious that the freedoms at issue are those of the parents concerned: in the relevant test cases (*Yoder* and *Mozert*) what was being argued was the right of *parents* to act in certain ways and have certain controls. But once we shift to the freedoms of parents, the argument used by multicultural liberals takes on a very different complexion, for freedoms of religion and association are being invoked to justify one set of individuals (parents) having control over another (children).

For the most part, people invoking freedom of association or religion do not acknowledge that this is what their position boils down to.[43] Some do, though. To take two examples: Charles Fried says that

> The right to form one's child's values, one's child's life plan and the right to lavish attention on that child are extensions of the basic right not to be interfered with in doing these things for oneself.[44]

Brenda Almond makes a similar point when she argues that

> [The] principle that cultural and religious freedom for people of mature years should carry with it freedom for those same adult people to bring up their children according to their own beliefs . . . Freedom of religion, then, together with freedom to maintain and perpetuate one's own culture, provides one kind of independent argument . . . for assigning ultimate authority in educational matters to parents.[45]

Now, we might worry Fried's point falls foul of inconsistency. If we spell out what he thinks the adult has a right to, it must be to form one's *own* values, and one's *own* life plan. Clearly, that is an appeal to autonomy; in which case, my argument in Section 4.3 holds, where I showed that if one takes *anyone's* autonomy to be valuable, then one must show equal concern for *everyone's*. That precludes treating the formation of a child's values and life plan as a means to the autonomy of their parents, as Fried implies, for while children are not themselves capable of autonomy, they are beings with an interest in living autonomous lives as adults.

Almond does not appeal explicitly to autonomy, and so her position does not automatically fall to the same charge. Of course, it might do insofar as she assumes something like a value of autonomy to explain why we should grant 'freedoms of culture and religion' to people of mature years in the first place. At the risk of repetition, it difficult to conceive of an alternative explanation, and despite asserting the existence of a 'prima facie' argument for her principle, she never actually gives it.[46] But let us be charitable, and think that some such argument can be made: I have no positive argument to show that there could not be one.[47]

This gives us the following conclusion. *If* someone wants to find an anti-autonomy perfectionistic liberalism based on freedoms of religion and association, then they must do the following two things. First, they must find a non-autonomy minded reason to think those freedoms valuable. Secondly, they must accept that the freedoms they appeal to are those of parents, rather than children; and they must further believe that claims based on the freedoms of those parents must have precedence over the interests of children in the future exercise of the very freedoms being appealed to as having normative force.

One of my tasks in this chapter is simply to make plain what must be believed if someone wants to avoid endorsing autonomy-minded liberalism. That task is fulfilled by the conclusion just reached. Going a little further, however, we might think that this conclusion is unattractive: certainly it is less attractive than before we made clear that it is the freedom of adults and control over children that is centrally required. Like Mill, we might think that a terrible mistake is made here:

> It is in the case of children, that misapplied notions of liberty are a real obstacle to the fulfilment by the State of its duties. One would almost think that a man's children were supposed to be literally, and not metaphorically, a part of himself, so jealous is opinion of the smallest interference of law with his absolute and exclusive control over them; more jealous than of almost any interference with his own freedom of action . . . [48]

If Mill and I are right about the unacceptability of this sort of attitude towards children, then there is good reason to reject a liberalism of this sort. And in that case, we will find in the appeal to freedoms of association and religion no grounds for a distinctive and plausible alternative to autonomy-minded liberalism.

5.4.2 Group Rights

I conclude with a discussion of the theory of group rights. Strictly speaking, multicultural liberalism based upon an appeal to group rights does not sit happily within my taxonomy: on the face of it, the appeal to such rights need not involve the presence of any particular value, the promotion of which is being advocated. Nevertheless, this discussion is useful because appeals to group rights are constantly made by multicultural liberals: an important strand of many attacks upon autonomy-minded liberalism is the claim that it ignores the rights of groups. Claims about group rights are also central to many defences of the *Yoder* judgment: on such a view, what justifies that judgment is precisely that it recognised the right for a *group* to ensure its survival by determining how its children are educated. To give a couple of examples: Vernon Van Dyke says that there are group rights that are not reducible to individual rights, and that groups should be acknowledged as 'right-and-duty-bearing units' alongside individuals.[49] Bhikhu Parekh says that there are group rights which can trump certain individual rights, and suggests (though it is unclear whether he endorses) 'the right of a group to enforce moral conformity or expel its members or deny them the right of exit.'[50] Such rights, on these views, are not reducible to the rights of individuals.[51]

In a sense, of course, I have already been discussing group rights: Kymlicka's theory, for example, suggests that we pass laws giving groups certain rights to preserve minority cultures. Such legal rights can be justified in various ways, including the appeals to the values of choice, diversity, or freedoms of association and religion already examined. To those discussions, I have nothing to add here. A final possibility remains, though, which is that such *legal* group rights are grounded in *moral* group rights. On such a view, groups are generators of rights in themselves that make claims on other people's actions, demanding that they treat the bearer in a certain way.

Any full account of group rights would need to give an explanation of *why* we should accord groups such rights. Assuming that such an explanation would ultimately appeal to some notion of value, we would be able then to work out where exactly in the anti-autonomy, perfectionistic terrain these accounts ought to go. For my present purposes that is not necessary: it is sufficient to say just that they must fit into that part of the philosophical terrain. In what follows, I show what an appeal to moral group rights entails, whatever the ultimate motivation of such an appeal might be.

Despite the frequency with which it is assumed that groups can be holders of moral rights, it is rare to find explicit argument for that claim. One exception is the work of Vernon Van Dyke, and so I here focus on him.[52] This does not mean that Van Dyke is especially prominent, just that his statement of the position is clear, and he is almost unique in giving it an explicit defence. So, concentrating upon Van Dyke gives me a stalking horse for my own arguments, but I take those arguments to have wider application to philosophers whose commitment to moral group rights lies more deeply hidden.

Van Dyke believes that there are some moral rights that are held by groups and are not reducible to moral rights held by individuals.[53] He offers three types of argument for the existence of moral group rights. I shall consider and comment on each one in turn, and suggest that none can bear any weight as part of a distinctive and plausible alternative to autonomy-minded liberalism.

First, Van Dyke says that in the natural environment humans naturally tend to form tribes and groups, rather than existing as completely independent individuals. Classic liberalism, though, is committed to a moral individualism that is untenable in the face of this fact. Since moral individualism is what stands in the way of recognising group moral rights, Van Dyke says that in the face of the historical evidence such refusal is unsustainable.[54]

This argument is invalid, not least because it relies on confusion about what sort of moral individualism liberalism is committed to. We can distinguish between three different positions that might be in Van Dyke's mind at this point:

Psychological individualism—This is the descriptive claim that people are able to be independent and self-sufficient, living happy and meaningful lives without dependency on other people or membership of groups.
Ethical individualism—This is the normative claim that people ought to be individualistic in the way just described. In the terminology I suggested in Chapter 3, this is the claim that *autarchy* is valuable.
Moral individualism—This is the meta-ethical claim that any human sources of moral claims must be individuals, rather than groups. Any moral claims (such as ascriptions of rights, duties or responsibility) that apparently ascribe such claims to groups should be taken as elliptical for claims about individuals.[55]

These varieties of individualism are independent. Therefore, we can ask two questions: 'which must liberals be committed to?' and 'which, if any, do Van Dyke's arguments threaten?'.

Now, autonomy-minded liberalism certainly is committed to the third claim (moral individualism); but any endorsement of the first two is certainly not essential to the autonomy-minded position. Indeed, the second—the commitment to autarchy—is ruled out by the commitment to autonomy, on the grounds discussed in the main argument of Chapter 3. At any rate, if Van Dyke wants to argue that groups can possess rights, and therefore be the source of moral claims, his attack must be upon the third claim.

In fact, though, Van Dyke's argument is directed only at the first two claims. To say that humans have generally lived in groups, and have thrived in situations of interdependency, does tend to undermine psychological individualism. The argument might also give us a weak reason to doubt ethical individualism, for observing that groups have always been important parts of human thriving suggests that we ought to be sceptical about an ethical theory that downplays the importance of groups. Even if this is so, however, the point is moot: being committed to autonomy means being committed only to moral individualism, and not to either psychological individualism or ethical individualism, which is the commitment to autarchy.

Van Dyke's second argument is that the existence of group rights is the best explanation of cases in which we grant *legal* rights to groups.[56] To this end, Van Dyke cites swathes of legal practice, including several judgments of the United States Supreme Court, the laws of multi-ethnic colonies under the British Empire, differing language rights for the two main communities in Belgium, and the partition of Cyprus. The fact that we are so happy to endorse the concession of legal group rights should be taken as evidence that we implicitly endorse the idea of moral group rights, because a commitment to the latter is the best explanation for our behaviour in respect of the former.[57] He does recognise that it might be possible to make the evidence fit 'liberal individualist theory', by which I presume he means that it is possible to find an account which justifies legal group rights on the basis that they are the best way to protect some individual moral rights. However, he regards such an attempt as merely 'Procrustean insistence', ignorant of the real complexities and irregularities of the situation.[58]

This argument relies on two assumptions, both mistaken. The first is that this is a case in which moral abduction works to take us from descriptive premises to a normative conclusion. Van Dyke's technique is to appeal to examples of past and present legal practice which, he says, imply a commitment to group moral rights. If his conclusion were just that legislators have relied on such a commitment and continue to do so, then this is a reasonable tactic (though I think it would fail even then, for reasons shortly to be made clear). However, he makes not only the descriptive claim that people *have been* guided by such a commitment but also the normative claim that they *should be*. For this further claim, he makes no argument at any point. However, that claim must be established if his account of group rights is to stand up as a normative theory (and therefore, amongst other things, justify the *Yoder* judgment).

Van Dyke's second assumption is that group moral rights are indeed the best explanation for our endorsement of the legal group rights that he cites. At no point does he provide an argument for this, save perhaps for the comment that alternative explanations are 'Procrustean'. Moreover, even if for the sake of argument we accept Van Dyke's assertion that some legal group rights cannot be justified on any grounds save the ascription of moral group rights, this will not show we must concede the existence of the latter. If one is sceptical about the existence of such rights, showing that a given legal practice implicitly assumes them could merely be taken as a reason to believe that the legal practice is incorrect. So, at best, Van Dyke's second argument for group rights establishes only a disjunctive conclusion: either we must say that groups can bear rights because some legal practice is only justifiable if they can, or we must say that some legal practice is unjustifiable.

The third argument for group rights comes from an analogy with states and nations. Van Dyke says that we are happy to concede that nations have a right to self-determination, and talk about such self-determination takes this to be a real moral right borne by the nation, rather than a placeholder for individual rights of self-government. However, if we are happy to accept that those (collective) entities have the right to self-determination, then we should be happy to attribute moral rights to other groups, for *a priori* there is nothing special about states and nations in this regard.[59]

Van Dyke's observation that most liberals have conceded some right of self-determination on the part of nations is true. However, Van Dyke is wrong to assume this *must* be a moral right ascribed to nations *qua* groups. There are other ways we might justify treating nations in this way, such as (for example) thinking that there is an individual right of freedom of association which implies that a group of people who demand to be treated as a corporate whole should be so treated. One might say, for example, that this is an example of a phenomenon that is quite widespread: that is, an individual moral claim that only becomes visible when we consider individuals as parts of groups.

Van Dyke does consider this sort of response, but rejects it on the grounds that it is very difficult to derive a right to self-determination from the sorts of rights we usually ascribe to individuals.[60] Even if that is so, it does not prove his point. Once again, his conclusion is more properly understood as disjunctive. In this case, it is a trilemma: we must accept *either* that there are non-derivative moral group rights, *or* face the difficulty of deriving a right of self-determination for nations from individual rights, *or* think that the idea of a right to self-determination is shown by this line of reasoning to be problematic.[61] Since we are not given a reason to grasp the first horn of the trilemma, the argument as it stands does not prove that there are moral group rights.

Of course, I have not yet said anything about why we should *not* grasp that horn. Nothing I have said shows that there might not be a successful positive argument for moral group rights. Hence, someone who believes in moral group rights could just stick to their guns, and insist that such rights exist, irrespective of the inconclusiveness of Van Dyke's arguments and the apparent explanatory eliminability that I have pointed to. What I have said does not prove that such a person is wrong. It does, though, mean they bear the burden of proof. Absent any positive argument for moral group rights, we should not complicate our moral universe by saying that there are such things.

CONCLUSION

In this chapter, I returned to the question left hanging at the end of Chapter 3, namely whether there is a liberal rival to my autonomy-minded theory. In that earlier chapter I showed that neither autonomy-minded perfectionistic liberalism nor anti-autonomy anti-perfectionistic liberalism is coherent, since each contradicts the Equivalence Claim there established. The only possible rival position is some form of anti-autonomy, perfectionistic liberalism, committed to a different value. Having noted that the only putative liberals actually holding this position all fall within a family we might call 'multicultural liberalism', I have argued that there is no distinct and plausible position for such a liberal to hold.

My argument has been inconclusive, for I have left open various possible positions that *are* consistent and distinct. I have suggested that they are so unattractive as to be implausible, but I have not *demonstrated* that they are untenable. These alternative possibilities are as follows.

First, following Kymlicka, one might endorse a liberalism founded on commitment to diversity, conceived of as *instrumentally* valuable, because it protects the necessary social context for freedom of choice. Taking this position involves shouldering a burden of proof: we must be shown that there is a non-autonomy-based reason to think that freedom of choice is valuable. It also means being committed to saying that conflicts between the freedom-based interests of adults and of children must be resolved in the interests of adults.

Secondly, one might be a diversity-minded liberal who holds that diversity is *intrinsically* valuable. Holding that means conceding that there is a real possibility that we might be required to force people, against their will, to live a certain way of life so as to promote diversity.

Thirdly, I have left open the possibility of an anti-autonomy perfectionistic liberalism based on commitment to freedoms of association or religion. Holding either position incurs a burden of proof: as with Kymlicka's position, we must have a non-autonomy-based reason to think those freedoms valuable. A defender of such a position would also have to accept that the freedoms they appeal to are those of parents, rather than children. Further, they must believe that claims based on the freedoms of those parents trump the interests of children, not only in living autonomous lives, but even in the future exercise of those very freedoms that are being appealed to as having normative force.

Fourthly, and finally, there may be variants of these positions—or ones appealing to values that I have not considered—that are committed to the existence of non-derivative moral group rights. Taking this position once again incurs a burden of proof, to show that we should believe in such rights, and that they are sufficient to override individual rights in cases like that of *Yoder*.

Each of these represents a distinct and consistent position within anti-autonomy perfectionistic liberalism, and hence a potential rival to my own theory. A modest conclusion is that I have made plainer the nature of the choices left open in this part of the philosophical terrain. A liberal political theory must be either committed to the promotion of autonomy, as mine is, or one one of the options listed previously.

I take it, though, that the auxiliary commitments each entails are rather hard to accept: certainly they are more contentious than the advocates of these forms of liberalism generally admit. For that reason I suspect that in this chapter I have given the grounds for a more ambitious conclusion. The costs of the positions considered are such as to provide good reason for a liberal to endorse the alternative to those positions, which is to say the autonomy-minded liberal theory which is the subject of this book.

Conclusion

At the start of this book, I said that there is a need for a clear and attractive theory of liberalism, to bring order to a rather chaotic and ill-managed debate concerning the deep foundations of liberalism on the one hand, and the details of liberal policy on the other. My offering is a theory of autonomy-minded liberalism: the state should promote autonomy, understood as a value which consists of an agent deciding for herself what is valuable and living her life in accordance with that decision. What I have shown is that, if one is inclined to hold a position within the territory of liberalism, this theory is the best way of finding a set of coherent and attractive commitments. To finish, I shall briefly summarise my main conclusions, explaining what I take myself to have established (with varying degrees of certainty). I shall also explain what questions have been left open, and sketch the shape that I expect any answers would have to take.

My case has had three main elements. The first has been to elucidate a conception of autonomy, and show what sort of a political theory emerges if one takes the promotion of autonomy so understood as a central concern. On my conception—which is inspired both by Joseph Raz's discussion of autonomy itself, and by von Humboldt's and Mill's earlier accounts of individuality—autonomy is an ideal of individuals deciding for themselves what is a valuable life, and living their lives in accordance with that decision. Deciding for oneself what is valuable consists in satisfying two conditions. The Endorsement Condition is satisfied when an agent has a disposition such that if she reflects (or were to reflect) upon what putative values she ought to pursue in her life, she judges (or would judge) of some such things that they are valuable. And the Independence Condition is satisfied when she is in a state where her reflection is, or would be if it took place, free from factors undermining her independence. Finally, in addition to satisfying these two conditions, an agent must make her decisions effective: that is, the ideal of autonomy is not just for her to decide what is valuable, but for her to live her life in accordance with that decision, bearing responsibility for the shape her life takes.

I have also explained something of the political morality that is entailed by the commitment to autonomy. I came to three main conclusions. Firstly, being committed to promoting autonomy means being committed to anti-perfectionism about state action. Secondly, the autonomy-minded liberal will have a conditional commitment to giving people *freedom*, by which I mean a range of choices for their actions. However, the reason to do that is also a reason to ensure that people are well-informed about their options and that those options are such that they could be chosen voluntarily. Thirdly, I also showed that the autonomy-minded liberal has some commitments in terms of *equality*. Autonomy-promoting action must show equal concern for everyone's autonomy, which is to say that we must aim for equal access to autonomy for all. This entails a further egalitarian commitment to the provision of equal opportunities for as wide a range of ways of life as possible, and also places autonomy-minded education policy at the heart of my theory of liberalism.

These two strands—making clearer a conception of autonomy, and showing what are the political consequences of taking it to be worthy of promotion—tell us something about what autonomy-minded liberalism looks like. The third and final strand has been to show why I take that theory to be superior to its competitors. An important part of this was my argument for the Equivalence Claim: the state should promote autonomy if and only if anti-perfectionism is true. This gave reasons to endorse autonomy-minded liberal by showing that the commitment to autonomy can be tied into a web of other positions likely to be attractive to liberals. It also served another important function, by eliminating two principal rivals to my own position. Neutrality-based liberals endorse anti-perfectionism and deny that the state should promote autonomy; perfectionistic autonomy-minded liberals have the converse commitments. My argument for the Equivalence Claim shows these positions to be seriously mistaken: each affirms one and denies the other of a pair of claims that must be accepted or rejected together. For this reason, I concluded that liberals of those colours must either accept my autonomy-minded theory, or reject those claims which they take to be constitutive of their theories. My argument left open taking the latter course, but I take it to be sufficiently unattractive as to give them good reason to reconceive their own positions in something closer to my terms.

The argument for the Equivalence Claim also left open the question of whether there might be an attractive and defensible liberal position which is both anti-autonomy and perfectionistic. I argued that many such positions fail, either because they are inconsistent or because they fail to be a distinctive alternative to my own theory. I also showed that certain such positions are left open, but predicted that they are so unattractive as to be implausible, even if they are distinct and consistent alternatives to my own. So, I suggested that we have good reason to endorse the only alternative left open to those positions, which is to say the autonomy-minded liberalism that is the subject of this book.

Inevitably, this book raises various questions that have yet to be answered. These mostly concern the policy implications of my views: I have not, save in a perfunctory and incidental manner, given much in the way of clear and practical guidance for liberal policies. To provide that, we need more than an account of the foundations of liberalism, such as I gave in Chapters 2 and 3, or the political morality developed in Chapter 4. To return to a familiar distinction, we also need an autonomy-minded theory of institutions if we are to know what needs to be done on a practical level. That theory would complete the task I set myself at the start of this book, namely to formulate a coherent and attractive liberal political theory that gives clear practical direction. However, providing such a theory is far beyond the scope of the present volume.

It may seem odd to finish a work like this with the ultimate conclusion still existing only as a promissory note. But, as I said, the lack of such direction was a symptom of confusion at the foundations. Here, I hope I have shown at least one way of making those foundations firm.

Notes

NOTES TO THE INTRODUCTION

1. Giovanni Pico della Mirandola, *de hominis dignitate*, translated into English C. G. Wallis into English as *On the Dignity of Man* (Indianapolis: Bobbs-Merrill, 1965), pp. 4–5.
2. Wilhelm von Humboldt, *Ideen zu einem Versuch, die Gränzen der Wirksamkeit des Staats zu bestimmen*, published in 1810. Edited and translated by J.W. Burrow as *The Limits of State Action* (Cambridge: Cambridge University Press, 1969).
3. John Stuart Mill, *On Liberty*, published in 1859. Reprinted in *On Liberty and Other writings*, ed. by Stefan Collini (Cambridge: Cambridge University Press, 1989), p. 60.
4. J. Raz, *The Morality of Freedom* (Oxford: Clarendon Press, 1986), p. 369.

NOTES TO CHAPTER 1

1. J. Christman, 'Constructing the Inner Citadel', *Ethics* 101 (1988), 505–520.
2. I. Kant, *Groundwork of the Metaphysics of Morals*, trans. by M. Gregor (Cambridge: Cambridge University Press, 1997), §3.
3. J. Jacobs, 'Some Tensions between Autonomy and Self-Governance', *Social Philosophy and Policy* 20(2) (2003): 221–244. Jacobs uses the term 'self-governance' to make his contrast with autonomy; but to avoid muddying the waters I have called it 'free and voluntary action', since that is what 'self-governance' amounts to on his view.
4. D.A.J. Richards, 'Rights and Autonomy', *Ethics* 92 (1981): 3–20, at 9.
5. J. Rawls, *Political Liberalism* (New York: Columbia University Press, 1993): p. xliv.
6. e.g, her *Autonomy and Trust in Bioethics* (Cambridge: Cambridge University Press, 2002); and 'Autonomy: The Emperor's New Clothes', *Proceedings of the Aristotelian Society: Supplement* 77 (2003): 1–21.
7. e.g., J. Waldron 'Moral Autonomy and Personal Autonomy', in J. Christman and J. Anderson eds. *Autonomy and the Challenges to Liberalism* (Cambridge: Cambridge University Press, 2005), pp. 307–329.
8. R.F. Ladenson, 'A Theory of Personal Autonomy', *Ethics* 86 (1975): 30–48, at 43.
9. M.J. Meyer, 'Stoicism, Rights and Autonomy', *American Philosophical Quarterly* 24 (1987): 267–271, (at 269).

10. e.g., J.M. Cooper, 'Stoic Autonomy', *Social Philosophy and Policy* 20(2) (2003): 1–29.
11. G. Sher, *Beyond Neutrality* (Cambridge: Cambridge University Press, 1997): p. 48.
12. K. Lehrer, 'Reason and Autonomy', *Social Philosophy and Policy* 20(2) (2003): 177–198.
13. J. Benson, 'Who is the Autonomous Man?', *Philosophy* 58 (1983): 5–17.
14. L. Haworth, *Autonomy: An Essay in Philosophical Psychology and Ethics* (New Haven: Yale University Press, 1986): p. 39. Haworth is somewhat ambiguous about whether full rationality on his definition is a sufficient condition for autonomy or merely a necessary one: here, I follow Christman (1988: 115) in interpreting him the former way.
15. See H. Frankfurt, 'Freedom of the Will and the Concept of a Person', *Journal of Philosophy* 68 (1971): 5–20; G. Dworkin, 'Autonomy and Behaviour Control', *Hastings Center Report* 6 (1976): 23–28; and G. Dworkin, *The Theory and Practice of Autonomy* (Cambridge: Cambridge University Press, 1988) ch. 1.
16. G. Dworkin, 'The Concept of Autonomy' in R. Haller, ed. *Science and Ethics* (Amsterdam: Rodopi, 1981), pp. 203–213, at 212.
17. G. Dworkin, 'Autonomy and Behaviour Control'.
18. G. Dworkin, *Theory and Practice of Autonomy*, pp. 15–17.
19. ibid. p. 20.
20. G. Watson, 'Free Agency', *Journal of Philosophy* 72 (1975) 205–220; I. Thalberg 'Hierarchical Analyses of Unfree Action', *Canadian Journal of Philosophy* 8 (1978) 211–226.
21. M. Friedman 'Autonomy and the Split-Level Self', *Southern Journal of Philosophy* 24 (1986) 19–35.
22. I should add that, as a matter of exegesis, I am sure that this is *not* Frankfurt or Dworkin's motivation, since neither writes about rationality as one of their central concerns. However, it might be a reason why someone else would adopt their position.
23. Raz, *The Morality of Freedom,* p. 369.
24. ibid. p. 385.
25. I will discuss in more detail what this vague condition might actually amount to.
26. References here are to the edition translated and edited by J.W. Burrow (Cambridge: Cambridge University Press, 1969).
27. Humboldt, p. 28.
28. I discuss the value of freedom more generally in Chapter 4. There, I give reasons to be suspicious about the claim that freedom is necessary for autonomy. So, if Humboldt does take freedom to be necessary for individuality, I disagree with him to that extent.
29. Humboldt, p. 16.
30. ibid. p. 21.
31. ibid. pp. 28–29.
32. Mill, p. 59.
33. ibid. p. 63.
34. ibid. pp. 59–61.
35. ibid. p. 58.
36. ibid. p. 61.
37. This latter point, that individuality must involve the determination of values rather than just the satisfaction of desires, is one that will be central to the notion of autonomy that I shall use, as we will see. However, in its emphasis upon occurrent reflection, it harkens back to the rationalist notions

considered in Section 1.1. As we shall see, I depart somewhat from Mill's company on this point: for my ideal, a *disposition* to reflect is sufficient. I will explain my reasons for this in more detail, but the basic point is that I take the reason we care about actual reflection to be that it tracks a certain relationship between individuals and their commitments, but that reflection is not *necessary* for that relationship to obtain.

38. Mill, p. 60.
39. Humboldt, pp. 28–29.
40. Raz, *The Morality of Freedom*, p. 395.
41. Mill, p. 62.
42. ibid. 57.
43, ibid. pp. 63–64.
44. ibid. p. 14.
45. ibid. p. 57.
46. For example, J.F. Stephen, *Liberty, Equality, Fraternity* (London: Smith, Elder, 1873). Reprinted ed. by R.J. White (Cambridge: Cambridge University Press, 1969) from which page references are taken. Henry Sidgwick concurred in his review essay '"Liberty, Equality, Fraternity" by James Fitzjames Stephen', *The Academy* 4 (August 1 1873), 292–294; quoted in P. Nicholson 'The Reception and Early Reputation of Mill's Political Thought', in Skorupski, pp. 464–496.
47. J. Gray 'Mill's Conception of Happiness and the Theory of Individuality' in *J.S. Mill's 'On Liberty'* in *Focus* ed. By J. Gray & G.W. Smith (London: Routledge 1991), pp. 190–211, (p. 199). See also his *Mill on Liberty: A Defence* (London: Routledge 1983).
48. For example: W. Donner, 'Mill's Utilitarianism' in Skorupski, pp. 255–292 (p. 277); T.H. Irwin, 'Mill and the Classical World', pp. 423–463 in the same volume; R.F. Ladenson 'Mill's Conception of Individuality', *Social Theory and Practice* 4 (1977), 167–182; R. Young 'The Value of Autonomy', *Philosophical Quarterly* 32 (1982), 35–44 (p. 37).
49. T. Hurka 'Why Value Autonomy?' in *Social Theory and Practice* 13 (1987), 361–380 (p. 361); and *Perfectionism* (New York: Oxford University Press, 1993), p. 148.
50. S. Wall *Liberalism, Perfectionism and Restraint* (New York: Cambridge University Press, 1998), p. 128. See also his 'Freedom as a Political Ideal' in *Social Philosophy and Policy* 20 (2003): 307–331.
51. M. Oshana, 'How Much Should we Value Autonomy?', *Social Philosophy and Policy* 20(2) (2003), 99–126 (p. 100).
52. There are, of course, still objections that might be made, which I discuss in the next chapter.
53. In what follows, I shall refer interchangeably to autonomy so conceived as either a value or an ideal. In general, values need not be ideals: but the value of autonomy is such, and so nothing hangs on the difference between the terms.

NOTES TO CHAPTER 2

1. Raz, *The Morality of Freedom*, pp. 370–371.
2. Wall, *Liberalism, Perfectionism, and Restraint*, pp. 128–129.
3. ibid. p. 128.
4. Mill, p. 61.
5. M. Sandel, *Liberalism and the Limits of Justice* (Cambridge: Cambridge University Press, 1982), ch. 1.

6. C. Taylor, 'Atomism' in his *Philosophy and the Human Sciences* (Cambridge: Cambridge University Press, 1985), and *Sources of the Self: the making of the modern identity* (Cambridge: Cambridge University Press, 1989).

7. It might be objected that even this response misses the target. The problem is not that I fail to recognise that such commitments exist, but rather that I fail to take them seriously. The policies to which I am committed, by dint of my focus on individuals deciding for themselves what is valuable, are damaging to things that are valuable because of our essential embeddedness in communities, families and non-voluntary commitments. Rephrased in this way, the attack ceases to be that my conception of autonomy rests on a false view of the self, but rather that it would have unpalatable consequences when used as a basis for state action. Hence, it seems appropriate to defer discussion of the matter until Chapter 5, when I deal with several such criticisms.

8. These conditions, especially the Independence Condition, echo Dworkin's position, which I discussed in Section 1.2 of the previous chapter. This is one of the places where there is some practical convergence between my conception of autonomy and his, though—as I said there—there is still a great difference in the understanding of the concept of autonomy between the two. I say more about the relationship between *my* Independence Condition and Dworkin's subsequently.

9. Though note that *even if* in the past one has failed to satisfy the Independence Condition in respect of a given commitment, so long as one *now* does so (and the Endorsement Condition is met) following that commitment will contribute to our autonomy.

10. Dworkin, *The Theory and Practice of Autonomy*, p. 18.

11. The example is adapted from Christian Piller's discussion of content-insensitivity in 'Content-Related and Attitude-Related Reasons for Preferences', in *Preferences and Well-Being*, ed. by Serena Olsaretti (Cambridge: Cambridge University Press, 2006), pp. 155-182 (p. 172).

12. This may also be true in some cases of content-insensitivity, though it need not be so.

13. See especially Chapter 3 in his *Sour Grapes: Studies in the Subversion of Rationality* (Cambridge: Cambridge University Press, 1983). The comparison between values formed in this way and adaptive preferences is not precise—I take valuing to be a somewhat broader category of attitudes than preferring—but a parallel story can nevertheless be told, to illustrate more ways in which the Independence Condition might be undermined.

14. Elster, *Sour Grapes*, pp. 127–128. It is unclear why Elster thinks this undermines autonomy, because it is unclear what he means when he talks about autonomy. One thing that is clear is that autonomy on Elster's view is a property of particular preferences, and not of complete lives (as it is on mine). What this property is, and why we should care about it, though, is never specified, beyond the rather vague statement that autonomy is 'for desires what judgment is for belief.' (p. 20). Precisely what this amounts to need not concern us here.

15. Elster notes the difficulty for his account of distinguishing between adaptation—which he takes to be problematic—and the closely-related phenomenon of character planning, which involves an agent voluntarily seeking to mould their preferences to fit their circumstances, and seems to be unproblematic (pp. 114–120). My account of autonomy provides a simple way of distinguishing these, which Elster himself could endorse. Character planning, unlike adaptation, consists in the adoption of particular values—in this case certain character ideals that one wants to embody—and then perhaps altering (in light of the opportunities one has) the things that one wants to

pursue. One can be entirely aware of this process, with no part of the causal mechanism being hidden; hence, I suggest, it is compatible with the Independence Condition. So long as the character ideal concerned is one which we endorse (or would endorse), it is clear to see how the process is compatible with autonomy. By contrast, in cases of adaptation, there seems to be no ideal or value actually informing the changes in preferences or value commitments, let alone an ideal which is endorsed under conditions of independence.

16. Both Raz and Wall identify this aspect of coercion as something peculiarly problematic for autonomy. See Raz, *The Morality of Freedom*, p. 155, and Wall, *Liberalism, Perfectionism and Restraint*, pp. 133–135.

17. F. A. Hayek, *The Constitution of Liberty* (London: Routledge and Kegan Paul, 1960), p. 21.

18. This is suggested by Serena Olsaretti, who also points out that this relation of dominance is not exclusive to coercion, but is also shared by other types of forcing where it is another agent that is exerting the force. See Olsaretti, *Liberty, Desert and the Market* (Cambridge: Cambridge University Press, 2004), pp. 141–148.

19. T. Scanlon, *What We Owe To Each Other*, (Cambridge, MA: Harvard University Press, 1998), ch. 6, esp. pp. 248–251 and p. 290.

20. e.g, Olsaretti, *Liberty, Desert, and the Market*, pp. 139–141, and pp. 152–156.

21. ibid. pp. 159–160.

22. Humboldt, pp. 28–29.

23. Raz, *The Morality of Freedom*, p. 395.

24. In many of these imaginary cases, I use religious commitment as a convenient example. That these deep and serious commitments are religious, however, is not essential to any of the cases involved. The point could be made just as well if we imagine that Caradoc was wholeheartedly committed to some non-religious value, such as an important scientific goal like the cure for cancer.

25. A third point emerges if we consider someone whose life goes the opposite way to Denise's: that is, someone who starts with deep religious convictions and arranges their life accordingly, and then has a crisis of faith and ceases to feel that life to be valuable. Such cases dictate that the autonomy-minded state is obliged to protect the exit rights of those who live within particular religious or cultural associations, which is to say that no legal penalty must be imposed on people who wish to leave, and groups must be prevented from attempting to prevent apostasy by coercion. I should emphasise that this is not because such associations necessarily damage autonomy, but because we must be sensitive to the possibility that people's commitments might change.

26. What follows is a shorter version of an argument I give in 'Forbidden Ways of Life', *The Philosophical Quarterly* 58 (2008), 618–629.

27. The argument appears in its clearest form in the writings of Chandran Kukathas and William Galston, both of whom argue that ruling out such ways of life is incompatible with a commitment to protecting diversity. See, for example: C. Kukathas, 'Are There Any Cultural Rights?', *Political Theory* 20 (1992) 105–139 (p. 122); and W. Galston, 'Two Concepts of Liberalism', *Ethics* 105 (1995) 516–534 (pp. 527–528). In a more indistinct and unreflective form, it often appears in literature which applies philosophical analysis to areas of political policy. For example, in the context of discussion of the education system, see Neil Burtonwood, 'Liberalism and Communitarianism: A Response to Two Recent Attempts to Reconcile Individual Autonomy with Group Identity', *Educational Studies* 24 (3) 295–304; Yael

Tamir, *Liberal Nationalism* (Princeton: Princeton University Press, 1995); Eamonn Callan *Creating Citizens: Political Education and Liberal Democracy* (Oxford: Clarendon, 1997) p. 11. In Chapter 5 I examine the multicultural liberalism of Kukathas and Galston in more detail, and argue that the position is untenable. However, that conclusion is not needed at present: it suffices to show that the argument of theirs under consideration here is based on a misunderstanding.

28. Once again, I follow Raz, who says that people have been autonomous 'whether or not they themselves or others around them thought of this as an ideal way of being.' Raz, *The Morality of Freedom*, p. 370.
29. This point anticipates my discussion of education in Chapters 4 and 5. The present brisk comments are thus not intended to provide a conclusive argument that such an education system is indeed something that the autonomy-minded liberal is committed to, though I hope it seems plausible that this is correct. If the reader is skeptical, however, it does not matter. So long as being committed to autonomy involves *some* practical commitments in terms of state policy, there will be some ways of life which we are biased against: namely those that cannot develop given the discharge of those practical commitments.
30. It would be the sort of upbringing demanded, for example, by the parents in the famous case of *Mozert v. Hawkins County Board of Education*, 827 F.2d 1058 (6th Cir. 1987). The *Mozert* parents argued that a primary school reading programme contravened their right to freedom of religion, because it exposed the children to a variety of points of view, and this variety denigrated the truth of their religious views.
31. I say more about this, and the possible sources of these intuitions, in the next chapter.

NOTES TO CHAPTER 3

1. For more detailed discussion of political perfectionism and its denial, see Hurka (1993); Raz (1986), especially Chapters 5 and 6; and G. Sher *Beyond Neutrality* (Cambridge: Cambridge University Press, 1997).
2. e.g., C. Larmore, *Patterns of Moral Complexity* (Cambridge: Cambridge University Press, 1987) pp. 52–53; Rawls, *Political Liberalism*; and Rawls, 'The Idea of Public Reason Revisited', *University of Chicago Law Review* 64 (1997), 765–807. I will argue that Rawls is in fact committed to the Autonomy Claim on my understanding; however, he does seem explicitly to reject that claim (see, for example, his 'Justice as Fairness: Political not Metaphysical' in *Philosophy and Public Affairs* 14 (1985), 245–246.) For the moment I use 'neutrality-minded' just as a label, but I define neutrality further in Section 3.3.3.
3. For example Raz, Wall and Hurka. Later I consider a group that I call multicultural liberals, who believe that liberalism is committed to the state protection of diversity or culture. In a sense, these too might be called 'perfectionistic'. In what follows, however, I shall use the term to refer only to autonomy-minded positions.
4. Larmore, *Patterns of Moral Complexity*, pp. 52–53, and pp. 128–130. Larmore makes the same point in his 'Political Liberalism', *Political Theory* 18 (1990): 339–360, at 345 and 356. Strictly speaking, Larmore talks not of anti-perfectionism but of neutrality, but he means the former as well. Another example of someone who affirms anti-perfectionism and makes it clear that he would also deny the Autonomy Claim on my conception is P. De

Marneffe, 'Rawls' Idea of Public Reason', *Pacific Philosophical Quarterly* 75 (1994): 232–250.

5. Wall, *Liberalism, Perfectionism, and Restraint*, p. 146.
6. ibid. p. 146.
7. This point is dealt with at more length in my discussion of Raz's Social Forms argument in the next section.
8. Raz, *The Morality of Freedom*, pp. 390–395. The theory of well-being concerned is expounded in Chapter 12, with crucial argument about the importance of social forms located specifically in pp. 307–313. Raz also has a more general argument in pp. 378–390 that autonomy is instrumentally valuable insofar as it can promote well-being, but since he takes the Social Forms argument to be the most developed version of this thought, it is with that argument that I deal principally here.
9. Of these, Wall is the most recent and most formidable. He devotes almost an entire chapter to developing a more robust version of the Social Forms argument. See *Liberalism, Perfectionism, and Restraint*, pp. 165–182.
10. For example, D. McCabe, 'Joseph Raz and the Contextual Argument for Liberal Perfectionism', *Ethics* 111 (2001), 493–522. Two reviewers of Wall's book also make the observation: the broadly sympathetic T. Hurka in *Mind* 110 (2001), 878–881; and the broadly hostile A. Tucker in *Ethics* 111 (2001), 651–653.
11. Raz, *The Morality of Freedom*, pp. 288–294. This is a slight simplification, since Raz believes that there are certain biologically determined factors whose presence or absence may affect an agent's well-being regardless of whether she herself holds those things as goals. However, Raz gives limited scope to those goals, and makes it clear that the part that depends upon an agent's own goals is considerably greater: thus he says 'barring a person's biologically determined needs and desires his well-being depends, at the deepest level, on his action reasons and his success in following them' (p. 308).
12. Raz, *The Morality of Freedom*, p. 308.
13. ibid. pp. 391–395.
14. McCabe's article is concerned with a detailed discussion of precisely these points.
15. This makes Raz's argument irrelevant for my purposes. What I say seems also to vitiate his own use of the argument, since he also seems to need autonomy to be able to justify liberalism in this way. It *may* be that Raz could justify his brand of perfectionistic liberalism simply by reference to his theory of well-being without appealing to autonomy at all, in which case my criticism is not damning for his general project. Since I am not interested in justifying liberalism in that way, I will not explore such a possibility—I am content to observe just that, if I am correct, the Social Forms argument is a spare wheel in Raz's general theory of liberalism.
16. Wall, *Liberalism, Perfectionism, and Restraint*, p. 164.
17. Raz, *The Morality of Freedom*, p. 157.
18. Ibid. p. 161.
19. ibid. p. 108.
20. ibid. p. 162. Admittedly, this only produces a full *reductio* if we take Raz also to think that such a commitment to autonomy is the only possible motivation for anti-perfectionism; but the general tenor of the argument is clearly in that direction.
21. For example: Cooper, 'Stoic Autonomy'; Ladensen, 'A Theory of Personal Autonomy'; and Oshana, 'How Much Should We Value Autonomy?'.
22. Hurka, 'Why Value Autonomy?', 361; Raz, *The Morality of Freedom*, p. 370.

23. This does not mean that I reject the possibility that autarchy might be valuable. Indeed, *prima facie* we might imagine that it could be derivatively valuable because living an autarchic life is a good way of living an autonomous life. I do not, however, intend to deal directly with the value of autarchy in what follows.

24. So, for example, Brian Barry says in *Culture and Equality* (Cambridge: Polity, 2001) that the ideal of autonomy is 'a vision of a state of affairs in which all the members of a society devote a great deal of time and effort to such activities as questioning their basic beliefs and probing the rationale of the institutions and practices within which they live' (pp. 120–121). Barry then takes the demandingness of this ideal to motivate merely providing the opportunity for autonomy, not promoting it.

25. For the sake of simplicity, the examples I have given all use direct reference to someone else's judgments of value in order to illustrate what I take to be second-order variables. It is somewhat easier to conceive of the features I intend to highlight in these cases. The appeal to third parties is not essential, though. In the following section, I discuss the example of autonomy, which (I argue) is a second-order value, but *not* because of reference to third parties.

26. For example, in *Political Liberalism* (p. 37) Rawls gives three examples of comprehensive doctrines of value which the state should not promote: orthodox medieval orthodox medieval Catholicism, utilitarianism, and the 'liberalisms of Kant or Mill', based on ideals of individuality or reason. That which Rawls identifies as impermissible in each case is commitment to values which are first-order, as the term was defined previously.

27. In what follows, I will almost always be talking about first-, rather than second-order anti-perfectionism. Hence, unless I explicitly state otherwise, I shall use the unqualified label to refer only to the former position.

28. For a different—and rather more Rawlsian—argument to the same conclusion, see M. Clayton, *Justice and Legitimacy in Upbringing* (New York: Oxford University Press, 2006): pp. 13–19, 24–27.

29. Once again, by 'deciding' here I mean something deliberately ambiguous between a notion of epistemic determination and a notion of choice-based action.

30. It does seem to me, however, that even if it were correct, truth-relativism would fail to provide a motivation for anti-perfectionism, for relativism is entirely compatible with a state being intolerant. Anti-perfectionism consists in saying that it is *true* that the state ought to refrain from promoting first-order values: and this is a claim that the relativist, if sincere, cannot possibly endorse.

31. This point is a familiar one—the best formulation of it is probably in Bernard Williams, *Morality* (Cambridge: Cambridge University Press, 1976), pp. 20–26.

32. My point is not that providing people with access to artificial insulin is inconsistent with either anti-perfectionism or the injunction to promote autonomy, since it could presumably be justified on the grounds that an adequate level of health is necessary for autonomy. The example is meant just to illustrate that apparently relativised claims like this are in fact just elliptical unrelativised claims.

33. Isaiah Berlin is one of the principal defenders of Strong Pluralism (which he calls 'value-pluralism'. See, for example, the introduction to his *Four Essays on Liberty* (Oxford: Oxford University Press, 1969) p. x. Amongst others, Raz endorses a similar position, though for different reasons. See *The Morality of Freedom*, p. 395.

34. See, for example: S. Scalet, 'Liberalism, Skepticism, and Neutrality', *The Journal of Value Inquiry* 34 (2000): 207–225; and G. Dworkin, 'Non-neutral principles', *The Journal of Philosophy* 71 (1974): 491–506 (pp. 503–505). Dworkin argues that Rawls too is committed to this line of argument if the veil of ignorance in his original position is to be justified. Raz suggests that scepticism lies behind Rawl's later concern for finding a theory of justice that is *epistemically abstinent*: that is, which avoids claiming that any particular comprehensive conception of the good is true. See J. Raz, 'Facing Diversity: The Case of Epistemic Abstinence', *Philosophy and Public Affairs* 19 (1990): 3–46 (pp. 9–10). Neither Dworkin nor Raz seem right in this interpretation of Rawls, to my mind. As I note in the next section, where I discuss it in depth, Rawls' position was not based on scepticism, but on the thought that we must be *neutral* for reasons of legitimacy, and hence avoid pronouncing on the truth of conceptions of the good. The sceptical argument is also discussed, though not endorsed, in J. Hampton, 'Should Political Philosophy be Done Without Metaphysics?', *Ethics* 99 (1989), 791–814.

35. There is a sense in which anti-perfectionism itself might also be called a form of neutrality, which is to say neutrality of aim: but that is distinct from the neutrality of justification I consider here. For more discussion of these types of neutrality, see J. Rawls, 'The Priority of Right and Ideas of the Good', *Philosophy and Public Affairs* 17 (1988), 251–276 (pp. 260–261); and also A. D. Mason, 'Autonomy, Liberalism and State Neutrality', *The Philosophical Quarterly* 40 (1990), 433–452.

36. Rawls, especially in *Political Liberalism*, is the dominant defender of this line; but see also B. Ackerman, *Social Justice in the Liberal State* (New Haven: Yale University Press, 1980), and his 'Political Liberalisms', *The Journal of Philosophy* 91 (1994), 364–386; J. Cohen 'Moral Pluralism and Political Consensus' in *The Idea of Democracy*, ed. by D. Copp, J. Hampton & J.E. Roemer (Cambridge: Cambridge University Press, 1993), pp. 270–291; Larmore *Patterns of Moral Complexity*; T. Nagel, 'Moral Conflict and Political Legitimacy', *Philosophy and Public Affairs* 16 (1987), 215–240; and L. Wenar, 'Political Liberalism: An Internal Critique', *Ethics* 106 (1995), 32–62.

37. Rawls, *Political Liberalism*.

38. The conclusion of this argument—though not the detail—is similar to those in Raz, 'Epistemic Abstinence', especially at 26; and in W. Galston, 'Pluralism and Social Unity', *Ethics* 99 (1989): 711–726 (pp. 712–714).

39. Rawls, *Political Liberalism*, p. 4.

40. If it weren't, then it would be incoherent, simultaneously aiming to promote some putative value and refusing to endorse its being valuable.

41. Rawls, *Political Liberalism*, p. 19.

42. ibid. pp. 202–203.

43. ibid. pp. 313–314, 322.

NOTES TO CHAPTER 4

1. See, for example, Raz, *The Morality of Freedom*, p. 3.

2. This is an adaptation of the familiar tripartite formulation of freedom which has gained wide usage from Gerald MacCallum's 'Negative and Positive Freedom', *The Philosophical Review* 76 (1967): 312–334; though MacCallum acknowledges earlier writers who used a similar characterisation, such as T.D. Weldon in *The Vocabulary of Politics* (Penguin: Baltimore, 1953)

and F. Oppenheim in *Dimensions of Freedom* (St Martin's Press: New York, 1961). The view that we should understand freedom in this way can be found in Ian Carter's *A Measure of Freedom* (New York: Oxford University Press, 1999), especially pp. 1–7.

3. See Berlin, *Four Essays*. Berlin identifies negative liberty as the notion running through much of the liberal tradition, including Hobbes, Locke, Humboldt and Mill. The same point is made by Carter, at pp. 221–222 and 237–245.

4. Raz, *The Morality of Freedom*, p. 408. Raz also refers to negative liberty, which he takes to be not the central notion of freedom, since it is only instrumentally valuable. As I shall say, I agree with him about the latter claim, but still believe that negative liberty is the appropriate notion to use when discussing freedom.

5. Raz, *The Morality of Freedom*, p. 409. Many writers on freedom and autonomy take a similar stance, and this is often because they—either explicitly or implicitly—use a similar positive conception of freedom, and thereby make trivial the question of the relationship between freedom and autonomy. To take a few examples: Hurka (in 'Why Value Autonomy?') takes a challenge to the value of freedom to be the same as a challenge to the value of autonomy; James Stacey Taylor says that the phrase 'acts freely' is synonymous with the phrase 'is autonomous with respect to her actions' ('Autonomy, Duress, and Coercion' in *Social Philosophy and Policy* 20 [2] [2003]: 129); and Wall ('Freedom as a political ideal', 307) says that 'individual freedom is best understood in terms of personal autonomy'. Finding any relevant discussion of the relationship between freedom and autonomy within the negative liberty tradition is surprisingly difficult, though there are several writers like Berlin who take negative liberty to be the fundamental value, and therefore consider any tensions between freedom and autonomy to cast doubt on the value of the latter. See Berlin's 'Two Concepts of Liberty', pp. 118–172 in *Four Essays on Liberty*; his discussion of Rousseau in particular in *Freedom and Its Betrayal: Six Enemies of Liberty* ed. H. Hardy (London: Chatto & Windus, 2002); and also Carter pp. 163–165.

6. This is not necessarily to say that there may not be other reasons; just that any other reason would not be based on the claims of autonomy.

7. G. Dworkin, 'Is More Choice Better than Less?' in *Midwest Studies in Philosophy* 7 (1982) ed. P. French (Minneapolis: University of Minnesota Press), 47–61. Reproduced in his *Theory and Practice of Autonomy*. For similar points, see N.K. Malholtra, 'Information Overload and Consumer Decision Making', *The Journal of Consumer Research* 8 (1982), 419–430; and M. Shapiro, 'Illicit Reasons and Means for Reproduction: On Excessive Choice and Categorical and Technological Imperatives', *Hastings Law Journal* 47 (1994), 1081–1218.

8. I don't mean that this is the *only* necessary condition, but I need point out only one to make the argument that increasing freedom need not always support our autonomy.

9. G. Dworkin ('Is More Choice Better than Less?') also argues this, saying that the costs of decision-making I discussed previously can become so great in some circumstances that greater freedom will lead to great mental stress, the which will actively hinder autonomy (rather than just failing to support it). I am unconvinced that this is a realistic scenario, so I refrain from discussing Dworkin's argument in what follows.

10. Some of what follows coincides with Elster's discussion of Odysseus' case; see his *Ulysses Unbound* (Cambridge: Cambridge University Press, 2000).

11. Some philosophers (e.g. H. Steiner in *An Essay on Rights* (Oxford: Blackwell, 1994) and R. Nozick in 'Coercion' in *Philosophy, Politics and Society*, 4th series, ed. by P. Laslett, W.G. Runciman & Q. Skinner (Oxford: Blackwell, 1972): pp. 101–135) have argued that this does not count as a restriction on his freedom since he consented to it, and nothing can be a restriction of freedom if we consent to it. I reject that position because it seems to elide an important distinction between freedom and voluntariness, as I explain in the next section.

12. Of course, Odysseus' restriction of freedom is a temporary one. Many permanent restrictions of freedom—such as selling oneself into slavery, perhaps—would seem to involve entering into a relation of dominance, and hence to be incompatible with autonomy for the reasons I gave in Section 2.1.2. My point still stands, though—it is not the loss of *freedom* that makes slavery problematic.

13. See, for example, Olsaretti, *Liberty, Desert, and the Market*, p. 139. As I noted in the section mentioned, none of the argument here depends upon any particular position concerning what is and is not acceptable; though I do say something further about the position that I take.

14. Olsaretti also suggests that a concern for voluntariness is grounded in a concern for autonomy, though she says little to tease out the nature of this connection: I take it that the analysis described here is consistent with her view. See her 'The Value of Freedom and Freedom of Choice', *Politeia* 56 (2000): 114–121, at 117.

15. See Olsaretti *Liberty, Desert, and the Market*, p. 139, pp. 140–141, and pp. 152–156. Earlier versions can be found in 'Freedom, Force and Choice: Against the Rights-Based Definition of Voluntariness', *The Journal of Political Philosophy* 6 (1998), 53–78; and in 'The Value of Freedom and Freedom of Choice'.

16. That is, so long as the choices available are not all trivial: I discuss the need for broad opportunities in Section 4.5.2 below.

17. There are other examples of this phenomenon which admit of the same interpretation. For example, G. Dworkin considers a scenario in which a university, which previously had only single-sex accommodation, institutes some mixed accommodation, and allows students to choose between the two types ('Is more choice better than less?', p. 69). In such situations, Dworkin states, students come under new pressures: 'by allowing cohabitation, the social pressures from one's peers to act in a similar fashion [that is, by living in a mixed dormitory rather than a single-sex one] increases and the easy excuse formerly available to those not so inclined vanishes.' Dworkin's point is that, for a given individual, increasing freedom can alter the nature of the options that one already has. If doing so makes those options worse, from that individual's perspective, and thereby makes it more difficult for her to pursue what she considers to be a valuable life, then such an increase will impair her autonomy.

18. Olsaretti, *Liberty, Desert, and the Market*, p. 139. I argue for an amendment to this proposal in 'The Concept of Voluntariness', *The Journal of Political Philosophy* 16 (2008), 101–111, saying that unacceptable options are those which involve serious prudential harm, but the details are not relevant to our purposes here.

19. Olsaretti, *Liberty, Desert, and the Market*, p. 154. Olsaretti's reason for this is the connection between voluntariness and responsibility that I noted above in Section 2.2: if voluntariness is indeed what underwrites ascriptions of responsibility, taking acceptability to be a subjective matter would also render responsibility subjective, and that is implausible.

20. Meir Dan-Cohen also gives various examples of such unfree voluntary choices, though he calls them instances of a concept of 'choice as election' (as opposed to 'selection' from a range of options). See 'Conceptions of Choice and Conceptions of Autonomy', *Ethics* 102 (1992), 221–243 (p. 228).
21. B. Williams, 'The Idea of Equality', in *Politics, Philosophy and Society, 2nd series*, ed. by P. Laslett and G. Runciman (Oxford: Blackwell, 1962). Reproduced in Williams' *Problems of the Self* (New York: Cambridge University Press, 1973), from which page references are taken.
22. ibid, p. 234.
23. Galston, 'Two Concepts', 522; Kukathas, 'Are There any Cultural Rights?', 122.
24. B. Parekh, *Rethinking Multiculturalism: Cultural Diversity and Political Theory* (Basingstoke: Palgrave, 2000), pp. 92–93.
25. *Congressional Record*, 27 July 1978, H754.
26. This is not to say that the content of their demands was autonomy-minded. The Longest Walkers sought the right to punish members of their community who dissented from elements of the group culture, and also to bring up their children so as to ensure their continuing commitment to that culture. Neither measure is warranted by the claim of autonomy.
27. So, for example, I do not see much hope in an argument that appeals to our being equally moral agents (for example, Williams, 'The Idea of Equality', pp. 235–236).
28. Williams, 'The Idea of Equality', p. 241. Raz also discusses—though does not offer a justification for—a principle of this sort. See 'Principles of Equality', *Mind* 87 (1978), 321–342 (pp. 331–333).
29. Williams, 'The Idea of Equality', p. 234.
30. A similar point is made by Brian Barry (p. 100 of *Political Argument*, London: Routledge & Kegan Paul, 1965) and S.I. Benn and R.S. Peters (p. 124 of *Social Principles and the Democratic State*. London: Allen & Unwin, 1959). Of course, one would have to be right about the difference being relevant. The point is just that it is not impossible, in respect of some goods, that there may be differences which are relevant and which therefore ground very unequal distributions.
31. Wall, *Liberalism, Perfectionism, and Restraint*, pp. 183–189.
32. Raz *The Morality of Freedom*, ch. 9.
33. Hurka, *Perfectionism*, p. 161 and p. 189.
34. ibid. p. 166.
35. ibid. p. 167.
36. ibid. p. 176, and ch. 13.
37. ibid. p. 189.
38. The first seems also to me problematic, since Hurka adduces no evidence in its favour, but showing that is unnecessary for my purposes here.
39. Hurka, *Perfectionism*, p. 176.
40. There are also practical limitations, such as limitation of resources and considerations of efficiency—but since these afflict *any* political theory, and thus do not argue in favour of any particular understanding of what equal concern for autonomy amounts to, I do not discuss them here.
41. This leaves open the possibility that there may be actions which are paternalistic on the definition I have given, but which are not ruled out by autonomy-minded concerns because they do not work by undermining the Independence Condition. For a discussion of types of paternalism like this, see Cass R. Sunstein and Richard H. Thaler, 'Preferences, Paternalism, and Liberty', in Olsaretti *Preferences and Well-Being*, pp. 233–264.

42. See 'Equality and Equal Opportunity for Welfare', *Philosophical Studies* 56 (1989), 77–93; 'Liberalism, Distributive Subjectivism, and Equal Opportunities for Welfare', *Philosophy and Public Affairs* 19 (1990), 158–94; and 'Equal Opportunity for Welfare Defended and Recanted', *The Journal of Political Philosophy* 7 (1999), 488–97. I should note that Arneson no longer holds the view I discuss here, and also that I take Arneson as my example just because the argument is especially clear in his writings. Other defenders of responsibility-sensitive egalitarianism include G.A. Cohen, whom I discuss below, and L.S. Temkin in *Inequality* (New York: Oxford University Press, 1993), esp. at p. 13.
43. Arneson, 'Equality and Equal Opportunity for Welfare', 82.
44. ibid., p. 83.
45. Arneson 'Equal Opportunity for Welfare Defended and Recanted', 490.
46. G. A. Cohen, 'On the Currency of Egalitarian Justice', *Ethics* 99 (1989): 906–944, at 907 and 916–917. Cohen himself defends equal access to what he calls 'advantage', rather than welfare or autonomy, though the concept is never clearly very clearly defined: he suggests that it will have as components preference-satisfaction, and resources, and need-satisfaction, and maybe more. See ibid. 907, and 'Expensive Taste Rides Again' in *Dworkin and His Critics,* ed. by J. Burley (Oxford: Blackwell, 2004), pp. 3–30 (p. 19).
47. This information requirement is, as I will show below, more stringent than that required just for voluntariness.
48. So, for example, having decided that I want to be a rhodium jeweller, I might voluntarily choose to sell many of my belongings to buy rhodium. That alone would not justify my being held responsible for my consequence impoverishment, since—amongst other things—I would need to have been in a position where I should have known just how expensive the necessary supply of rhodium would be.
49. Note that it is the *impossibility* of living autonomously without assistance that is crucial here, and marks a qualitative difference between other less severe cases where a momentary vitiation of someone's responsibility for their actions would lead to a greater chance of living an autonomous life thereafter. Reimbursing me for non-catastrophic amounts of money I recklessly spend on train journeys to Scotland would give me ample opportunity to pursue more things that I deem valuable (more trips to Scotland, for example). Assuming that the cost of train tickets to Scotland does not leave me in a position where it is impossible for me to live autonomously, however, such intervention could not be justified on the grounds given previously, which is that there would be *no* chance of my living an autonomous life without it.
50. E. Anderson, 'What is the Point of Equality?', *Ethics* 109 (1999), 287–335 (pp. 298–303). Others who take a similar line include Samuel Scheffler, who endorses Anderson's argument, and Jonathan Wolff, who arrives at a similar conclusion via the thought that respect for individuals should sometimes trump considerations of fairness, which is in his view what grounds a concern for responsibility. See S. Scheffler, 'What is Egalitarianism?', *Philosophy and Public Affairs* 31 (2003), 5–39 and J. Wolff 'Fairness, Respect, and the Egalitarian Ethos', *Philosophy and Public Affairs* 27 (1998), 97–122.
51. See, for example, his 'Equality of Resources', Chapter 2 of *Sovereign Virtue,* pp. 65–119.
52. See 'Equality of Opportunity Defended and Recanted', his response to K. Lippert-Rasmussen 'Arneson on Equal Opportunity for Welfare', *The Journal of Political Philosophy* 7 (1999), 478–487.
53. By 'bad brute luck' I mean what Dworkin means when he uses the term—that is, bad outcomes that are not the result of deliberate gambles or something

that is appropriately similar to a deliberate gamble. See *Sovereign Virtue*, pp. 73–83.

54. See, for example, Arneson, 'Equality of Opportunity Defended and Recanted', 489–490; Cohen, 'On the Currency of Egalitarian Justice', 937; and Cohen 'Expensive Taste Rides Again', p. 11. For examples of others whom I have not discussed but who hold a similar view, see: E. Rakowski, *Equal Justice* (New York: Oxford University Press, 1991), e.g. at pp. 74–75; J.E. Roemer, 'A Pragmatic Theory of Responsibility for the Egalitarian Planner', *Philosophy and Public Affairs* 22 (1993), 146–166 (pp. 147, 149–150); and Temkin *Inequality*, p. 13.

55. B. Barry, *Why Social Justice Matters* (Cambridge: Polity Press, 2005), pp. 136–137.

56. J. Feinberg, 'The Child's Right to an Open Future', in *Whose Child? Children's Rights, Parental Authority, and State Power*, ed. by W. Aiken and H. LaFollette (Totowa, NJ: Rowman & Littlefield, 1980). Reproduced in J. Feinberg *Freedom and Fulfillment* (Princeton: Princeton University Press, 1992), pp. 76–97.

57. The twin concerns of specialisation and of allowing children control over what they study are rather too complex to deal with here. The correct approach to these concerns will involve respecting two important autonomy-minded considerations. On the one hand, promoting autonomy demands we allow the young control over their lives as early as possible: the later we leave it, the bigger the danger of treating someone paternalistically when they are capable of exercising autonomy in an adult way. On the other hand, respecting autonomy also demands that we design education so as to increase the ability of future adults to live autonomous lives, and that may well not best be done by allowing them, too early, choices that seriously restrict the ways they might live in the future. I have no substantial suggestion as to how to strike the balance between these two considerations, save that they seem to require a smooth transition. As children grow older, it will be right to grant them more control over what they do, both because we recognise the importance of their burgeoning capacity for autonomy, and because giving (circumscribed) power over their learning is the best way of encouraging them on the road to becoming the sorts of agents who can exercise that capacity effectively. Precisely what this means in practical terms, though, is an issue to be dealt with at another time.

58. The point that what might count as minimal basic training is relative is made by Alexander Brown, though his concern is with ensuring *self-respect* rather than autonomy. See A. Brown, 'Equality of Opportunity for Education: One-off or Lifelong?', *Journal of Philosophy of Education* 40 (2006), 63–84.

59. See, for example, H. Brighouse, *School Choice and Social Justice* (Oxford: Oxford University Press, 2000), especially pp. 65–82. Brighouse himself denies that education should be autonomy-promoting, instead saying that it should be 'autonomy-facilitating' (p. 82), but his reasons for this seem to be that he has in mind a notion of autonomy that demands actual reflection (hence somewhat different to mine). The specifics of educational policy he suggests, however, will all apply to the promotion of autonomy understood as I suggest. So, for example, he proposes a combination of a traditional academic curriculum with training for recognising forms and fallacies in argument, knowledge about a variety of ethical views, and about the various ways in which people have dealt with moral and religious conflict (pp. 74–75).

60. I say '*prima facie*' because there may well be autonomy-minded claims based on the value to the children and the parents of a certain type of family rela-

tionship that might override this reason, especially in the case of practices where the danger to autonomy is not great.

61. Matthew Clayton in *Justice and Legitimacy in Upbringing* discusses these matters in great depth, and from a theoretical standpoint rather close to mine (that is, an autonomy-minded and anti-perfectionistic liberalism).

62. As I argued above, against the requisite educational background we can take people to be *at least* partially responsible for making their decisions in a way sensitive to their own talents; so, it is not necessary that opportunities be provided without conditions upon talent and competence. Of course, there is an independent reason to have only skilled people in certain roles: the general autonomy-promoting functions of the state would be ill-served if there weren't competency requirements for being a doctor or a teacher.

63. I assume, for the sake of simplicity, that their decision to be a teacher is not influenced by knowledge that it is the only option they have.

64. Raz, *The Morality of Freedom*, pp. 384–385.

65. Once again, I leave aside the question of whether we might find some more direct autonomy-minded argument against the invasions of privacy such a monitoring policy would involve.

NOTES TO CHAPTER 5

1. That is, so long—as I suggested—as they understand autonomy in the way that I do.

2. Galston, 'Two Concepts of Liberalism', and later in his *Liberal Pluralism: The Implications of Value Pluralism for Political Theory and Practice* (Cambridge: Cambridge UP, 2002).

3. C. Kukathas, *The Liberal Archipelago* (New York: Oxford UP, 2003), p. 4, and pp. 74–116. See also his 'Do We Have any Cultural Rights?', and 'Cultural Toleration' in *Ethnicity and Group Rights: NOMOS XXXIX*, ed. by I. Shapiro & W. Kymlicka (New York: New York UP, 1997), pp. 69–104.

4. W. Kymlicka, *Multicultural Citizenship: A Liberal Theory of Minority Rights* (Oxford: Clarendon, 1995).

5. For reasons already stated in Section 3.1.1, I myself am reluctant to rely on such arguments to do serious justificatory work. However, many multicultural liberals *do* rely on those arguments to justify their positions.

6. Admittedly, it might often be prudent for an autonomy-minded state to allow parents a large measure of control even in those cases where this will result in a less effectively autonomy-promoting education than might otherwise be enjoyed, because the alternative might incur punitive financial and psychological costs for state and families respectively. Nevertheless, believing that the state has authority to override parental wishes when they conflict with provision of an autonomy-promoting education is characteristic of the position I defend.

7. e.g. Galston 'Two Concepts of Liberalism, 529; Parekh *Rethinking Multiculturalism,* pp. 216–217.

8. *Wisconsin v. Yoder*, 406 U.S. 205 (1972); *Mozert v. Hawkins County Board Of Education*, 827 F.2d 1058 (6th Cir. 1987).

9. Kymlicka, *Multicultural Citizenship*, ch. 5.

10. Mill pp. 20–21, 30–31, 35–55.

11. ibid. p. 55.

12. ibid. p. 106.

13. A. Gutmann, 'Civic Education and Social Diversity', *Ethics* 105 (1995), 557–579.

14. S. Macedo 'Liberal Civic Education and the Case of God v. John Rawls', *Ethics* 105 (1995): 468–496 (p. 471). Macedo is not, incidentally, a multicultural liberal himself, being instead a political liberal on Rawlsian lines. However, the argument he suggests is a possible grounds for an anti-autonomy, perfectionistic position. See also G.W. Dent Jr., 'Religious Children, Secular Schools' in *Southern California Law Review* 61 (1988), 863–941 (p. 924).

15. e.g. Kymlicka *Multicultural Citizenship*, ch. 5; also his *Liberalism, Community and Culture* (Oxford: Clarendon, 1989), ch. 7–8. In saying this, Kymlicka echoes Raz, who—in his Social Forms argument—also places great importance upon the existing community practices as a context of choice and autonomy. See Raz, *The Morality of Freedom*, pp. 307–313. Kymlicka's concern with autonomy makes it unclear whether it is strictly correct to classify him as an anti-autonomy, perfectionistic thinker. I do so here because he shares many practical prescriptions with the other multicultural liberals I examine, and because—regardless of how we interpret him on autonomy—he is a perfectionist with regard to state action aiming at the preservation of diversity.

16. See, for example, Barry, *Culture and Equality*, pp. 128–129; and B. Parekh, 'Cultural Diversity and Liberal Democracy' in *Democracy, Difference and Social Justice*, ed. by G. Mahajan (Delhi: Oxford UP, 1998).

17. Rawls, *Political Liberalism*, p. 222. Kymlicka also makes this point himself (*Multicultural Citizenship*, p. 85).

18. Galston, 'Two Concepts of Liberalism', 521.

19. Admittedly, this glosses over the fact that people are sometimes able to mould their beliefs over a period of time—some beliefs are susceptible to being changed by an act of will. However, the point still stands that at a given moment, a strongly held belief will not be so susceptible, and so the fact that there are several such beliefs that one could hold does not constitute a range of options in the way that, say, the existence of several varieties of beer does. Admittedly, a variety of cultures might be a source of inspiration concerning possible values we might adopt. However, as I noted in Section 5.2.1, such an argument will only work if that diversity is in a context where people are able to decide for themselves and experiment with ways of living; and that possibility is precisely what the multicultural liberal is committed to preventing in the crucial test case of *Yoder*.

20. Kymlicka, *Multicultural Citizenship*, p. 121.

21. ibid. p. 83.

22. R. Dworkin, *A Matter of Principle* (London: Harvard UP, 1985), pp. 232–233.

23. Kymlicka, *Multicultural Citizenship*, p. 84.

24. ibid. p. 52.

25. Kukathas notes, incidentally, that Kymlicka's discussion of freedom seems to rely upon an implicit appeal to a value of autonomy. See 'Are there any cultural rights?', 241.

26. Kymlicka, *Multicultural Citizenship*, p. 84.

27. J. Waldron, 'The Civil Society Argument' in 'Minority Cultures and the Cosmopolitan Alternative' in *University of Michigan Journal of Law Reform* 25/3 (1992) (p. 762).

28. Kymlicka, *Multicultural Citizenship*, p. 85.

29. ibid. p. 85.

30. Incidentally, it is worth repeating the observation I made at the end of Section 5.1, that this argument is not restricted to justifying complete parental control over education. The Kymlicka-style justification of the *Yoder* judgement

I have sketched rests on the claims of those adults whose culture would be threatened by children growing up within the majority culture, and those adults need not be those children's parents—indeed, they need not be personally related at all.

31. Galston, 'Two Concepts of Liberalism', 521.
32. I.M. Young, *Justice and the Politics of Difference* (Princeton: Princeton UP, 1990): p. 158.
33. Parekh, *Rethinking Multiculturalism*, p. 12, and pp. 126–136.
34. Galston, 'Two Concepts of Liberalism', 521.
35. Here, neither the multicultural liberal nor the autonomy-minded liberal can appeal to intuitions in the *Yoder* case without begging the question, since it is how that case should have been decided that is at issue.
36. See, for example, T. Robinson, *Stones of Aran: Pilgrimage* (London: Viking, 1989); J.M. Synge, *The Aran Islands* (Dublin, 1912).
37. As I will discuss, that is not to say that such an advocate would have to think that an *overall* reason must obtain.
38. They cannot, for example, argue that the intrinsic value of diversity will never in practice override the choices of individuals. This would hand victory to the autonomy-minded liberal by default. If considerations of individual autonomy always trump diversity-based claims, there can be no scope for a diversity-minded defence of *Yoder*, or indeed any substantial practical alternative to autonomy-minded liberalism. Roughly, if the reason to preserve diversity is only palatable if it could never be effective, it is no sort of reason at all.
39. Kukathas, *The Liberal Archipelago*, p. 4.
40. Kukathas, 'Are There Any Cultural Rights?', 116–117.
41. ibid. 122.
42. To echo a point made in Section 5.1, I think that we might also talk about the freedom of other adults in the community at large, but in what follows I shall talk only about parents to simplify the argument.
43. Kukathas (in 'Are There Any Cultural Rights?') always remains vague, slipping without comment between talking about the freedom of association held by individuals themselves (e.g. 116–117) and about parental rights over children (e.g. 126–127).
44. C. Fried, *Right and Wrong* (Cambridge, MA: Harvard UP, 1978), p. 153.
45. B. Almond, 'Education and Liberty: Public Provision and Private Choice', *Journal of Philosophy of Education* 25 (1991), 193–202 (pp. 200–201).
46. These points echo Brighouse's response to Almond. See *School Choice*, p. 91.
47. Brighouse attempts to do so by pointing out that we take there to be limits on how an individual's freedoms of religion and association can confer rights over other people in other areas. So, he says that we don't think that the right to consensual sexual relations between adults extends to relations between adults and children or among children; and 'the right to free association does not support claims to associate with those who wish to avoid your company.' (*School Choice*, p. 83.) However, Brighouse's argument is too weak for my purposes here, since at best it only establishes that rejecting Almond's position would be consistent with our practice in other areas.
48. Mill, p. 105.
49. V. Van Dyke, 'The individual, the state, and ethnic communities in political theory' in *World Politics* 29 (1977): 344–369.
50. Parekh, *Rethinking Multiculturalism*, p. 216.
51. There are others who assume that there exist group rights. See, for example, B. Singh, 'Liberalism, parental rights, pupils' autonomy and education' in

Educational Studies 24 (1998), 165–82, and J. W. Nickel, 'Group Agency and Group Rights' in Shapiro & Kymlicka, pp. 235–256.

52. The principal argument can be found in 'The Individual, the State, and Ethnic Communities'. Different versions of the same argument are laid out in 'Justice as Fairness: For Groups?', *American Political Science Review* 69 (1975), 607–614; and in 'Collective Entities and Moral Rights', *Journal of Politics* 44 (1982), 21–40.

53. Van Dyke, 'The Individual, the State, and Ethnic Communities', 343.

54. 'Collective Entities and Moral Rights', 39.

55. I say 'human sources' because such moral individualism is not committed to saying that there are no non-human sources of moral claims. For example, it is compatible with moral individualism to say that there are moral claims generated by the environment.

56. e.g. 'Justice as Fairness: For Groups?', 611–614; 'The Individual, the State, and Ethnic Communities', 350–357.

57. 'The Individual, the State, and Ethnic Communities', 356.

58. ibid.

59. 'The Individual, the State, and Ethnic Communities', 357; 'Collective Entities and Moral Rights', 39.

60. 'Collective Entities and Moral Rights', 26.

61. Note that this third horn of the trilemma does not require that we reject the notion of self-determination as a proper political aim entirely: it is consistent with advocating it on other grounds, such as stability.

Bibliography

Ackerman, B., *Social Justice in the Liberal State* (New Haven: Yale University Press, 1980).

———. 'Political Liberalisms', *The Journal of Philosophy* 91 (1994), 364–386.

Almond, B., 'Education and Liberty: Public Provision and Private Choice', *Journal of Philosophy of Education* 25 (1991): 193–202.

Anderson, E., 'What is the Point of Equality?', *Ethics* 109 (1999): 287–335.

Arneson, R.J., 'Equality and Equal Opportunity for Welfare', *Philosophical Studies* 56 (1989): 77–93.

———. 'Liberalism, Distributive Subjectivism, and Equal Opportunities for Welfare', *Philosophy and Public Affairs* 19 (1990): 158–194.

———. 'Egalitarianism and Responsibility', *Journal of Ethics* 3 (1999): 224–247.

———. 'Equal Opportunity for Welfare Defended and Recanted', *The Journal of Political Philosophy* 7 (1999): 488–497.

———. 'Luck Egalitarianism and Prioritarianism', *Ethics* 110 (2000): 339–247.

Arneson, R.J. & Shapiro, I. 'Democratic Autonomy and Religious Freedom: A Critique of *Wisconsin v. Yoder*'. In *NOMOS XXXVIII*, ed. by R. Hardin and I. Shapiro (New York: New York University Press, 1996), pp. 367–411.

Arrow, K., *Social Choice and Individual Values*, 2nd edition (New Haven: John Wiley & Yale University Press, 1963).

———. 'Gifts and Exchanges', *Philosophy and Public Affairs* 1 (1972): 343–362.

Barry, B., *Political Argument* (London: Routledge & Kegan Paul, 1965).

———. *Culture and Equality* (Cambridge: Polity Press, 2001).

———. 'The Muddles of Multiculturalism', *New Left Review* 8 (March-April 2001): 49.

———. *Why Social Justice Matters* (Cambridge: Polity Press, 2005).

Benn, S.I. & Peters, R.S., *Social Principles and the Democratic State* (London: Allen & Unwin, 1959).

Benson, J., 'Who is the Autonomous Man?', *Philosophy* 58 (1983): 5–17.

Benson, P., 'Free Agency and Self-Worth', *The Journal of Philosophy* 91 (1994): 650–668.

Berlin, I., *Four Essays on Liberty* (Oxford: Oxford University Press, 1969).

———. *Freedom and Its Betrayal: Six Enemies of Liberty*, ed. H. Hardy (London: Chatto & Windus, 2002).

Berofsky, B., 'Identification, the Self, and Autonomy', *Social Philosophy and Policy* 20(2) (2003): 199–200.

Bratman, M., 'Autonomy and Hierarchy', *Social Philosophy and Policy* 20(2) (2003): 156–176.

Brighouse, H., 'Is There a Neutral Justification for Liberalism?', *Pacific Philosophical Quarterly* 77 (1996): 193–215.

———. 'Civic Education and Liberal Legitimacy', *Ethics* 108 (1998): 719–745.

———. *School Choice and Social Justice* (Oxford: Oxford University Press, 2000).

Brighouse, H. & Swift, A., 'Defending Liberalism in Education Theory', *Journal of Education Policy* 18 (2003): 355–373.

Brink. D., 'Moral Conflict and its Structure', *The Philosophical Review* 103 (1994): 215–247.

Brison, S.J., 'The Autonomy Defence of Free Speech', *Ethics* 108 (1998): 312–339.

Brown, A., 'Equality of Opportunity for Education: One-off or Lifelong?', *Journal of Philosophy of Education* 40 (2006): 63–84.

Burley, J. ed., *Dworkin and His Critics* (Oxford: Blackwell, 2004).

Burtonwood, N., 'Beyond Culture—Reply', *Journal of Philosophy of Education* 30 (1996): 295–299.

———. 'Culture, identity, and the curriculum', *Educational Review* 48 (1996), 227–235.

———. 'Liberalism and Communitarianism: A Response to Two Recent Attempts to Reconcile Individual Autonomy With Group Identity', *Educational Studies* 24 (1998): 295–304.

———. 'Isaiah Berlin, Diversity Liberalism, and Education', *Educational Review* 55 (2003): 323–331.

Burtt, S., 'In Defence of Yoder: Parental Authority and the Public Schools'. In *NOMOS XXXVIII*, ed. by R. Hardin and I. Shapiro (New York: New York University Press, 1996), pp. 412–437.

Callan, E., *Creating Citizens: Political Education and Liberal Democracy* (Oxford: Clarendon Press, 1997).

———. 'The Great Sphere: Education against Servility', *Journal of Philosophy of Education* 31 (1997): 221–232.

———. 'Liberal Legitimacy, Justice, and Civic Education', *Ethics* 111 (2000): 141–155.

Carter, I., *A Measure of Freedom* (New York: Oxford University Press, 1999).

———. 'Choice, Freedom, and Freedom of Choice', *Social Choice and Welfare* 22 (2004): 61–81.

Christman, J., 'Constructing the Inner Citadel—Recent Work on the Concept of Autonomy', *Ethics* 101 (1988): 505–520.

———. 'Autonomy and Personal History', *Canadian Journal of Philosophy* 21 (1991): 1–24.

———. 'Defending Historical Autonomy: A Reply to Professor Mele', *Canadian Journal of Philosophy* 23 (1993): 281–289.

Christman, J. & Anderson, J. eds., *Autonomy and the Challenges to Liberalism* (Cambridge: Cambridge University Press, 2005).

Choudhry, S., 'National Minorities and Ethnic Immigrants: Liberalism's Political Sociology', *The Journal of Political Philosophy* 10 (2002), 54–78.

Clayton, M., 'The Resources of Liberal Equality', *Imprints* 5 (2000), 63–84

———. 'Liberal Equality and Ethics', *Ethics* 113 (2002), 8–22.

———. *Justice and Legitimacy in Upbringing* (New York: Oxford University Press, 2006).

Cohen. G.A., 'On the Currency of Egalitarian Justice', *Ethics* 99 (1989), 906–944.

———. *Self-ownership, Freedom, and Equality* (Cambridge: Cambridge University Press, 1995).

———. 'Expensive Taste Rides Again'. In *Dworkin and His Critics*, ed. by J. Burley (Oxford: Blackwell, 2004), pp. 3–30.

Cohen, J. 'Moral Pluralism and Political Consensus'. In *The Idea of Democracy*, ed. by D. Copp, J. Hampton and J.E. Roemer (Cambridge: Cambridge University Press, 1993), pp. 270–91.

Colburn, B., 'The Concept of Voluntariness', *The Journal of Political Philosophy* 16 (2008), 101–111.

———. 'Forbidden Ways of Life', *The Philosophical Quarterly* 58 (2008), 618–629.

Congressional Record, 27 July 1978, H754.

Cooper, J.M., 'Stoic Autonomy', *Social Philosophy and Policy* 20(2) (2003), 1–29.

Dagovitz, A., 'When Choice Does Not Matter: Political Liberalism, Religion, and the Faith School Debate', *Journal of Philosophy of Education* 38 (2004): 165–180.

Dan-Cohen, M., 'Conceptions of Choice and Conceptions of Autonomy', *Ethics* 102 (1992): 221–243.

Daniels, N., 'Equality of What: Welfare, Resources, or Capabilities?', *Philosophy and Phenomenological Research* 50 (1990): Supplement, 273–296.

Darwall, S., *Equal Freedom* (Ann Arbor: University of Michigan Press, 1995).

De Marneffe, P., 'Rawls' Idea of Public Reason', *Pacific Philosophical Quarterly* 75 (1994): 232–250.

Dent, G.W., 'Religious Children, Secular Schools', *Southern California Law Review* 61 (1988): 863–941.

Donner, W. 'Mill's Utilitarianism'. In *The Cambridge Companion to Mill*, ed. by J. Skorupski (Cambridge: Cambridge University Press, 1998): pp. 255–292.

Downie, R.S. & Telfer, E., 'Autonomy', *Philosophy* 46 (1971): 293–301.

Dworkin, G., 'Acting Freely', *Noûs* 4 (1970): 367–383.

———. 'Non-neutral Principles', *The Journal of Philosophy* 71 (1974): 491–506.

———. 'Autonomy and Behaviour Control', *Hastings Center Report* 6 (1976): 23–28.

———. 'The Concept of Autonomy'. In *Science and Ethics* ed. by R. Haller (Amsterdam: Rodopi, 1981), pp. 203–213.

———. 'Is More Choice Better Than Less?' In *Midwest Studies in Philosophy 7* ed. by P. French (Minneapolis: University of Minnesota Press, 1982), pp. 47–61. Reproduced in G. Dworkin *The Theory and Practice of Autonomy*, pp. 62–84.

———. *The Theory and Practice of Autonomy* (Cambridge: Cambridge University Press, 1988).

Dworkin, R., 'What is Equality? Part One: Equality of Welfare', *Philosophy and Public Affairs* 10 (1981): 185–255. Reproduced in R. Dworkin *Sovereign Virtue*, pp. 11–64.

———. 'What is Equality? Part Two: Equality of Resources', *Philosophy and Public Affairs* 10 (1981): 283–345. Reproduced in R. Dworkin *Sovereign Virtue*, pp. 65–119.

———. *A Matter of Principle* (London: Harvard University Press, 1985).

———. 'The Foundations of Liberal Equality'. In *The Tanner Lectures on Human Values* vol. 11., ed. by G.B. Peterson (Salt Lake City: University of Utah Press, 1991): pp. 1–119.

———. *Sovereign Virtue: The Theory and Practice of Equality* (Cambridge, MA: Harvard University Press, 2000).

Elster, J., *Sour Grapes: Studies in the Subversion of Rationality* (Cambridge: Cambridge University Press, 1983).

———. *Ulysses Unbound* (Cambridge: Cambridge University Press, 2000).

Feinberg, J., 'The Child's Right to an Open Future'. In *Whose Child? Children's Rights, Parental Authority, and State Power*, ed. by W. Aiken and H. LaFollette (Totowa, NJ: Rowman & Littlefield, 1980). Reproduced in Feinberg *Freedom and Fulfillment*, pp. 76–97.

———. *Harm to Self*, vol. 3 of *The Moral Limits of the Criminal Law* (New York: Oxford University Press, 1986).

———. *Freedom and Fulfillment* (Princeton: Princeton University Press, 1992).

Fitzmaurice, D., 'Autonomy as a Good: Liberalism, Autonomy, and Toleration', *The Journal of Political Philosophy* 1 (1993): 1–16.

Frankfurt, H., 'Freedom of the Will and the Concept of a Person', *The Journal of Philosophy* 68 (1971): 5–20.

———. 'Equality as a Moral Ideal', *Ethics* 98 (1987): 21–43.

Freeman, S., 'Illiberal Libertarians: Why Libertarianism is Not a Liberal View', *Philosophy and Public Affairs* 30 (2001): 105–151.

Fried, C., *Right and Wrong* (Cambridge, MA: Harvard University Press, 1978).

Friedman, M., 'Autonomy and the Split-level Self', *Southern Journal of Philosophy* 24 (1986): 19–35.

Galston, W., 'Pluralism and Social Unity', *Ethics* 99 (1989): 711–726.

———. 'Civic Education in the Liberal State'. In *Liberalism and the Moral Life*, ed. by N. Rosenblum (Cambridge, MA: Harvard University Press, 1989), pp. 83–101.

———. *Liberal Purposes: Goods, Virtues and Duties in the Liberal State* (Cambridge: Cambridge University Press, 1991).

———. 'Two Concepts of Liberalism', *Ethics* 105 (1995): 516–534.

———. *Liberal Pluralism: The Implications of Value Pluralism for Political Theory and Practice* (Cambridge: Cambridge University Press, 2002).

Gray, J., *Mill on Liberty: A Defence* (London: Routledge, 1983).

———. 'Mill's Conception of Happiness and the Theory of Individuality'. In *J.S. Mill's 'On Liberty' in Focus* ed. by J. Gray and G.W. Smith (London: Routledge, 1991), pp. 190–211.

———. *Two Faces of Liberalism* (London: Polity Press, 2000).

Grether, D.M., Schwartz, A. and Wilde, L.L. 'The Irrelevance of Information Overload: An Analysis of Search and disclosure', *Southern California Law Review* 57 (1986): 277–307.

Gutmann, A., 'Children, Paternalism and Education: A Liberal Argument', *Philosophy and Public Affairs* 9 (1980): 338–358.

———. 'Communitarian Critics of Liberalism', *Philosophy and Public Affairs* 14 (1985): 308–322.

———. ed. *Multiculturalism: Examining the Politics of Difference* (Princeton: Princeton University Press, 1994).

———. 'Civic Education and Social Diversity', *Ethics* 105 (1995): 557–579.

Guyer, P., 'Kant on the Theory and Practice of Autonomy', *Social Philosophy and Policy* 20 (2) (2003): 70–98.

Halstead, J.M., 'Voluntary Apartheid? Problems of Schooling for Religious and Other Minorities in Democratic Societies', *Journal of Philosophy of Education* 29 (1995): 257–272.

Hampton, J., 'Should Political Philosophy be Done Without Metaphysics?', *Ethics* 99 (1989): 791–814.

Hardin, R. & Shapiro, I. eds. *Political Order: NOMOS 38* (New York: New York University Press, 1996).

Harrison, T.R., *Democracy* (London: Routledge, 1993).

Haworth, L., 'Autonomy and Utility', *Ethics* 95 (1984): 5–19.

———. *Autonomy: An Essay in Philosophical Psychology and Ethics* (New Haven: Yale University Press, 1986).

Hayek, F.A., *The Constitution of Liberty* (London: Routledge and Kegan Paul, 1960).

von Humboldt, W., *Ideen zu einem Versuch, die Gränzen der Wirksamkeit des Staats zu bestimmen*, originally published 1810. Ed. and trans. by J.W. Burrow as *The Limits of State Action* (Cambridge: Cambridge University Press 1969).

Hurka, T., 'Why Value Autonomy?', *Social Theory and Practice* 13 (1987): 361–380.

————. *Perfectionism* (New York, Oxford University Press, 1993).

————. Review of Wall *Liberty, Perfectionism and Restraint*, *Mind* 110 (2001): 878–81.

Irwin, T.H., 'Mill and the Classical World'. In *The Cambridge Companion to Mill*, ed. by J. Skorupski (Cambridge: Cambridge University Press, 1998), pp. 423–463.

Jacobs. J., 'Some Tensions between Autonomy and Self-governance', *Social Philosophy and Policy* 20 (2) (2003): 221–244.

Jonathan, R., 'Liberal Philosophy of Education—A Paradigm under Strain', *Journal of Philosophy of Education* 29 (1995): 93–107.

Joppke, C., 'The Retreat of Multiculturalism in the Liberal State: Theory and Policy', *British Journal of Sociology* 55 (2004): 237–257.

Kant, Immanuel., *Grundlegung zur Metaphysik der Sitten*, originally published 1785. Ed. and trans. by M. Gregor as *Groundwork of the Metaphysics of Morals* (Cambridge: Cambridge University Press, 1994).

Kukathas, C., 'Are There Any Cultural Rights?', *Political Theory* 20 (1992): 105–139.

————. 'Cultural Rights Again: a Rejoinder to Kymlicka', *Political Theory* 20 (1992): 674–680.

————. 'Cultural Toleration'. In *NOMOS 39*, ed. by I. Shapiro and W. Kymlicka (New York: New York University Press, 1997), pp. 69–104.

————. 'Multiculturalism as Fairness; Will Kymlicka's *Multicultural Citizenship*', *The Journal of Political Philosophy* 5 (1997): 406–427.

————. *The Liberal Archipelago* (Oxford: Oxford University Press, 2003).

Kymlicka, W., *Liberalism, Community and Culture*. (Oxford: Clarendon Press, 1989).

————. 'The Rights of Minority Cultures: Reply to Kukathas', *Political Theory* 20 (1992): 140–146.

————. *Multicultural Citizenship: A Liberal Theory of Minority Rights* (Oxford: Clarendon Press, 1995).

Ladenson, R.F., 'A Theory of Personal Autonomy', *Ethics* 86 (1975): 30–48.

————. 'Mill's Conception of Individuality', *Social Theory and Practice* 4 (1977): 167–182.

Larmore, C., *Patterns of Moral Complexity* (Cambridge: Cambridge University Press, 1987).

————. 'Political Liberalism', *Political Theory* 18 (1990): 339–360.

Lehrer, K., 'Reason and Autonomy', *Social Philosophy and Policy* 20 (2) (2003): 177–198.

Lippert-Rasmussen, K., 'Arneson on Equal Opportunity for Welfare', *The Journal of Political Philosophy* 7 (1999): 478–487.

McCabe, D., 'Joseph Raz and the Contextual Argument for Liberal Perfectionism', *Ethics* 111 (2001): 493–522.

MacCallum, G., 'Negative and Positive Freedom', *The Philosophical Review* 67 (1967): 313–334.

Macedo, S., *Liberal Virtues* (Oxford: Clarendon Press, 1990).

————. 'Liberal Civic Education and the Case of God v. John Rawls', *Ethics* 105 (1995): 468–496.

McLaughlin, T.H., 'Liberalism, Education, and the Common School', *Journal of Philosophy of Education* 29 (1995): 239–255.

Malholtra, N.K., 'Information Overload and Consumer Decision Making', *The Journal of Consumer Research* 8 (1982): 419–430.

Marx, K., *The Paris Notebooks*, originally published 1844. Reproduced in *Marx: Early Political Writings*. Ed. and trans. by J. O'Malley (Cambridge: Cambridge University Press, 1984), pp. 71–96.

Mason, A.D., 'Autonomy, Liberalism and State Neutrality', *The Philosophical Quarterly* 40 (1990): 433–452.

Mele, A., *Autonomous Agents: From Self-Control to Autonomy* (New York: Oxford University Press, 1995).

Meyer, M.J., 'Stoicism, Rights and Autonomy', *American Philosophical Quarterly* 24 (1987): 267–271.

Meyers, D.T., 'Personal Autonomy and the Paradox of Feminine Socialization', *The Journal of Philosophy* 84 (1987): 619–628.

Mill, J.S., *On Liberty*, originally published 1859. Reprinted in *On Liberty and Other Writings*, ed. by Stefan Collini (Cambridge: Cambridge University Press, 1989).

Mozert v. Hawkins County Board of Education. 1987. 827 F.2d 1058 (6th Cir. 1987).

Mullhall, S. & Swift, A., *Liberals and Communitarians*, 2nd edition (Oxford: Blackwell, 1996).

Nagel, T. 'Moral Conflict and Political Legitimacy', *Philosophy and Public Affairs* 16 (1987): 215–240.

Nicholson, P. 'The Reception and Early Reputation of Mill's Political Thought'. In *The Cambridge Companion to Mill*, ed. by J. Skorupski (Cambridge: Cambridge University Press, 1998), pp. 464–496.

Nickel, J.W. 'Group Agency and Group Rights'. In *NOMOS 39*, ed. by I. Shapiro and W. Kymlicka (New York: New York University Press, 1997) pp. 235–256.

Norman, W.J., 'Taking Free Action Too Seriously', *Ethics* 101 (1991): 505–520.

Nozick, R., 'Coercion'. In *Philosophy, Politics and Society, 4th series.*, ed. by P. Laslett, W.G. Runciman and Q. Skinner (Oxford: Blackwell, 1972), pp. 101–135.

Nussbaum, M., *Women and Human Development* (Cambridge: Cambridge University Press, 2000).

Olsaretti, S., 'Freedom, Force and Choice: Against the Rights-based Definition of Voluntariness', *Journal of Political Philosophy* 6 (1998): 53–78.

———. 'The Value of Freedom and Freedom of Choice', *Politeia* 56 (2000): 114–121.

———. *Liberty, Desert and the Market* (Cambridge: Cambridge University Press, 2004).

———. ed. *Preferences and Well-Being* (Cambridge: Cambridge University Press, 2006).

O'Neill, O., *Constructions of Reason* (Cambridge: Cambridge University Press, 1989).

———. *Towards Justice and Virtue* (Cambridge: Cambridge University Press, 1996).

———. *Autonomy and Trust in Bioethics* (Cambridge: Cambridge University Press, 2002).

———. 'Autonomy: The Emperor's New Clothes', *Proceedings of the Aristotelian Society: Supplement* 77 (2003): 1–21.

Oppenheim, F., *Dimensions of Politics* (New York: St Martin's Press, 1961).

Oshana. M., 'How Much Should We Value Autonomy?', *Social Philosophy and Policy* 20 (2) (2003): 99–126.

———. *Personal Autonomy in Society* (Aldershot: Ashgate, 2006).

Otsuka, M. 'Luck, Insurance, and Equality', *Ethics* 113 (2002): 40–54.

Parekh, B. 'Superior People; the Narrowness of Liberalism from Mill to Rawls', *Times Literary Supplement*, 25 Feb 1994, 11–13.

———. 'Cultural Diversity and Liberal Democracy'. In *Democracy, Difference and Social Justice*, ed. by G. Mahajan (Delhi: Oxford University Press, 1998).

———. *Rethinking Multiculturalism: Cultural Diversity and Political Theory* (Basingstoke: Palgrave, 2000).

Pico della Mirandola, Giovanni, *De hominis dignitate*, originally published 1486. Translated by C. G. Wallis into English as *On the Dignity of Man* (Indianapolis: Bobbs-Merrill, 1965).

Piller, C., 'Content-Related and Attitude-Related Reasons for Preferences'. In *Preferences and Well-Being*, ed. by S. Olsaretti (Cambridge: Cambridge University Press, 2006), pp. 155–182.

Rakowski, E., *Equal Justice* (New York: Oxford University Press, 1991).

Rawls, J., 'Two Concepts of Rules', *The Philosophical Review* 64 (1955): 3–32.

———. *A Theory of Justice*, revised edition (Oxford: Oxford University Press, 1999).

———. 'Kantian Constructivism in Moral Theory', *The Journal of Philosophy* 77 (1980): 515–572.

———. 'Social Unity and the Primary Goods'. In *Utilitarianism and Beyond*, ed. by A. Sen and B. Williams (Cambridge: Cambridge University Press, 1982), pp. 159–186.

———. 'Justice as Fairness: Political not Metaphysical', *Philosophy and Public Affairs* 14 (1985): 233–251.

———. 'The Idea of an Overlapping Consensus', *Oxford Journal of Legal Studies* 7 (1987): 1–25.

———. 'The Priority of Right and Ideas of the Good', *Philosophy and Public Affairs* 17 (1988): 251–276.

———. *Political Liberalism* (New York: Columbia University Press, 1993).

———. 'The Idea of Public Reason Revisited', *University of Chicago Law Review* 6 (1997): 765–807.

Raz, J., 'Principles of Equality', *Mind* 87 (1978): 321–342.

———. *The Morality of Freedom* (Oxford: Clarendon Press, 1986).

———. 'Facing Diversity: The Case of Epistemic Abstinence', *Philosophy and Public Affairs* 19 (1990): 3–46.

Richards, D.A.J., 'Rights and Autonomy', *Ethics* 92 (1982): 3–20.

Ripstein, A., 'Equality, Luck and Responsibility', *Philosophy and Public Affairs* 23 (1994): 3–23.

Robinson, T., *Stones of Aran: Pilgrimage* (London: Viking, 1989).

Roemer, J.E., 'A Pragmatic Theory of Responsibility for the Egalitarian Planner', *Philosophy and Public Affairs* 22 (1993): 146–166.

Ryan, A., 'Mill in a Liberal Landscape'. In *The Cambridge Companion to Mill*, ed. by J. Skorupski (Cambridge: Cambridge University Press, 1998), pp. 497–540.

Sandel, M., *Liberalism and the Limits of Justice* (Cambridge: Cambridge University Press, 1982).

Scalet, S., 'Liberalism, Skepticism, and Neutrality', *The Journal of Value Inquiry* 34 (2000): 207–225.

Scanlon, T., 'Equality of Resources and Equality of Welfare: A Forced Marriage?', *Ethics* 97 (1986): 111–118.

———. 1988. 'The Moral Significance of Choice'. In *The Tanner Lectures on Human Values* vol. 8, ed. by S.M. McMurrin (Cambridge: Cambridge University Press, 1988), pp. 149–216.

———. *What We Owe To Each Other* (Cambridge, MA: Harvard University Press, 1998).

Schaller, W.E., 'Is Liberal Neutrality Insufficiently Egalitarian?', *The Journal of Philosophy* 101 (2004): 639–650.

Schapiro, T., 'What is a Child?', *Ethics* 109 (1999): 715–738.

Scheffler, S., 'Responsibility, Reactive Attitudes, and Liberalism in Philosophy and Politics', *Philosophy and Public Affairs* 21 (1992): 299–323.

———. 'What is Egalitarianism?', *Philosophy and Public Affairs* 31 (2003): 5–39.

Sen, A. 'Equality of What?'. In *Tanner Lectures on Human Values, Vol. 1.*, ed. by S. McMurrin (Salt Lake City: University of Utah Press, 1980). Reproduced in

Equal Freedom, ed. by S. Darwall (Ann Arbor: University of MichiganPress, 1995), pp. 309–330.

———. 'Well-being, Agency and Freedom', *The Journal of Philosophy* 82 (1985): 169–221.

———. *Inequality Reexamined* (Cambridge, MA: Harvard University Press, 1992).

———. 'Justice: Means versus Freedoms', *Philosophy and Public Affairs* 19 (1996): 111–121.

Shapiro, I. & Kymlicka, W. eds., *Ethnicity and Group Rights: NOMOS 39*. (New York: New York University Press, 1997).

Shapiro, I. 'Democratic Justice and Multicultural Recognition' in *Multiculturalism Reconsidered*, ed. by P. Kelly (Cambridge: Polity Press, 2002), pp. 174–183.

Shapiro, M., 'Illicit Reasons and Means for Reproduction: On Excessive Choice and Categorical and Technological Imperatives', *Hastings Law Journal* 47 (1994): 1081–1218.

Sher, G., *Beyond Neutrality* (Cambridge: Cambridge University Press, 1997).

Sidgwick, H. 'Review of *Liberty, Equality, Fraternity* by James Fitzjames Stephen', *The Academy* 4 (August 1 1873): 292–294.

Singh, B., 'Shared Values, Particular Values, and Education for a Multicultural Society', *Educational Review* 47 (1995): 11–24.

———. 'Liberalism, Parental Rights, Pupils' Autonomy and Education', *Educational Studies* 24 (1998): 165–182.

———. 'Further Attempts to Balance Liberal Virtues with Claims for Cultural Identity within Traditional Non-liberal Communities. A reply to Neil Burtonwood', *Educational Studies* 26 (2000): 213–228.

Skorupski, J. ed., *The Cambridge Companion to Mill* (Cambridge: Cambridge University Press, 1998).

Spinner, J., *The Boundaries of Citizenship: Race, Ethnicity and Nationality in the Liberal State* (Baltimore: Johns Hopkins University Press, 1994).

Steiner, H., 'Individual Liberty', *Proceedings of the Aristotelian Society* 75 (1975): 33–50.

———. *An Essay on Rights* (Oxford: Blackwell, 1994).

Stephen, J.F. *Liberty, Equality, Fraternity* (London: Smith Elder, 1873). Reprint ed. by R.J. White (Cambridge: Cambridge University Press, 1969).

Sunstein, C.R. & Thaler, R.H., 'Preferences, Paternalism, and Liberty'. In *Preferences and Well-Being*, ed. by S. Olsaretti (Cambridge: Cambridge University Press, 2006), pp. 233–264.

Swaine, L.A., 'How Ought Liberal Democracies to Treat Theocratic Communities?', *Ethics* 111 (2001): 302–343.

Synge, J.M., *The Aran Islands* (Dublin: Dodo Press, 1912).

Tamir, Y., *Liberal Nationalism* (Princeton: Princeton University Press, 1995).

———. 'Two Concepts of Multiculturalism', *Journal of Philosophy of Education* 29 (1995): 161–172.

Taylor, C., *Philosophy and the Human Sciences* (Cambridge: Cambridge University Press, 1985).

———. *Sources of the Self: The Making of the Modern Identity* (Cambridge: Cambridge University Press, 1989).

———. 'The Politics of Recognition'. In Multiculturalism, ed. by A. Gutmann (Princeton: Princeton University Press, 1994), pp. 25–73.

Taylor, J.S., 'Autonomy, Duress, and Coercion', *Social Philosophy and Policy* 20(2) (2003): 127–156.

Temkin, L.S., *Inequality* (New York: Oxford University Press, 1993).

Thalberg, I. 'Hierarchical Analyses of Unfree Action, *Canadian Journal of Philosophy* 8 (1978): 211–226.

Titmuss, R., *The Gift Relationship* (New York: Pantheon, 1972).

Tucker, A. Review of Wall *Liberalism, Perfectionism and Restraint*, *Ethics* 111 (2001): 651–653.

Van Dyke, V. 'Justice as Fairness: For Groups?', *American Political Science Review* 69 (1975): 607–614.

———. 'The Individual, the State, and Ethnic Communities in Political Theory', *World Politics* 29 (1977): 343–369.

———. 'Collective Entities and Moral Rights', *Journal of Politics* 44 (1982): 21–40.

Van Parijs, V., 'Why Surfers Should Be Fed: The Liberal Case For An Unconditional Basic Income', *Philosophy and Public Affairs* 20 (1991): 101–131.

Waldron, J., 'Minority Cultures and the Cosmopolitan Alternative', *University of Michigan Journal of Law Reform* 25/3 (1992): 751–793.

———. 'Moral Autonomy and Personal Autonomy', In *Autonomy and the Challenges to Liberalism*, ed. by J. Christman and J. Anderson (Cambridge: Cambridge University Press, 2005), pp. 307–329.

Wall, S., *Liberalism, Perfectionism and Restraint* (New York: Cambridge University Press, 1998).

———. 'Neutrality and Responsibility', *The Journal of Philosophy* 98 (2001): 389–410.

———. 'Freedom as a Political Ideal', *Social Philosophy and Policy* 20(2) (2003): 307–331.

Waltzer, M., 'Response to Kukathas'. In *NOMOS 39*, ed. by I. Shapiro and W. Kymlicka (New York: New YorkUniversity Press, 1997), pp. 105–111.

Watson. G., 'Free Agency', *The Journal of Philosophy* 72 (1975): 205–220.

Weldon, T.D., *The Vocabulary of Politics* (Baltimore: Penguin, 1953).

Wenar, L., 'Political Liberalism: An Internal Critique', *Ethics* 106 (1995): 32–62.

Williams, A., 'Equality for the Ambitious', *The Philosophical Quarterly* 52 (2002): 377–389.

Williams, B. 'The Idea of Equality'. In *Politics, Philosophy and Society, 2nd series*, ed. by P. Laslett and G. Runciman (Oxford: Blackwell, 1962). Reproduced in B. Williams *Problems of the Self*, pp. 230–249.

———. *Problems of the Self* (Cambridge: Cambridge University Press, 1973).

———. *Morality* (Cambridge: Cambridge University Press, 1976).

———. 'Persons, Character and Morality'. In *The Identity of Persons*, ed. by A.O. Rorty (Berkeley: University of California Press, 1976), pp. 197–216.

———. 'Voluntary Acts and Responsible Agents', *Oxford Journal of Legal Studies* 10 (1990): 1–10.

Wisconsin v. Yoder, 1972. 406 U.S. 205.

Wolff, J., 'Fairness, Respect, and the Egalitarian Ethos', *Philosophy and Public Affairs* 27 (1998): 97–122.

Young, I.M., *Justice and the Politics of Difference* (Princeton: Princeton University Press, 1990).

Young, R., 'Autonomy and the 'Inner Self'', *American Philosophical Quarterly* 17 (1980): 35–43.

———. 'Autonomy and Socialization', *Mind* 89 (1980): 565–576.

———. 'The Value of Autonomy', *The Philosophical Quarterly* 32 (1982): 35–44.

Index

Page references in square brackets are to endnotes.